School Law's Evolution – Reflections of a Texas Lawyer

By Kelly Frels

EDUCATION LAW ASSOCIATION
www.educationlaw.org

Disclaimers

The Education Law Association (ELA) is a private, nonadvocacy, nonprofit, international member association. The opinions expressed in this publication are those of the author and do not represent official views of the Association.

2121 Euclid Avenue, LB 46, Cleveland, OH 44115-2214
Phone: (216) 523-7377 / Fax: (216) 687-6881
www.educationlaw.org

Printed in the United States of America.
ISBN 10: 1-56534-189-9
ISBN 13: 978-1-56534-189-0
EAN: 9781565341890

NOLPE/Education Law Association

The Education Law Association was established in 1954 as the National Organization on Legal Problems of Education. We provide unbiased information about history and precedents in education law; current legal issues affecting education; as well as the rights of those involved in both public and private K-12 schools and postsecondary higher education.

ELA's primary role is to provide high-quality, practical information that builds members' legal literacy and promotes professional growth. We cover key trends in education law and support research through cost-effective print and digital publications (books and monographs), periodicals, an annual conference, seminars, and webinars. Our website and social media allow members to share timely information. Members include attorneys, school administrators in K-12 and higher education, faculty in schools of education and law, consultants, and graduate students who represent the next generation of those pursuing careers in education or education law.

Preface

Writing these reflections began in response to students who were doing research and writing papers about the Houston Independent School District desegregation case. At the requests of others, I prepared histories of my involvement in the development of school law organizations. As I wrote, other historically significant stories came to mind which prompted me to write about them.

The result has been the production of these reflections so school lawyers and others who are interested can have some exposure to these events and to the early days of the school law practice, an exciting time when new issues seemed to arise daily. These reflections are also prepared so I will have contemporaneously written accounts available when people ask what happened on an issue or how a school law organization developed. I enjoyed being a part of something very interesting, and I want to share the stories.

Most of these stories are purely factual, but some near the end include my personal opinions on education policy issues. Being free to comment on policy matters is a luxury of being retired and not having clients who might be discomfited by my opinions. These stories and opinions are my personal recollections and views and are not those of Bracewell LLP, any client, former client, or other person. I have not included stories about my being managing partner of Bracewell, or president of the Houston Bar Association or State Bar of Texas. Nothing in this material is intended as legal advice, nor should it be considered legal advice.

These reflections are not presented as a historical narrative. I have chosen to reflect primarily on events or issues that most directly fashioned the school practice, especially those events that left a lasting impression on me. Some of these events are historically significant, while others are meaningful only to me or to those who were directly involved.

Each of these reflections is a story unto itself, so there is some replication throughout this series of self-standing stories. Readers can browse the Table of Contents to select stories of interest without reading all the reflections. The endnotes are limited and are intended to provide references to some historically relevant sources.

I know some events worthy of mention have not been included, so please forgive their omission. Likewise, I recognize that many of these stories are about the Houston Independent School District and its many dedicated people, but, keep in mind that the HISD was my central client focus for 38 years. These reflections are written in the first person because I can tell the stories better that way, and I think that makes for better reading. I apologize in advance for omitting what anyone feels should have been included, for what I say about someone, or how I remember what happened. After all, these are my reflections and my opinions.

By Kelly Frels

Table of Contents

The Setting....1
Starting at Bracewell & Patterson....2
My Evolution into a School Lawyer....3
The Creation of the Houston Community College in 1971....5
The Paul Kitchen Case....10
The Houston Independent School District Evolution Case....11
The Houston Independent School District Teacher Strike of 1971....12
Houston's Desegregation Case – The Beginnings, Magnets, Westheimer, Metropolitan, Unitary Status and Settlement....13
School Prayer – *Guild v. HISD*....26
Special Act Creating the Houston Independent School District of 1923 and Conflicts of Interest....27
Harry Patterson Gets Shot and the Birth of the Construction Manager....28
National Organization on Legal Problems of Education and Education Law Association....30
The Evolution of School Lawyer Organizations....32
The School Law Committee of the State Bar of Texas – Later, the School Law Section....33
The National School Boards Association's Council of School Attorneys....36
The Texas Association of School Boards Council of School Attorneys....37
The University of Texas School Law Conference – UT School of Law....39
Hearings Before The Commissioner of Education and The State Board of Education....40
Dealing with the HEW....41
School Finance – The Unending Saga....42
Dress Codes, Hair Regulations and Student Walkouts....45
"I Don't Like to Lose" – Dr. Tom Spencer....47
Here Is the File – *Green v. HBU*....47
Being Trumped by John Lewis....48
Immigration – Undocumented Aliens....48
Sovereign Immunity and Student Injuries....51
Open Meetings, Open Records and Privacy....51
Student Discipline – Suspensions, Corporal Punishment, and Search and Seizure....54
Greg Kite and the UIL....59
The Advent of the Fax Machine and More Technology....60

House Bill 72 and Teacher Testing Cases....61
No Pass – No Play – An H.B. 72 Issue....63
The Career Ladder Debacle – Merit Pay....63
Objecting to Judge DeAnda's Questions and Arguing the First Amendment with Judge Justice....64
Introduction to Due Process Hearings in Special Education....65
Introduction to AIDS....67
Home School Lawsuit....68
Exhaustion of Administrative Remedies – *Houston Federation of Teachers v. HISD*....69
Larry Watts Stories....70
More on the McAllen lawsuits....72
Tim Cooper Selected Tales....73
The Plane Ride to Eagle Pass....75
The "Heart Attack" – Texas Southmost College....76
Green Tee Terrace Goes to Pearland ISD....77
Steve Braun – The Law or Professional Basketball....78
Cars Driven by Superintendents and School Lawyers....79
Title IX, Education Amendments of 1972 – Gender Equality....79
Emergence of Women in the Law....80
David, Would You Consider Coming to Houston?....82
The Lopez Connection – David and Vianei....83
Cheerleader Cases....83
High School Graduation – To Walk or Not?....84
School District and College Police Departments....84
The Media – Friend or Foe?....85
Teacher Termination Issues – A Constant Throughout....87
The Gordon Cotton Principalship – An Example of School Leadership....89
Here Comes the City – Changes in Small Town Districts....90
Changing Superintendents – "Neal, Wait until after Midnight"....91
The Santa Fe ISD Prayer Case – How We Were Hired....91
Sexual Harassment and Sexual Misconduct....92
Transgender Issues....93
Pro Se Plaintiffs....94
Asbestos – What a Challenge....94
Joan Raymond – Trying Times....97
Frank Petruzielo, Rod Paige and Kaye Stripling....98

Lawsuits, and Avoiding Them......100
Road Trips with Associates......102
Other Desegregation Cases......102
Value of Humor......104
Lawyers Working Together......105
School Lawyers Must Be Astute Politicians and Must Avoid Partisan Politics......106
Speaking and Writing......107
Writing Editorials......109
Schools in Economically Diminished Areas......111
Governance – Fewer Business Leaders Now Serve as Trustees......113
Governance – Total Single Member Districts: Has Their Time Passed?......114
Leadership Counts......117
The Difference Between Schools in the 1950s and Today......118
Charter Schools......122
Motivated and Involved Parents......124
Commercialization, Monetization and Privatization of Public Education..126
Advice for Law Practice and Life......128
Which Projects Were the Most Fulfilling?......131
From Bracewell to Thompson & Horton and Beyond......132
Farewell to Jeff Horner......132
Thank You, Carmela......133
The Future......133
Conclusion......135

Appendices......137
Endnotes......173
Acknowledgements......177
Photos......182

The Setting

It was 1970. Two of the most defining events of the twentieth century, the Great Depression and World War II, had ended more than 25 years earlier. The Marshall Plan had redeveloped much of Europe, and we were seeing more goods with "Made in Japan" stamped on them. The Cold War with the Soviet Union was raging around the globe, with the Berlin Wall standing as the symbol of Soviet defiance.

World War II had caused Americans to unite to fight common enemies in the Pacific and Europe. When the troops came home, the war effort turned to strengthening America's infrastructure and producing consumer goods. Businesses, law firms (such as Bracewell & Tunks), and civic clubs were founded in the years immediately following the war. America was becoming more mobile, as President Eisenhower persuaded Congress to approve the development of the interstate highway system.

The world conflict had also fueled the recognition that the separation of races in the United States must come to an end. The quest for civil rights for America's African-Americans became a movement that was highlighted by the end of the "separate but equal" doctrine in education through the Supreme Court's *Brown v. Board of Education*[1] in 1954, as well as by the passage of the Civil Rights Act of 1964[2] and the Voting Rights Act of 1965[3]. The battle for equal rights and fair treatment which continues today has, of course, extended to issues beyond the scope of these historical laws and cases.

As a result of the Pacific and European conflicts, the United States armed forces and our country's presence was felt virtually worldwide. As a recognized superpower and preserver of a new world order, America was drawn into conflicts and disputes to prevent the spread of communism, including Indochina and in particular, Vietnam. Americans, who had historically gotten their news from newspapers and radio, were enthralled with television—which brought the Vietnam conflict into our living rooms. Even though the United States put a man on the moon in 1969, the war in Vietnam divided Americans.

The Vietnam War led to clashes between students and authorities on college campuses and in the streets of our cities. The public schools best reflect our society, so it was not surprising that students in Des Moines, Iowa, donned black armbands to protest the Vietnam War. The discipline these students received for protesting caused the Supreme Court to bring the Constitution to the high school campus through *Tinker v. Des Moines*[4] in 1969. With *Brown* and *Tinker*, the civil rights era began to be reflected in the educational institution cases brought in the nation's federal courts. Times were changing dramatically and quickly!

By Kelly Frels

I was born in the small community of Lolita, Texas, near the end of World War II to parents who had experienced the brunt of the Great Depression. My World War I veteran dad, having lost his business of operating cotton gins during the depression, farmed and ran a small herd of cattle. My mother taught school at the junior high school across the street from our house. I graduated with my 43 classmates from Industrial High School in 1962. After brief attempts at playing baseball and kicking the football at Southwest Texas State University, I turned to student politics and my fraternity.

My next educational step was graduate school in government at The University of Texas, where we studied a lot about what lawyers did. I decided I would rather do what lawyers did, so I went to law school at The University of Texas in the fall of 1967. Three experience-filled years of law school later, I was looking for a job. (There were no summer clerkships at law firms then, so I continued working summers as a cotton ginner at the Farmers Co-op Gin in Edna. After my second year in law school, I served as an assistant to Senator William "Bill" Patman in the Texas Legislature.)

The entire partnership of Bracewell & Patterson showed up to interview at The University of Texas in the fall of 1969, and I knew that I had found my next home—with Bracewell in Houston, Texas. Houston was a city on the move where one's future depended more on hard work and ingenuity than on birth. Bracewell & Patterson was committed to becoming a significant law firm.

During the last year of law school, I met Carmela Madden, who had become the first assistant dean of women at Southwest Texas State University. I actually saw her picture in the Southwest Texas *University Star,* and I vowed to meet her. We met and got married in September 1970. We moved to Houston, where I began my career as a lawyer and Carmela taught English at Westchester High School in the Spring Branch ISD. Little did I know that many of my experiences growing up would prepare me so well for the changing times that lay ahead.

Starting at Bracewell & Patterson

I was the 23rd lawyer at Bracewell & Patterson when I arrived on the 18th floor of the First City National Bank building on August 1, 1970. Having taken the Texas Bar Exam and incurring some debts finishing law school, I was ready to do what was asked to earn my beginning salary of $1050 per month.

With no attorney office available, I was given partner William Key "Bill" Wilde's well-appointed office while he was on vacation. My bubble burst after two weeks when Bill returned. I was then assigned to the first office for all new Bracewell lawyers of the time—"the" library. The library was located next to "the" conference room where all lawyers met each Monday morning at 7:30

a.m. to review the new client matters opened the prior week. After the general meeting of lawyers, the partners met alone.

I was assigned to work half-time for Bill Wilde, the senior trial lawyer and head of the trial group. The other half of my time was devoted to working with Harry W. Patterson, the former president of the Houston Bar Association, who, as of January, 1970, became responsible for serving the legal needs of the Houston Independent School District ("HISD").

The firm, established in 1945, was then known as Bracewell & Tunks. When Bracewell, Reynolds & Patterson split in 1966, Joe Reynolds took the HISD desegregation case and the school representation with him to Reynolds, White, Allen & Cook. Joe resigned as the HISD attorney when the new HISD Board majority called Citizens for Good Schools ("CGS") was elected in December 1969. The CGS majority pledged to desegregate the schools, accept federal money for school lunches, and offer half-day kindergarten. Jim Kronzer, former president of the Houston Bar Association and one of the state's outstanding plaintiffs' lawyers, headed the HISD desegregation trial team, with Ernie Cannon serving as his assistant. Kronzer was a close friend of Harry Patterson and both had served as president of the Houston Bar Association.

About a year after my arrival, I was moved from the library to a small office down the hall from firm controller Dolores Dutton, who had typed the original answer in the HISD desegregation case on a manual typewriter in January 1957. My office was also next door to the coffee room, where everyone who drank coffee contributed to the purchase of coffee and supplies.

The youngest lawyer of the firm had to take cold calls from people who asked questions the receptionist could not handle. The youngest trial lawyer also had to attend the Friday "docket call," where the state court ancillary judge would call a long list of cases and give them numbers for assignment to random judges for trial during the following two weeks. If a motion had to be argued or a continuance was sought, the lawyer on the file also might actually attend docket call. Upon the conclusion of docket call, the lawyer who attended would get out a dime and find a public telephone to report any case given a number for trial (cell phones were only available to James Bond in the early 1970s). I was the youngest trial lawyer for over two years, so I grew really tired of docket call.

My Evolution into a School Lawyer

When the Constitution came to the campus in 1954 through *Brown v. Board of Education of Topeka, Kansas* (desegregation), and in 1969 with *Tinker v. Des Moines* (student free speech), school districts generally called upon community trial lawyers to represent districts in an occasional lawsuit. With a few exceptions, like *Fromen v. Goose Creek ISD*[5] (teacher tenure) and *Braun v. Trustees of Victoria ISD*[6] (sovereign immunity), much of a school lawyer's work involved real estate, construction, and tax collections.

With desegregation and the emergence of student and employee rights cases, such as *Ferguson v. Thomas*,[7] outstanding trial lawyers representing school districts gradually began to handle a wider variety of school-related litigation. Joe Reynolds and Grant Cook represented the Houston Independent School District until 1970, Warren Whitham represented the Dallas Independent School District, Cecil Morgan represented the Fort Worth Independent School District, and Ralph Langley represented the San Antonio Independent School District. Morris Galatzan was El Paso Independent School District's lawyer. Rick Peebles had the Goose Creek Independent School District as a client, and J. W. Gary represented the Corpus Christi Independent School District. Earl Luna represented a number of Dallas-area districts.

J. C. Hinsley, who had been an assistant attorney general and represented the state of Texas in school-related cases, and then practiced as an independent Austin lawyer, pulled together school laws that were spread throughout the state's statutes. He published these statutes in a hardbound book with annotations prior to the adoption of the Texas Education Code in 1969. With the codification of the state's school laws in 1970 (the first substantive Texas laws on one subject to be codified), plus the development of student and employees' rights and the application of due process for discipline or expulsion, the representation of school districts really began to change. It was a time for the evolution of the school law specialist, so when I became licensed on September 18, 1970, I found myself on the cutting edge of something challenging and exciting. Bracewell & Patterson became the Houston Independent School District's lawyers in January 1970, and I was the only lawyer hired by the firm that year. The associate at Bracewell & Patterson doing much of the school work at the time did not want to do it, so upon my arrival, he gladly handed off the school matters and became a real estate lawyer. I hit the practice of law at just the right time to dig in and learn from the start to be a school lawyer. My first endeavor to do so was to read the newly codified Texas Education Code from beginning to end.

Several civil rights cases against the HISD had been pretty much resolved before my arrival, including a school prayer case brought by attorney Lynn Hughes in United States District Judge John Singleton's court. Another case involved student discipline was brought by attorney Robert E. Hall in United States District Judge Woodrow Seals' court. I dived right into the existing cases against the HISD, as well as the new ones filed on student discipline, teaching evolution as a religion, and several teacher terminations.

Riding to the state courthouse on the city bus one morning in early January 1971, Bill Wilde asked if I was interested in working on the HISD's desegregation case. At the next HISD Board meeting, the board hired Bracewell to take over the case. (Interestingly, the HISD Board, in a statement of openness, did not conduct closed sessions to discuss anything, not even litigation strategy.) I immediately went to Jim Kronzer's and Ernie Cannon's office to get the desegregation files, which were literally spread everywhere.

An amended order concerning how the HISD was to be operated, dated September 18, 1970, had been entered by United States District Judge Ben C. Connally, but no one knew of it because the United States District Clerk apparently did not send a notice of the order's entry to any of the lawyers. I found the order quite by accident when comparing the docket sheet in the United States District Clerk's office with the pleadings and orders I had retrieved from Jim Kronzer's office. (The amended order was entered to conform Judge Ben C. Connally's 1969 desegregation order with the August 25, 1970 opinion of the Fifth Circuit Court of Appeals.)

The Creation of the Houston Community College in 1971

In 1965, the leaders of Tarrant and Dallas Counties called successful elections to establish countywide community colleges. A 1969 election to create a community college in the Houston area failed—in large part because of anti-taxers. Yes, anti-taxers were a part of Houston politics in the 1960s, and they had great influence on local elections. Many of the people who opposed the creation of a Houston-area community college in 1969 were instrumental in attempting to create the proposed Westheimer Independent School District in 1973, and again in 1976.

As noted earlier, the HISD Board experienced a major change in leadership through the 1969 trustee election. Eleanor Tinsley, George Oser, Leonard Robbins, and Rev. D. Leon Everett were elected to the seven-member board on the Citizens for Good Schools ("CGS"} reform slate. HISD Superintendent George Garver, who was hired by the CGS Board from Livonia, Michigan, urged the HISD Board to find a way to create a community college. An HISD community college would provide terminal educational opportunities in vocational (technical) areas, and provide transitional opportunities between high school and senior colleges. Eleanor Tinsley, a college classmate of Edith Patterson (wife of Bracewell Patterson's Harry Patterson) at Baylor, and Shell Oil Company physicist, board member George Oser, were the board's leaders who wanted to find a way to create an HISD community college.

I had been a lawyer for a little over a month when HISD Superintendent George Garver called me on October 27, 1970, stating that the HISD wanted to establish a community college. Dr. Garver wanted Bracewell & Patterson's legal advice regarding HISD's authority to create and operate a community college, and how to fund the college's operation. Dr. Garver felt that funding from the state of $695 per student per year, plus a $50 per semester tuition, could cover the operating costs. If the HISD facilities were used by the college for classes after school and in the evenings, there would be no immediate need for capital expenditures.

Dr. Garver and I discussed the 1969 effort to create a community college in Houston and that the University of Houston had evolved from the former junior college operated by the HISD. (The University of Houston was once an HISD junior college that became a four-year state university. The history of the University of Houston is the subject of Patrick J. Nicholson's book, *In Time*.)[8] Dr. Garver and I talked about using Chapter 51 of the Texas Education Code, which provided for the creation of a community college under the control of an independent school district's board. Recognizing that the Texas Higher Education Coordinating Board had broad powers over the creation and operation of community colleges, Dr. Garver and I determined that our contacting the Coordinating Board was a necessary first step in the creation of an HISD community college.

There was agreement among HISD Board members, administrators, and community supporters that the keys to securing a successful college vote would be the removal of additional taxes from the creation proposal and the college's use of HISD facilities. At the HISD Board's direction and under Harry Patterson's supervision, I drafted the petition to call an election to create the Houston Community College. After sufficient signatures were obtained, the petition was presented to the Harris County Commissioner's Court with the request that the court call an election. The anti-tax people, and those who opposed just about anything the HISD's board proposed, began voicing their opposition.

The opposition's main complaint was that the HISD Board could not use Chapter 51 of the Texas Education Code to create a community college. Instead, the opponent's asserted that a special statute enacted in 1969—Article 2815h-2a, which provided a procedure for the creation of a Houston community college district with boundaries coextensive with those of the HISD—was the only means to create a college. Using Article 2815h-2a process would have required twice the number of petition signatures (10%) to call an election than Chapter 51 (5%), and the proposition would have to include a vote on an immediate tax. Senator Chet Brooks, who authored Article 2815h-2a, provided an affidavit that Article 2815h-2a was not intended to be the sole means to establish a community college with boundaries coextensive with those of the HISD. Senator Brooks stated that the HISD could use Chapter 51 of the Texas Education Code. On March 28, 1970, the Harris County Commissioner's

Court approved HISD calling of an election on the creation of the Houston Community College for May 18, 1971.

The opponents made the same argument to the Texas Higher Education Coordinating Board. The Commissioner of Higher Education, Dr. Bevington Reed, requested an opinion of Attorney General Crawford Martin to resolve the legal issue of which statute was applicable. We provided the Attorney General with a brief in support of the HISD using Chapter 51 of the Texas Education Code. Even though Commissioner Reed had not yet received an opinion from the Attorney General, the Coordinating Board issued an order on April 23, 1971 approving the election.

An interesting constitutional issue arose when I was preparing the petition to call the election and the instructions for signing the petition. The Texas Constitution required that a person own property as a condition of voting in these types of local elections. The United States Supreme Court had recently held that property ownership as a condition of voting in a New York local election and in an Arizona school election violated the Equal Protection Clause of the United States Constitution. In deciding the Arizona case, the Supreme Court cited Texas and ten other states with similar restrictive provisions. We opined that property ownership could not be required to sign the petition or vote in the election. Interestingly, those who opposed of the creation of the community college never raised the issue of who could sign the petition or vote in the election.

Houston's business and education community leaders favored the HISD's efforts to create the college. The Houston Chamber of Commerce supported the proposal, with business leaders like S. I. Morris and Hines Baker stepping forward. The League of Women Voters and the Houston Junior Bar signed on in support. University of Houston President Philip Hoffman and South Texas Junior College President W. I. Dykes led the education community supporters, which included the Houston Teachers Association and HISD school administrators. Mayor Louie Welch and future Houston mayors Robert C. Lanier and Fred Hofheinz, plus State Senators Barbara Jordan and Chet Brooks, spoke out in favor of the college.

Many other notables, like Bishop John L. Markowsky of the Galveston-Houston Diocese, Judson Robertson, Jr., John E. Castillo, Frank Penedo and AFL-CIO Secretary Don Horn urged people to vote for the creation. Of course, the members of Citizens for Good Schools (CGS) coalition, which had supported Robbins, Oser, Tinsley and Everette in the 1969 HISD School Board election, were big supporters. The *Houston Post* editorialized in support of the creation.

Opposition to the creation was led by Rev. L. E. Equia, a minister who said he supported a community college, but one that required a larger number of petition signers and a vote on a tax base as required by Article 2815h-2a. Naturally, Clymer Wright and the *Houston Tribune* opposed the proposition. Just before the election, the Committee for Sound American Education (CSAE) urged a "no" vote and issued a harsh criticism of Dr. Garver and trustees Robbins, Oser and Tinsley, whom CSAE had opposed in the 1969 trustee election. CSAE's opposition was akin to asking the HISD residents to vote "no" as a referendum of the leadership of the CGS's slate to integrate the HISD schools and make other changes in school operations. The *Houston Tribune* and *Houston Chronicle* editorialized urging voters to reject the proposal, both papers saying they supported a community college but just not as proposed.

Dr. Garver put J.B. Whiteley, the HISD Assistant Superintendent responsible for vocational education in charge of coordinating HISD's efforts to create the community college. Whiteley was assisted by Assistant Superintendent Dr. Britton (Britt) Ryan. Dr. Joseph "Joe" Champagne, Assistant Dean of the University of Houston Business School, took a leading role on behalf of higher education.

The creation of the Houston Community College was approved by the voters on May 18, 1971, by a vote of 61.32% to 38.6%. On May 28, 1971, ten days after the election, Attorney General Crawford Martin issued Opinion M-876 in which he opined that the HISD could use the process set out in Chapter 51 of the Texas Education Code to create the community college. Attorney General Martin agreed there was no conflict between Chapter 51 and Article 2815h-2a.

The HISD Board chose Dr. Joe Champagne as the College's administrator to be responsible for the HCC's startup. Later, Dr. Champagne became the president of the HCC. J.B. Whiteley ultimately became HCC's President and then Chancellor, a position in which he served until his retirement. Dr. Britt Ryan became the equivalent of Whiteley's chief of staff and served in that position until his retirement.

The HCC began to conduct limited vocational classes in the fall of 1971. A more complete schedule, including academic offerings, began in January 1972. The HCC explored the purchase of the facilities and operations of the private South Texas Junior College, but without a tax base, purchasing facilities was not viable. Ultimately, the University of Houston purchased South Texas Junior College's facilities for what has become the University of Houston-Downtown.

Without additional property tax revenues, securing funds to provide the basics needed to develop a college was challenging. J.B. Whiteley was a master in securing federal, state and other funding, and he was very adept at applying unspent budget funds from the prior year to meet urgent needs. Providing quality services to students on a shoestring budget was difficult.

Harry Patterson was especially helpful to Whiteley in securing some basic facilities such as the first real administrative building at 22 Waugh Drive, a building previously occupied by the funeral company, Service Corporation International (SCI). Patterson took great pleasure in telling of their initial visit to 22 Waugh Drive when it was still occupied by SCI, and having to visualize college offices replacing the velvet drapes and the caskets.

The Houston Community College System ("HCCS") has grown from its humble beginnings into the fifth-largest community college in the country. Through the capable legal work of Bracewell partner, Arturo Michel, the HCCS got a board separate from the HISD in 1989. The HCCS is now governed by a nine-member board, elected through single member districts. I continued to serve as the HCCS's counsel through its separation from the HISD. After the separation, Arturo, who had developed a close relationship with the HCC Board, incrementally took over the general counsel role. When Arturo became the City Attorney for the city of Houston in 2004, Bracewell partner Jarvis Hollingsworth became the primary lawyer for the HCCS, a role in which he continues to serve. The HCCS now also has an in-house general counsel and several assistants.

The San Jacinto Junior College in Harris County was the community college where the taxing powers of junior colleges for facilities was solidified. San Jacinto College District, established in 1961 with the territory of six school districts (Pasadena, Deer Park, La Porte, Galena Park, Sheldon, and Channel View), conducted a tax election to build facilities. The election was judicially contested by those who asserted that San Jacinto could not levy taxes for facilities. The Texas Supreme Court opened the door for today's operation of junior and community colleges by ruling that junior colleges could levy ad valorem taxes for facilities.[9]

The HCCS's facilities are now separate from those of the HISD. HCCS and HISD have moved forward together to create dual-credit courses so high school students can gain college credit while in high school. Some students now graduate from high school with an associate degree from HCCS, and many more move on to four-year colleges with a year or more in college credit. The HCCS has agreements with The University of Texas at Tyler, Texas A&M University, and the University of Houston Downtown to provide cooperative programs leading to degrees in engineering.

HCCS, San Jacinto College, Lone Star College, and Lee College have become increasingly active in coordinating with the Houston-area business community in identifying and preparing students for current and future workforce needs. All these Harris County community colleges provide programs leading to certifications required for certain jobs and providing lifetime learning opportunities for all of us. School districts in Texas are either in the territory of a community college, or their territory is served by virtue of being in the service area of an existing community college.

By Kelly Frels

The Paul Kitchen Case

The first really big case I got to work on was filed by Robert E. "Bob" Hall, of Dixie, Wolf & Hall, with Eric Nelson, who was carrying Bob's briefcase —just as I was doing for my mentor, Bill Wilde. A high school student, Paul Kitchen, had not followed the recently revised and adopted HISD rules for his distribution of *Space City News* at the entrance to Waltrip High School, where Gordon Cotton was the principal. These new rules were developed by a student, faculty, and community committee led by attorneys Jonathan Day, Bill Coats, David Redford, Travis Broesche, and Marc Grossberg. The community committee was formed after an injunction was issued by United States District Court Judge Woodrow Seals in an earlier suit brought by attorney Bob Hall on behalf of a Sharpstown high school student named Sullivan. The injunction prohibited the HISD from doing certain things with respect to the distribution of material by students and required procedural due process before suspending students for misbehavior. *Space City News* was an independently produced paper typical of the early 1970s, with lots of anti-war and anti-authority articles laced with four-letter words.

The first hearing before Judge Seals was an attempt by Bob Hall and Eric Nelson to get Paul Kitchen back in school, which Judge Seals seemed pleased to do. After the injunction hearing, we had a meeting of counsel in Judge Seals' chambers, where I met the judge for the first time. I still had red hair and was wearing one of two suits I owned; this one had three buttons and a vest. Judge Seals asked Bill Wilde, "Wilde, who is this you have with you? He looks like a John Bircher." (The John Birch Society, headquartered in Dallas, was the country's best known ultraconservative organization of the times.) Bill responded, "I assure you he is not, your honor." Thus began my long relationship with Judge Seals.

The *Kitchen* case had all the First and Fourteenth Amendment issues a first-year lawyer could want. What fun I had! Judge Seals, a traditional liberal activist before becoming a federal judge, seemed predisposed to rule against the HISD, and that is exactly what he did. One of the times Judge Seals seemed to grasp the need for order in school was when newly appointed Deputy Superintendent Larry Marshall (later, after retirement, an HISD Board member) testified, "Before learning can take place, you have to secure the environment." That was true then, and it may be even more true today.

After Judge Seals' adverse ruling, we appealed to the Fifth Circuit on the First Amendment issue of prior restraint, the use of suspension as discipline, the failure of Judge Seals to abstain from ruling, plus other grounds. The Fifth Circuit proceeded to hold our case and rule on less-complex First Amendment cases from other school districts involving some of these issues. Interestingly, the Fifth Circuit used the reasoning, even some of the language, of our brief in deciding these other cases. By the time the court got to ruling on our appeal, most of our issues had been decided in our favor through the other cases. Of critical independent impact in our case was Kitchen's defiance of Gordon Cotton's demand that he comply with Board policy; when confronted with the Board policy and newspaper distribution, he shouted at Cotton "the common Anglo-Saxon vulgarism for sexual intercourse." Kitchen also shouted as he slammed the door to Cotton, within the hearing of school staff members, "I don't want to go to this goddamn school anyway" as Cotton suspended him. This independent reason was the Fifth Circuit's easy way out in reversing Judge Seals. The Fifth Circuit simply referred to their prior decisions for guidance on the other First Amendment issues.[10]

During the preparation of the appellate brief, I began to be known among our firm staff as the "dirty dictator" because I had to use the four-letter words of *Space City News* in memos and briefing. I would give our MTST operator a Dictaphone tape with the apology up front that I hoped she would not be offended by my having to use the four-letter and hyphenated words. (The MTST was a giant machine that used magnetic memory tape, but it was a significant step from the advanced Selectric typewriter, which was succeeded by the mag card, on the journey to word processing on the computer.) The MTST had a memory stored on tape and would also print multiple copies, so carbon paper was no longer necessary. The *Kitchen* case also gave me a preview of how parents, many of whom previously paid little attention to their children's school activities, would "come in on the white horse" and take the side of their children without hearing the school teacher's or administrator's side of the issue.

The Houston Independent School District Evolution Case

In 1971, the HISD had its own evolution case that was also randomly assigned to Judge Woodrow Seals, a devout Methodist. It was a shade of Scopes, because Rita Wright's next friend from the Solid Rock Refuge for Women, Leona Weber, alleged that evolution was humanism, and that humanism was in fact a religion. She asked Judge Seals to prevent the HISD from teaching evolution in its schools.

The HISD voluntarily accommodated Rita Wright and others of like views by giving them a self-study option when evolution was being taught as a scientific theory in classes. That was not enough for the plaintiffs, because they appealed Judge Seals' dismissal of the case to the Fifth Circuit. The Fifth Circuit affirmed by treating the 12(b) motion as one for summary judgment, and the Supreme Court denied certiorari.[11] Jim Kelly, a religiously conservative trial lawyer who worked closely with Dick Sedgley, an ad valorem tax collection lawyer who represented the Spring Branch Independent School District and a number of smaller school districts on school law matters, represented Leona Weber and Rita Wright.

The Houston Independent School District Teacher Strike of 1971

The movement to have collective bargaining for teachers swept the country in the late 1960s and early 1970s. As an attempt to avoid collective bargaining with school employees, the Texas Legislature adopted a statute allowing school boards to "consult" with teacher and other employee groups on "wages, hours and conditions of work."[12] The legislature of 1967 also authorized school districts to adopt what amounted to tenure for teachers through the use of probationary and continuing contracts. The consultation statute contemplated that school administrators, acting on behalf of boards, would meet with employees and get their views on policy issues, but the authors of the statute never envisioned collective bargaining or the development of an "agreement" whereby the board would relinquish its authority to change policy without having employee groups agree. Such a result would be collective bargaining. Texas also had, as it currently has, a strong right-to-work law that prohibits strikes or work stoppages by public employees.[13]

The 1971 school year was about to begin, and the consultation meetings between the administrators and the teachers, represented by the Houston Teachers' Association ("HTA"), got hot and heavy at 3830 Richmond, the HISD administration building. A large basket of fruit was sent to the administrative team on which I was participating. We were reluctant to eat it for fear it was doctored with a laxative—what intrigue in a right-to-work state! We sent the fruit on to the teachers' team, for whom we later learned it was intended. Meetings continued several days through Saturday, when the HTA declared that there was an "impasse," and after a much-publicized meeting in an athletic stadium on Sunday, the teachers voted to strike. In classic labor union fashion, the teachers' union had already prepared picket signs.

Despite warnings that a strike was illegal, a good number of teachers picketed the administration building and individual schools on Monday. A substantial number of teachers did not report for work. At our suggestion, the administration took pictures of the teachers who were on the picket lines. It would later prove difficult for a teacher shown holding a picket sign in a photo to argue that he or she was not involved in the strike.

The HISD Board called an emergency meeting. Harry Patterson publicly reviewed with the board a report prepared by fellow associate Ron Dougherty and me on the application of the no-strike law and another law which provided that striking teachers could have their teaching certificates revoked. When this information was revealed at the meeting and reported in the press, the teachers realized they had exceeded their boundaries, even with the teacher-friendly CGS Board. The board agreed to grant amnesty to any teacher who returned to school the next day, but the board voted that teachers who continued to strike would be fired and the Texas Education Agency ("TEA") would be notified so their certificates could be revoked. Afterwards, the teacher group met again and voted to end the strike. After the strike ended, the "consultation agreement" was concluded and approved by the board.

The job security of teachers having probationary and continuing contracts, plus the teacher-friendly "consultation agreement" provisions, prompted the Houston Principals Association ("HPA") and the two other teacher organizations to file a complaint with the Commissioner of Education contesting the teacher agreement as an illegal collective bargaining agreement. While this proceeding was ongoing at the TEA, the new Citizens Alliance for Responsible Education ("CARE") school board majority was elected to the HISD Board (Erwin Herman, William F. "Bill" Russell, Hazel "Shug" Bracken, and John Mullins). The CARE Board instructed us to draft administrators' contracts which were as self-perpetuating as legally possible, so the administrators would have the same protections teachers enjoyed through their probationary and continuing contracts. We dutifully drafted these contracts, which were "evergreen" in that any contract took an affirmative vote by the board not to continue an administrator's employment.

Ultimately, virtually all provisions of the teachers' "consultation agreement" were placed in board policy with the provision that the board alone had the authority to make policy. The administrators' evergreen contract form was changed, with the aid of a Commissioner of Education's decision. In the 1990s, the legislature authorized school districts that had adopted probationary and continuing contracts to issue term contracts to future teachers. Another change to the administrators' contracts was made in the 1990s to give the board and superintendent more control of administrators' employment. The no-strike laws reviewed earlier remain in application and effect.[14] This strike, and the assertion of power by teachers and their unions here and nationally in the late 1960s and 1970s, have been factors in the teaching profession losing some of the prestige it historically enjoyed.

Houston's Desegregation Case – The Beginnings, Magnets, Westheimer, Metropolitan, Unitary Status, and Settlement

The Beginnings

No event or case has had more impact on me or the development of Bracewell's school law practice and my professional life than the HISD desegregation case, *Delores Ross, et al. v. HISD,* No. 10444, United States District Court for the Southern District of Texas.[15] The case began with the filing of a complaint in United States District Judge Ben C. Connally's court by black lawyers Weldon Berry and Francis Williams, in 1956. This was after the Supreme Court's 1954 decision finding a constitutional violation in "separate but equal" schools in *Brown v. Board of Education*, and the Supreme Court's 1955 decision where the remedy for the constitutional violation was addressed.[16] The Supreme Court directed that segregated schools must be desegregated "with all deliberate speed." (Weldon Berry and Francis Williams could not join the Houston Bar Association in 1956 because only whites could be members. The HBA became integrated in 1965 during the presidency of James Kronzer.)

The Houston desegregation case had five United States District Court judges preside over it during its pendency from 1956 through 1989: Judges Ben C. Connally, James Noel, Finis Cowan, Robert O'Conor, and John V. Singleton. The case finally terminated with a five-year settlement agreement in 1984, which expired in 1989. A case involving the desegregation of a major southern city like Houston cannot be fully addressed in reflections such as these, so I have attached a chronological listing of all orders, reported and unreported, entered in the case, plus relevant Supreme Court decisions, as Appendix A. Copies of all the orders are included in bound volumes in my possession.

It is fair to say that historically the HISD Board of Education actively resisted the desegregation of its schools, then dragged its feet in the years preceding the 1969 school board election. Houston's public schools, and those throughout the South, had always been segregated by race, white and black, so integrated schooling presented a significant social change. In 1968, the United States Supreme Court in *Green v. Board of Education*,[17] rejected freedom of choice as an acceptable desegregation technique and declared that desegregating with "all deliberate speed" meant "now." After extensive hearings in 1969, Judge Connally found that the HISD continued to be illegally segregated, so real change became inevitable.

After the CGS slate, Dr. George Oser, Eleanor Tinsley, Dr. Leonard Robbins, and Rev. D. Leon Everett won the 1969 school board election, it was clear that the HISD would be desegregated. Attorney Joe Reynolds, who had facilitated the HISD's board policies on desegregation, resigned as HISD's attorney, and Jim Kronzer was hired to represent the HISD in desegregation matters. Bracewell & Patterson was hired in January 1970 to represent the HISD in all other matters, and in January 1971, we took over the desegregation case. Little did I know that my involvement in the desegregation of the HISD would be my career case, lasting until the expiration of a five-year settlement agreement on September 10, 1989.

Judge Connally's 1969 desegregation plan, which significantly changed school attendance zones, was modified by the Fifth Circuit on August 25, 1970 to include the pairing or clustering of eleven black schools with eleven white schools to reduce the number of one-race black schools (more than 90 percent black). Pairing would require busing—and to make matters worse, the schools identified as white schools were overwhelmingly Hispanic. Hispanics had been historically regarded as white in the HISD. Furthermore, many Anglos had moved from the "paired schools" to other HISD schools, or to the Houston suburbs. As a result, many of the paired schools the trial record reflected as being majority white schools were largely Hispanic or had become one-race black schools.

The CGS Board, new Superintendent George Garver, and all segments of the community, including blacks and Hispanics, were not enthusiastic about the pairings of largely black and Hispanic students. The pairings probably created the greatest disruption ever in Houston's desegregation efforts which, for a southern city, were not particularly disruptive due to the presence of Judge Connally and the leadership of the business community and African-American leaders. Some in the Hispanic community boycotted HISD's schools after the pairings were ordered and started "huelga," or strike schools. The pairings were slowly implemented, but they were destined to last only a short time as no party or political segment in the community wanted busing, especially to mix black and Hispanic students.

A hotbed of discontent over the desegregation order and other actions of the CGS-controlled school board centered on those living in a geographic area running from Loop 610 W (the Galleria area) along Buffalo Bayou to the western boundary of the district (Highway 6). People from this area circulated a petition to create the proposed Westheimer Independent School District ("WISD"). It was widely believed that the proposed district was primarily an effort by its organizers of the then-90% white area to avoid having their children go to school with black students and having their children taught by black teachers. Lower taxes and higher property values may have motivated others. Some probably really believed a smaller district would improve education.

The Harris County Board of Education (one of only two county boards remaining in the state at the time, Dallas being the other) conducted hearings on the proposed district's creation at Second Baptist Church on Woodway. The Harris County Board approved the proposed district's creation, but Judge Connally stopped it for three years through an injunction. We had no idea that a different judge would be presiding three years later who would attempt to give the proposed district new life. More on that later.

As noted earlier, the CGS board, elected in 1969, was voted out of office in 1973 by the CARE slate of Erwin Heinen, William "Bill" Russell, Hazel "Shug" Bracken, John Mullins, and Rev. D. Leon Everett (who switched from the CGS slate to CARE). These trustees' main focus was quality education, economic stability, and getting rid of the "Singleton Ratio," which was a provision all Fifth Circuit desegregation orders were required to have by virtue of its decision *Singleton v. Jackson Municipal School District.*[18] In

1970, two-thirds of the students were white in the HISD's segregated system, and two-thirds of the teachers were also white. When the black teachers were reassigned throughout the district, it resulted in historically black schools having two-thirds of their black teachers replaced by two-thirds white teachers. A large number of the white teachers assigned to teach mostly black children were inexperienced and unprepared to teach in predominately black schools. The African-American community felt that the laws designed to help them had again disadvantaged them.

The CARE-controlled board elected in November 1973, with Rev. D Leon Everett as its president, set about making changes. These changes started with Superintendent George Garver. Board member John Mullins told me that my job was to get George to leave for a second time so the CARE trustees could choose their superintendent. Garver had been fired in 1971 when he proposed the termination of a long-term African-American high school principal who used the proceeds from the school vending machines for his private purposes. The principal was a friend of Rev. Everett's, and he was represented at the school board hearing by former HISD attorney Joe Reynolds. Rev. Everett switched sides, and the board voted four to three to not fire the principal. The board then turned around and voted four to three to fire George Garver, who was rehired after three members of the board who voted to fire him were defeated in the November 1971 school board election.

George and I had worked together since he first arrived at the HISD from Michigan. George was a professional who understood politics and what needed to be done, so we put together his modest (at least by today's standards) resignation and settlement agreement. Longtime HISD administrator, Dr. Charles Nelson, served as HISD's interim superintendent. Billy Reagan—the former superintendent of the North East ISD in San Antonio, who served in the HEW Office of Education and then at Region IV Education Service Center—was hired as the new HISD superintendent in 1974.

Billy was bright, energetic, and, above all, politically astute. Before long, we had the board of education understanding that getting rid of the "Singleton Ratio" was more of a legal problem than they thought. *Singleton* was the law, and its mandate to have racially mixed teaching staff at each school simply could not be eliminated. We did get Judge Connally to add some flexibility in assigning teachers to school by race, and a longitudinal study of student achievement was launched to determine if the race of the teacher had any impact on the achievement of students by race. The longitudinal study (one following the same students over the years and not classes of students), led by HISD's Michael Say and Ronnie Veselka, and Texas A&M University Professor James McNamara, did not reveal any statistically significant differences in achievement by students based upon the race of their teachers. The study did show lower student achievement by students taught by the less-experienced teachers and by students taught by very senior teachers nearing retirement.

The Magnet School Program

I received a call from Billy Reagan early one Friday afternoon that ultimately offered me one of my most rewarding opportunities as a lawyer, the creation of the magnet school program. I arrived at Superintendent Reagan's office about 1:00 p.m., where he announced that he had the solution to end the pairing of the twenty-two elementary schools.

Billy said he wanted to use magnet schools whereby a specialty program offered at a school would attract students like a magnet. He said the schools should be open to anyone. When I said that wouldn't work under the desegregation order, Billy challenged me to come up with something that would work. "I appreciate your telling something won't work legally, but your job is to find a way for this plan to be legally acceptable." I reminded him of the Vanguard Elementary at River Oaks Elementary, the High School for the Performing Arts, the High School for Health Professionals, and the Barbara Jordan Institute, specialty schools which had been developed in 1971 by the previous administration and board. To avoid these open enrollment campuses from having racially identifiable student bodies, we had set up pretty strict racial goals for students attending each specialty campus. Some student seats reserved by race were held open all year to ensure that the campus principals would not fill the slots with dominant-race children after the initial enrollment was completed and the racial restrictions were lifted.

Billy called different administrators in and out of his office all afternoon, testing various aspects of the proposed concept. Billy knew magnet schools, or any other desegregation program, would only be acceptable by the community as an alternative to the paired schools if it was examined by and came from a community task force whose members included some harsh critics of the HISD. Deputy Superintendent Gonzalo Garza, a longtime and well-respected HISD administrator, chaired the Quality Integrated Education ("QIE") Task Force composed of a broad and diverse group of community members. The task force conducted hearings, called upon consultants, and looked at all alternatives to the pairing. Under the Fifth Circuit's 1970 decision, any substitute plan for pairing would have to provide the same or greater degree of desegregation as contemplated by the pairing of the elementary schools. With three dissenters who filed a short report, the QIE Task Force recommended the adoption of a comprehensive Magnet School Plan. The board of education approved the appointment of the QIE Administrative Task Force to develop an implementation plan.

Little did I realize that Billy's masterful inclusion of people with different views but with a commitment to a common goal—the elimination of the pairings of the twenty-two schools—was what we hail today as a "collaborative" effort. I have used this process many times over the years to develop solutions to challenges and for strategic planning. Consultants have refined this model of bringing people with different backgrounds and interests together to achieve a common goal; they call the result generated by the collaborative process a "collective impact."

An administrative team headed by Deputy Superintendent Faye Bryant developed the QIE Magnet Plan using the concepts of a whole school being a magnet, adding a specific program to the school's regular program and establishing a school of transfer students to study a focused program within one existing school. Free transportation was offered for magnet transfers. The magnet schools were chosen to integrate one-race schools and to stabilize schools whose student populations were trending toward becoming one-race. These schools had classroom space available and their principals were supportive of the effort. To ensure a more comprehensive mixing of students on at least a part-time basis, cluster centers were developed whereby students from one-race white and black schools were brought together to address a special issue, such as ecology, literature, or world trade, for a week.

It was a challenge getting the implementation plan developed and documented so we could seek the approval of the Justice Department and the NAACP Legal Defense and Education Fund. We ultimately received consent from the Justice Department and the NAACP, and, in July 1975, Judge James Noel signed the order to implement the Magnet School Plan in lieu of the pairings beginning with the 1975-76 school year. This comprehensive HISD Magnet School Plan was a first for the nation. Many have told me, and I firmly believe, that the magnet schools have over the succeeding decades provided attractive, quality programs. These programs have kept many engaged families of all races and ethnicities, but especially Anglos, in the Houston public schools. Our children, Jonathan and Catherine, both attended Lamar High School, the business magnet, and Catherine attended the Lanier Vanguard Middle School.

Billy Reagan always had a cadre of people working with him. He thought so quickly and moved ahead so rapidly that he left a wake of unfinished tasks. He inundated board members with reams of paper covering many subjects. People commented that trees quaked when Billy Reagan got an idea or saw something he wanted to share. These fine people—Mike Say, Ronnie Veselka, Pat Shell, Maureen Singleton, Trudy Herolz and others—would follow up on what was needed to implement whatever Billy had fashioned. History has proven that in many cases, Billy was a man ahead of his time. Maureen ultimately went to law school and became a stalwart in Bracewell's public law practice, before leaving with others to form Thompson & Horton.

The Proposed Westheimer Independent School District

The movement to create the proposed Westheimer Independent School District ("WISD") in the then-90% white area, including the Galleria and along Buffalo Bayou and south to Westheimer Road, was the most divisive and intense of the desegregation issues. Buffalo Bayou had changed course over the years and was reconstructed upstream by the U.S. Army Corps of Engineers. Some segments of the Spring Branch ISD, and a very small part of the Katy ISD, were left on HISD's south side of the reconstructed bayou. By using the reconstructed bayou as the proposed boundary, the proponents could technically comply with the state statutory requirement to take territory from "two contiguous districts."

The proponents easily secured the required signatures to present a petition to the Harris County Board of Education whose members were also supportive of the proposed district. The Harris County Board's lawyer, Dick Sedgley, was openly supportive of the proposed district. The Spring Branch administration was also openly supportive of the creation. Dr. H. M. Landrum, the SBISD superintendent, at first refused to provide Mike Say and me with the SBISD Iowa test scores, but finally did so after threats of a lawsuit. The Iowa test scores of the HISD elementary schools in the Westheimer area of HISD proved to be higher than the SBISD elementary Iowa test scores just across Buffalo Bayou. So much for the arguments that SBISD schools were better, but the Harris County Board's vote to allow creation of the district was a foregone conclusion. In 1973, Judge Connally enjoined the proposed district's creation for three years.

Judge Connally retired and Judge James Noel took over the case. Judge Noel had approved in 1975 the comprehensive magnet school plan discussed earlier, and, through an agreed motion and order, changed the number and composition of the court-appointed Biracial Committee to reflect the growing Hispanic student population. The reconstructed Tri-Ethnic Committee had four Anglos, four African-Americans, and two Hispanics, a reflection of the then-HISD student population. (In 1973, the HISD Board recognized Hispanics as a separate ethnic group for student assignment and other remedial purposes). The HISD Board specifically denied that Hispanics had ever been the subject of intentional discrimination, and no court ever found that Hispanics had suffered intentional discrimination in HISD.

The Tri-Ethnic Committee evaluated HISD's compliance with the desegregation order and reported twice annually to the court. The Tri-Ethnic Committee proved to be an effective safety valve where citizens could ask questions or present concerns concerning the implementation of the desegregation order.

In 1976, the three-year injunction prohibiting the proposed WISD from going forward needed to be extended to prevent the proposed new district from proceeding. We sought an extension of the injunction from Judge Noel, who was noticeably supportive of the proposed district. We could not persuade Judge Noel to continue the injunction, so we ultimately filed suit in state court on state court issues, engaged the TEA, and even asked United States District Judge William Wayne Justice of Tyler to stop the effort. Judge Justice had jurisdiction of the statewide desegregation order under *U.S. v. Texas* (known as Civil Action No. 5281.) Since territory from three districts (Houston, Spring Branch and Katy) was involved, we felt Judge Justice should intervene. There were no children in the Spring Branch or Katy territory proposed to be taken, so Judge Justice deferred to Judge Noel. The Texas Supreme Court also denied HISD any relief on the state law issues.

During this phase of the desegregation case, I needed help. Fortunately, Woodie Jones came to the firm to work in the trial section for Bill Wilde. I'll always remember, as does Woodie, my taking him to lunch on his first day and telling him, "Welcome to the firm and to Westheimer." Woodie was an invaluable help for the duration of the Westheimer ordeal. Woodie's and my most memorable experience was our trip to Jackson, Mississippi. There we appeared before Fifth Circuit Chief Judge Charles Clark seeking a stay of Judge Noel's order allowing the proposed WISD to proceed with its operation. We flew from Houston to Shreveport to Jackson via Trans Texas Airway (later Texas International, then Continental, and now United) on a DC-3, one of the aircraft flown in the June 6, 1944 Normandy invasion.

Judge Clark took little time in declining to enter a stay in the case. We had a night flight back to Houston, so Woodie and I went across the street to a Greek restaurant where we had the best fried oysters I have ever tasted. Our return flight was "highlighted" by flying in another DC-3 through a really bad lightning storm. (This flight occurred soon after a wind shear caused a major plane crash, and it was my most frightening flying experience ever.) Years later, I met the daughter of the Jackson, Mississippi restaurant owner at a dinner party at a neighbor's home after telling my "best ever" oyster story. Woodie later moved to Austin, where he ultimately became a state appellate judge. Although Woodie lost a reelection bid in 2002, he ran again in 2008 and won. He is now a "retired" judge in private practice.

HISD's effort to defeat the proposed WISD was supported by the United States Department of Justice; the NAACP Legal Defense and Education Fund; the Mexican-American Legal Defense and Education Fund; the state of Texas through the TEA; and an important group of citizens led by attorney Bill Pannill, who contested the effort in another federal court proceeding based on the proponents failing to comply with the Voting Rights Act of 1965. The challenges to the creation of the proposed WISD brought these diverse groups together to battle a common foe.

In the middle of the Westheimer controversy, HISD called a bond election. The New York rating agencies, Moody's and Standard & Poor, were following the legal maneuverings through their newspaper clipping service and were concerned with how much of the property tax base the HISD would lose if the Westheimer district split off. How would the loss of that tax base affect the ability of HISD to service bonds, and what rating should the new bonds receive? The bond ratings by Standard & Poor and Moody's would have a huge impact on the interest rate of the bonds. In the dead of winter, I made the bond rating trip to New York, where my job was to explain the legal status of the dispute and to project where I thought we would end up.

We made a weather-delayed arrival at the Waldorf Astoria Hotel with snow and ice everywhere. Due to the miserable weather, few people were guests at the hotel, so the school board members who were along got corner suites. One of the more playful board members had a lady of the night knock on President Bill Harwell's door of the General McArthur Suite late in the evening. Bill was a deeply religious man and the joke was not initially well-received. The novelty of the event soon prevailed and everyone—including Bill, who had a sense of humor—appreciated the practical joke. I made my presentation to the newly minted MBAs who made up the reviewing committee of Standard & Poor and Moody's and returned to the legal battle in Houston. Gene Shepard, of Greer, Moreland, Fosdick & Shepard, the District's financial advisors, and Bill Stapp of Vinson & Elkins, the public finance lawyer, along with Superintendent Billy Reagan, Business Manager Linus Wright, and the school board members continued the discussions. Fortunately, the HISD retained its AAA bond rating.

Everywhere we turned, we were met with the answer that Judge Noel had jurisdiction of the issue and other judges would not get involved. Judge Noel remained committed to the proponents of the proposed WISD despite the clear evidence that the creation of the proposed WISD would harm HISD's desegregation efforts. Why was Judge Noel so supportive of the proposed district? A radio station reporter who was investigating a number of issues in the Westheimer area told me he was pulled off his inquiries of why Judge Noel favored Westheimer's creation by his station's management—he was getting "too close."

The election to create the proposed WISD was conducted in December 1976, with one of the polling places being in a garage at the end of the block in the Briarcroft subdivision where Carmela and I lived. The *Houston Chronicle* reporter who covered the HISD and education and who favored the proposed district was a salty old fellow named Elmer Bertelsen. On election day, Elmer drove by our house toward the polling place and, pointing to me (as I worked in my yard), loudly proclaimed to his wife, "There is the enemy." Carmela and I were referred to as communists and spoken of negatively behind our backs in the community. People felt so strongly about Westheimer and so negatively about my representing the HISD that Carmela and I stopped attending Christmas parties in 1976. In fact, none of us, Bill Wilde, Harry Patterson, nor I, were very popular figures because we were fighting "freedom of choice" and "quality education," and we were losing at every turn.

A second incident with Elmer Bertelsen occurred when he called our home trying to find me one Sunday night in early 1977 when I was in Billy Reagan's office. Carmela told Elmer she did not have a number for me in Billy's office, which she did not. He became belligerent and accused her of lying. She was furious, yet frightened, due to all the community flack we were receiving and to her reading *The Godfather* at the time. She called Searcy Bracewell, Harry Patterson, and Fentress Bracewell to tell them what happened and to seek their intervention. She then talked with a "cub" *Chronicle* reporter, Janet Sanders, who was dating a former Bracewell lawyer, Chip DeWitt. Janet apparently went to work on the issue because when I saw Elmer later that week at an HISD Board meeting, he was angry and belligerent to me about Carmela's calling Janet, and told me that a "cub" reporter had no stroke at the *Chronicle*. Interestingly, that was the last time I ever saw Elmer Bertelsen, as he left the education beat and soon retired from the *Chronicle*. Janet's father was United States District Judge Barefoot Sanders of Dallas, who later became the federal judge responsible for the Dallas ISD desegregation case.

After much digging, we found a reason we felt Judge Noel was so partial to the proposed WISD. Immediately after the HISD was ordered to fully desegregate in 1969, Judge Noel secured a transfer for his son from HISD's Lamar High School to the Spring Branch ISD's Memorial High School. The judge asserted in his transfer request to the Texas Education Agency that his son should have access to the best education in Houston. Judge Noel stated that such was not available at Lamar, which was recognized by most as one of the finest high schools in the state. The transfer was granted by the TEA.

Should we file a sworn motion to disqualify Judge Noel from hearing the case based upon his lack of impartiality? Bill Wilde and Harry Patterson ultimately decided that we owed the duty to our client, the HISD, so we filed it. The filing of the motion to disqualify was followed by a long period of silence and inactivity from Judge Noel, who ultimately wrote an 80-plus-page memorandum opinion denying our motion while stating why he was not prejudiced. Soon after releasing the lengthy opinion, Judge Noel retired and relinquished the HISD desegregation case, which was assigned to newly appointed Judge Finis Cowan, a former Baker Botts trial partner.

The Fifth Circuit vacated Judge Noel's order allowing the proposed WISD to proceed and dismissed as moot our mandamus to disqualify Judge

Noel. Judge Cowan went right to work, and, after an extensive hearing, he permanently enjoined the creation of the proposed WISD. At one point in the hearing, Billy Reagan was enthusiastically expounding from the witness chair about the damage the proposed WISD would inflict on HISD's desegregation effort. As he continued to talk, Billy lifted his empty water glass, whereupon Judge Cowan got up, moved down from the bench, and filled the glass with water. Billy did not miss a beat as he continued to speak.

A "moment in history" that sticks in my mind occurred at an earlier hearing in Judge Noel's court when Bill Bednar, general counsel of the TEA at the time and a Marine reserve captain who had served in Vietnam, was standing tall while being confronted by Judge Noel. Bill's co-counsel, Lynn Taylor of the Texas Attorney General's Office, wrote Bill Wilde and me a note saying, "If Bill squeezes any harder, he is going to hurt himself." We could not laugh, but it was valuable humor at a tense time. Bill has always assured us that we, as civilians, just did not know what the position of attention looked like as executed by a Marine.

Several other proposals to detach territory from the HISD surfaced in the late 1970s. Foremost among them was city of Stafford Mayor Leonard Scarcella's proposal to create the Stafford Municipal School District. Except for two blocks of HISD territory, the remaining city of Stafford was within the Ft. Bend ISD. After expressing initial objections to the idea of removing any of its territory, the HISD dropped its opposition to the district's creation. The Stafford Municipal School District was created in 1977, and Leonard Scarcella, who was first elected mayor in 1969, continued as the city of Stafford's mayor in 2018.

Two other groups expressed an interest in creating new school districts from HISD territory. One proposal was to create an east end school district that would take the downtown tax base plus the area centered along and south of the Houston Ship Channel. The other was for the cities of Bellaire and West University Place to create a municipal school district. Neither of these efforts generated sustained interest, and neither progressed beyond the discussion stage.

From late 1976, the beginning of this second effort to create the proposed WISD, to the Fifth Circuit's late 1977 ruling vacating Judge Noel's go-ahead order and sending the case back to Judge Cowan, Bill Wilde, Woodie Jones and I appeared before more than fifteen courts or tribunals on more than fifty occasions.

After enjoining the proposed WISD from proceeding, Judge Cowan told all lawyers that either the HISD was unitary or some further action had to be taken. HISD took the position that the district was unitary, meaning that the HISD had done all that was practicable in the circumstances to desegregate the school district. The judge's comment also resulted in breaking up the parties' united front we had forged to defeat the proposed WISD. The plaintiffs and defendants were back in their traditional positions of opposing each other, but with a new and profound respect for each other.

Judge Cowan left the bench to return to private practice at Baker Botts, and Judge Robert O'Conor of Laredo moved to Houston. As the newest federal judge in Houston, he took over the case. Judge O'Conor directed the TEA to evaluate options in urban education, including voluntary inter-district transfers, and also appointed lawyers Joe Jamail, Sidney Ravkind, and Ed Mallett to represent the children of the HISD. Jamail made only one loud and active appearance. Mallett attended several hearings, but said little. Ravkind came up with the idea that the HISD should be teaching in English in a different way so African-American children would feel positive about themselves. We enlisted the advice of experts in linguistics from The University of Texas Health Science Center and Baylor Medical School. Their opinions were that this different type of English was not a language but an aberration of English, and its use was not in children's best educational interests since it would not prepare them to be successful in our society. Judge O'Conor did not accept Ravkind's proposal.

Metropolitan Case

A big event for the HISD and the other Harris County school districts was the NAACP Legal Defense and Education Fund's and the Justice Department's 1979 motion to create an inter-district metropolitan case by adding as defendants to the HISD case the other twenty-two Harris County districts, plus the TEA, the Harris County Department of Education, the city of Houston, and Harris County. There was some scattered evidence of districts having sent students to other districts during the days of state law-mandated segregation. For example, Alief sent all its high school students, black and white, to HISD until the mid-1960s because it did not have a high school. Spring Branch ISD at one time had a school for black students on Clay Road. There was one African-American teacher, who also served as the principal and maintained the school, which was referred to as her school. Judge O'Conor denied the eleventh-hour motion to make the HISD suit a metropolitan one in 1980, and the Fifth Circuit affirmed in 1983. The Fifth Circuit stated that the metropolitan issues would have to be addressed in a separate suit, which was never filed.

Unitary Status

In 1980 and 1981, we presented evidence that the HISD had attained unitary status. This was disputed by the NAACP Legal Defense and Education Fund and, to a lesser extent, the Justice Department. In 1981, Judge O'Conor found that the HISD was unitary because the district had done all that was practical in the circumstances to remove the vestiges of the dual-school system. Judge O'Conor issued an order declaring the HISD unitary. The Fifth Circuit affirmed Judge O'Conor's ruling in 1983, but ordered that the case be placed on the inactive docket for three years from Judge O'Conor's 1981 ruling.

Settlement

When the three years on the inactive docket expired in 1984, we filed a motion to dismiss the case. This action was opposed by a group of six young lawyers for the "Original Plaintiffs." After extensive hearings and difficult negotiations, the parties agreed to enter into a settlement agreement wherein the case was dismissed, but with the existing remedial orders remaining in effect for five years. During the negotiations, we had one HISD Board member who would leave the HISD Board's executive session where we discussed our settlement issues and tell the plaintiffs' lawyers what we were going to propose and the strategy we were going to employ. We began to meet with individual board members to discuss strategy and were pretty general when we met with the entire board.

One of the original named plaintiffs, Delores Ross, returned to the HISD Administration Building for a ceremonial signing of the settlement agreement on September 10, 1984. We settled the attorney fees with the plaintiffs' lawyers for a reasonable amount without resorting to the court. The original plaintiffs' lawyers, Weldon Berry's and Francis Williams' estates, did not file claims for attorney fees. The settlement agreement finally expired on its own terms on September 10, 1989—ironically, my wife Carmela's birthday. What a nice present for all! After thirty-four years in the courts and eighteen years of my professional life, the last of the case was gone.

Even though the issues involved in the desegregation of a major school system evoked strong community feelings, the lawyers representing all parties, with the exception of one of the WISD lawyers, always treated each other with respect. In addition to the lawyers mentioned earlier, Joe Rich represented the United States through the Justice Department from the government's intervention in 1967 forward. Joe was the consummate professional who was a steady presence through the changes in White House administrations. Norma Cantu (Austin), Abe Ramirez (Houston) and Ricardo DeAnda (Laredo) represented the interests of Hispanics through the Mexican-American Legal Defense and Education Fund (MALDEF). In addition to Weldon Berry and Frances Williams, the original plaintiffs were represented in the end by a group of lawyers led by Lonnie Knowles and Ray Shackelford, who interestingly became co-counsel with Bracewell several years later on a major piece of litigation for the city of Houston.

Some have asked me why the Houston desegregation case was not marked with acrimony, significant demonstrations, and marches. Judge Connally was a judge who, while firm, had the ability to follow the law as it developed and constructively guide the parties. The Houston business community, led by Bob Dundas, Foley's vice president, with the help of the city's ministers and the cooperation of the press, integrated downtown lunch counters voluntarily on August 25, 1960. This was earlier than other southern cities, and doing so helped avoid extreme racial unrest. The leadership of the HISD Board, beginning with the CGS election in 1969 and continuing with those elected on the CARE slate provided constructive leadership working with all races and ethnic groups. African-American community leaders like Rev. Bill Lawson worked relentlessly within the "system" to peacefully achieve the integration of Houston's schools. Superintendent George Garver was a dedicated and creative change agent, and Billy Reagan was not only creative, but he was also a master at getting people to work together in pursuit of a common goal. To some extent, our lawyering skills and our ability to work with the other parties— plus the other lawyers' skills and willingness to do the same—played a part. These factors all worked together for the HISD to achieve unitary status while avoiding overt racial strife.

School Prayer – *Guild v. Houston Independent School District*

I began my school practice in the fall of 1970 after *Tinker* applied the First Amendment's free speech provision to students wearing black armbands to protest the United States' involvement in the Vietnam War. As recounted in another section of these reflections, I immediately became involved with a student free speech case at Waltrip High School in the HISD. On December 28, 1970, United States District Judge John V. Singleton introduced me to another aspect of the First Amendment, the Establishment Clause, when he entered an injunction against the HISD concerning prayer and other religious activities.

Guild v. HISD[19] was filed on behalf of parents at Hamilton Junior High School who did not want their child to be subjected to readings from the Bible and other religious activities, such as the Gideon Society passing out bibles at school. The case was brought by attorney Lynn N. Hughes, and it was tried on stipulated facts and oral argument. Judge Singleton' s order was predicated on the Supreme Court's 1962 and 1963 decisions in *Engel v. Vitale,*[20] and the combined cases of *School District of Abington Township, Pennsylvania v. Schepp* and *Murray v. Curlett.*[21]

Judge Singleton's order in *Guild* was never published, and he wrote no opinion. In the order, the judge prohibited school-sponsored prayer and bible reading, and forbade the distribution of bibles by the school or outside groups. Judge Singleton acknowledged that objective courses on comparative religion or the history of the Bible and similar religious books could be taught as a part of the school history curriculum. He also recognized the right of individual students and school employees to engage in personal prayer, so long as the school district did not organize or sponsor it.

As with other social changes ordered by the courts, there was unhappiness and grumbling in many parts of the community (remember that in 1970, the HISD was also implementing a comprehensive desegregation court order, and, as a result of another court order, the rules for disciplining students had just changed dramatically). We included discussions of what Judge Singleton's order meant and how it had to be followed in our legal in-services with administrators who had the responsibility for compliance. Over time, the prohibitions in the order became accepted as a part of how schools were to be conducted after the Constitution's somewhat dramatic arrival on HISD's school campuses through these various court orders.

Several Supreme Court decisions have tweaked Judge Singleton's 1970 order a bit, with many of them focusing on the application of the Free Exercise Clause and its relationship to the Establishment Clause. Nevertheless, the judge's care in following the existing law, and his foresight in not exceeding the scope of Supreme Court precedent, have made his work somewhat timeless.

Special Act Creating the Houston Independent School District of 1923 and Conflicts of Interest

When I began practicing in 1970, determining when a board member of the district had a conflict of interest in a business matter was simple: Did the trustee have a "direct or indirect pecuniary interest" in the matter? If the trustee did, the HISD could not contract with the contractor or other vendor. This absolute prohibition on the district contracting with any entity in which one trustee had a pecuniary interest was a holdover from the *Special Act Creating the Houston Independent School District of 1923.*[22]

Before the Texas Constitution was amended in 1925 to prohibit special acts, thousands of Texas school districts under the control of a city, like Houston, or county boards, were made independent of city or county control by special legislative acts. After the 1925 constitutional amendment, independent school districts were created and received their powers from the legislature by general laws. There were 4,500 school districts in Texas before the massive consolidation into about 2,900 occurred as a result of the Gilmer-Akin Act of 1949. (The Gilmer-Akin Act also dramatically changed how Texas public schools were financed.)[23] With the codification of the Texas Education Code in 1969, most of the special act-created independent school district statutes were totally repealed, while others, like the HISD' s Special Act of 1923, were repealed insofar as statutes were adopted that conflicted with or superseded provisions of the special acts. Interestingly, the HISD' s Special Act' s conflict-of-interest provision was left intact, and it was only with the adoption of Chapter 171 of the Texas Local Government Code in 1987 that the provision changed.[24]

Chapter 171 of the Texas Local Government Code is a general conflict-of-interest law that applies not only to school districts and community colleges but to cities, counties, and certain other local governmental entities. Unlike the absolute prohibition of a school district doing business with a vendor in which a trustee, or relative within the first degree by blood or marriage, has an economic or beneficial interest, the Chapter 171 conflict-of-interest statute allows a district to do business with a vendor in which a trustee, or a relative within the first degree by blood or marriage, has such an individual interest or a substantial interest through a business entity (defined in the statute). The statute requires a trustee who has a "substantial" interest (also defined in the statute) to file an affidavit disclosing that interest with the board and abstain from participating in discussions concerning the issue to be voted upon and then abstain from voting. Out of an abundance of caution, we advised our client districts that a trustee who had a substantial interest should leave the room during any discussions and vote on an issue where the trustee was required to file an affidavit.

We prepared manuals for our clients on the conflict-of-interest law and provided sample affidavits that could be used to disclose any substantial interest. The Texas Association of School Boards Policy BBFA (Legal) provides a statement of the conflict-of-interest law and related statutes with which trustees must comply, along with helpful information on compliance with the laws.[25]

Harry Patterson Gets Shot and the Birth of the Construction Manager

Splitting my time working with Harry Patterson on general school matters and Bill Wilde on school and general litigation was a challenge. After a short time, the HISD workload required my full attention. While Bill probably would have preferred that I continue to work more on non-school cases, he accommodated my need to focus on the HISD trial and general school matters.

The "no new tax" group residing in the HISD, coupled with a reaction to the election of the CGS Board in 1969, made increasing taxes through bonds to repair and renovate schools in the early 1970s impossible. An extensive bond proposal would have had no chance of passage. Furthermore, the HISD continued to lose students to the suburbs through "white flight" and the construction of more affordable housing in those areas. Finally, the condition of the HISD school facilities deteriorated to the point that the need to spend money reconditioning the schools was obvious, except to the core tax opponents and those who just did not want to support the HISD. The election of the "conservative" CARE candidates in 1973 (especially retired Ernst & Young accountant Erwin Heinen and the owner of Russell and Smith Ford, William F.

Russell) set the stage for the passage of a bond election and the development of a "pay as you go" tax set aside for planned repairs and renovations.

SpawGlass Contractors and Van Ness Architects formed a team to develop a "fast track" bid and construction system using a visionary concept they called a "construction manager." Harry Patterson began working on fitting this concept into the state's arcane school bid and construction laws. Having my hands full of lawsuits and other matters, and knowing nothing about construction law or finance, I kept my distance until the fateful night when Harry Patterson got shot. My life and practice changed forever when a robber at a fried chicken restaurant in Richmond, Texas shot Harry as he walked in to get some takeout chicken while the robbery was taking place.

Harry's wound was serious, and he was taken to Memorial Southwest Hospital. While Harry eventually recovered, he did not return to an active practice. During his long recovery, I learned about bid and construction law, and together with Frank Glass of SpawGlass, John Van Ness of Van Ness Architects, Superintendent Billy Reagan, Business Superintendent Linus Wright, Controller James Carlson, and with support from the Association of General Contractors and others, we put together the "Fast Track Bidding System." A construction manager served as the school district or owner's representative. Learning the law and how the construction industry worked while creating this system, along with the necessary legal documentation, was stressful, but I was told by the HISD Board, "Your job is not to say no but to find a way to make it work legally." I did just that, or Bracewell would probably have lost the school district's representation.

"Fast Track" was legally unassailable, and no lawsuits were ever filed to contest it. The absence of objection was aided by a lack of motivation on the part of a depressed construction market to seriously challenge a fair system where virtually all qualified companies got work. The system was efficient and cost-effective, and there was little duplication of effort. Buildings were remodeled and repaired using the funds that were set aside. "Fast Track" was very successful in quickly getting remodeling done at a low cost, while spreading the business around. As the economy improved, some construction companies wanted projects bid in bigger pieces, so they convinced the legislature to change the bid laws to disallow some key provisions of "Fast Track" bidding. By then, the school renovation objective had largely been achieved, and the HISD was ready to utilize more conventional methods of bidding dictated by the new legislation. The new laws permitted the use of a construction manager, but in a different form that is widely used today.

The adversary process was at the core of school district representation in the 1970s and 1980s, so I was trained to become a trial lawyer. Until my entry into the business side of school district representation with the construction manager and "Fast Track" bidding and construction, my school law experiences had been trial and policy development. The office practice and the trial practice were in constant conflict throughout my years of active practice. When in trial, the business side seemed to always demand attention, and vice versa.

National Organization on Legal Problems of Education and Education Law Association

As a neophyte lawyer in the fall of 1970, I was thrashing about for some source of information on school laws. There was no internet to tap into in 1970. The best I could find in Texas was J.C. Hinsley's compilation of school laws that he developed prior to the enactment of the 1969 Texas Education Code, the first legislative codification of Texas laws by specific subject matter. There were a few textbooks by lawyer/professors like Professor Reynolds Seitz, who I would later learn was a national giant in education law. The only local school law source for Texas school laws was a short pamphlet prepared by Dr. Richard "Dick" Strahan, the former president of Lee College, who had begun teaching school administration with some school law at the University of Houston. Dick, a lawyer, was also the Texas membership representative for the National Organization on Legal Problems of Education ("NOLPE").

Further inquiry led me to the national convention and annual seminar of NOLPE in New Orleans in November 1970. Carmela and I, married on September 5 of that year, attended the NOLPE meeting at the Roosevelt Hotel, now the Fairmont. What a bonanza I hit at NOLPE! This organization of lawyers, professors, board members, administrators, and labor union officials met and discussed all the current legal issues affecting school districts—and they had publications! NOLPE was organized after *Brown v. Board of Education* in 1954, largely under the leadership of Professor Martha Ware and primarily to have a forum to discuss the issues of collective bargaining and desegregation. Being the youngest attendees at NOLPE, Carmela and I were "adopted" by several older couples with whom we formed long friendships. They included Irving Evers and his wife Ronda, of Hackensack, New Jersey, and Marvin Jaffe and his wife Rhoda, of Connecticut.

Irving Evers shared his "education index," a binder in which he listed by key words the issues addressed in each school case or opinion he read. I took his system, composed mainly of New Jersey commissioners' decisions, deleted the New Jersey commissioners' decisions, and expanded it and adapted it to cover evolving cases involving education in the federal courts. After Bracewell took over the HISD desegregation case in January 1971, I created a separate index for desegregation cases. For years I used this index to find cases applicable to evolving issues by looking in the index for topics from cases I had read and recorded.

This index system ultimately became the basis for the education key word system used by Westlaw in its key number system for the *Education Law Reporter*. Now, of course, LexisNexis, Westlaw and the State Bar of Texas, as well as the internet itself, offer online research using the key word concept. While technology has taken quantum leaps since 1970, the concept of searching for key words has remained constant.

My involvement in NOLPE grew as the leadership of "older" professionals, mainly those 50 or older, were looking for younger members to do the grunt work and eventually evolve into leadership roles. As it turned out, I fit that profile and exhibited those characteristics—I came along at the right time. My first published article appeared in the *NOLPE School Law Journal*. The article "Exhaustion of Administrative Remedies," based upon my work in the HISD's Paul Kitchen experience, started a long and continuing publishing relationship for me and others at Bracewell with NOLPE, now named the Education Law Association ("ELA"). I eventually became the president of NOLPE, as have fellow Texans Bill Bednar and Bracewell partner Jeff Horner. Chris Borreca, a partner of mine at Bracewell, who is now a partner at Thompson & Horton, was ELA's president in 2008. Lynn Rossi Scott, also a former Bracewell partner in Dallas, now a partner in Brackett & Ellis of Fort Worth, was ELA's 2017 president. Wayne Haglund, of Lufkin, is ELA President for 2019. What a wonderful Texas and Bracewell legacy! Attached as Appendix-B is a list of all the presidents of NOLPE/ELA.

After writing articles came speaking at seminars, then election to the NOLPE Board in 1973. The first NOLPE board of directors' meeting I attended was at the "old" Biltmore Hotel in New Jersey, well before Atlantic City was rebuilt as a gambling mecca. This meeting exposed me to the concept of a shared bathroom down the hall of the hotel and a hamburger consisting of just a bun and meat. I wondered what I had gotten into. I soon found out that college professors and other educators could not afford to travel to higher-priced places, so they tried to go to unique, generally cheaper places, a trend that continues today under ELA Executive Director Cate Smith. (I first met Cate when she was executive director of my law fraternity, Delta Theta Phi.) Also, Marion "Mac" McGhehey, the executive director of both NOLPE and the Kansas Association of School Boards, was an expert on low-cost travel. Mac's personality and willingness to work for almost nothing was the reason the NOLPE headquarters was in Topeka, Kansas, the home of *Brown v. Board of Education*. (NOLPE, renamed Education Law Association in 1996, moved to Dayton, Ohio in 1997 and Cleveland, Ohio in 2013.)

Two memorable events occurred at separate NOLPE meetings at the Broadmoor Hotel in Colorado Springs before the Broadmoor was renovated and enhanced to become a premier national conference center. One involved two former Marines who both served as NOLPE presidents, Gus Steinhilber and Bill Bednar, who celebrated the Marine Corps' November 10 birthday at the Broadmoor bar until it closed. I stayed with them for a while, but it was clearly their birthday celebration and were they enjoying it!

The second event again involved drinking beer at the Broadmoor, but this time Carmela was with me at the Broadmoor's Golden Bee, a grand bar across the street from the hotel's main building. The national General Counsel for the American Federation of Teachers and I became engaged in a long discussion about two contentious AFT cases Houston Executive Director, Gayle Fallon, had filed against the HISD. We developed a real rapport, and several months later the two AFT cases against HISD got resolved. I'll never know if drinking beer at the Golden Bee with the AFT General Counsel was a factor in the dismissals, but NOLPE again provided the forum for professionals from different perspectives to meet and develop an understanding of each other's positions.

Several other NOLPE events occurred at the San Francisco meeting when our young son, Jonathan, accompanied us for a stay at the Hyatt. He and Carmela visited Alcatraz, and on the ferry back to the mainland, they were dive-bombed by a huge Pacific Coast gull who left its signature mark on Carmela's coat. The Hyatt cleaners, located in the depths of the hotel, did a magnificent job of restoration! The next morning, Bill Bednar and I engaged in an early morning run along a deserted Embarcadero. Bill and I were witness to the vision of a woman of almost mystical beauty running towards us in what seemed to be slow motion. Even today, Bill and I wonder if she was real or a product of two runners' highs.

Throughout the years, NOLPE/ELA meetings and publications continued to provide me with early access to breaking legal issues and knowledgeable professionals with whom to talk. Instant access through internet technology is now utilized by ELA in providing information on breaking education law news. ELA continues to emphasize the benefits of in-depth discussion of new issues and interdisciplinary and non-advocacy networking of professors, lawyers, and administrators.

The Evolution of School Lawyer Organizations

Attorneys representing school districts in the 1970s and 1980s had common needs. After the *Brown v. Board of Education* cases in 1954 and 1955, legal issues in the schools started a long boil that has only recently leveled off in the early twenty-first century. School district lawyers found they needed a forum to meet and discuss common issues without "the other side" being there. NOLPE had a non-advocacy, inclusive format, a forum where people on all sides of the issues could debate, discuss and network, so NOLPE did not meet this need. The National School Boards Association's Council of

School Attorneys ("COSA") was born in 1967 as a national school district advocacy organization under the leadership of San Diego's General Counsel Tom Shannon. (Tom, who was president of NOLPE in 1972, later became the executive director of the National School Boards Association and is now retired and living in Virginia.) Next is the story of how I got involved in the State Bar of Texas School Law Section and National School Boards Association's Council of School Attorneys.

The School Law Committee of the State Bar of Texas – Later, the School Law Section

Lawyers who represented Texas school districts in the 1970s were looking for an organization through which they could network, but the school lawyer leadership did not want to organize through the Texas Association of School Boards ("TASB"). The TASB was perceived as having too narrow a focus and being too controlling. A professional alternative was sought, and it was achieved by school district lawyers becoming a standing committee of the State Bar of Texas. Once the membership became large enough, the State Bar rules provided that the committee could evolve into a section.

The organizational meetings of the School Law Committee were called by Cecil Morgan in 1971. These meetings were held at Warren Whitham's and Franklin Spafford's Dallas offices in the Adolphus Hotel Building. The invitees were the lawyers for the major school districts who had met through a late 1960s lawsuit in Fort Worth federal court against the state of Texas over the calculation of property values by the state that adversely affected the amount of state money that flowed to urban districts. The urban districts kept their property values higher than rural districts and were correspondingly penalized when state funds were distributed based upon taxable values. The suit was ultimately dismissed after the Peveto Committee of the Texas House of Representatives made its report on appraisal practices and the legislature took corrective action to better equalize property values across the state for tax purposes. The Peveto Report resulted in the creation of county-wide appraisal districts and the State Property Tax Board.

Cecil Morgan of Fort Worth, Warren Whitham of Dallas, Ralph Langley of San Antonio, Grant Cook of Houston, Morris A. Galatzan of El Paso, and Harry Patterson of Bracewell were invited to the Dallas meeting. Harry Patterson was in Alice bird hunting on the day of the first meeting, so he sent me in his place. Bylaws were written, and after approval by the State Bar Board of Directors, the group became organized as the School Law Committee of the State Bar of Texas. The initial annual dues were set at $3.00. Cecil Morgan, the "Dean" of Texas school law, served as the first chair of the School Law Committee. The initial membership of the School Law Committee was exclusively school district attorneys, and the Committee's first seminar was presented at the State Bar's 1972 Annual Meeting in Houston.

A significant meeting that solidified the section's membership was held at the Executive Inn (now a Doubletree) at Dallas' Love Field to discuss the implementation of the 1973 Open Meetings Act and the legality of school districts purchasing liability insurance. It was at this meeting that Warren Whitham presented a draft of a sample meeting notice with a process for complying with the newly enacted Open Meetings Act; versions of Warren's original notices continue to be used by school districts and other governmental entities today. By 1974, the Section had 236 members. Each of the founders, Cecil Morgan, Warren Whitham, Ralph Langley, Grant Cook, Morris Galatzan, and I, served as the chair of the School Law Section. Everyone who has served in that position is listed on Appendix-C.

Early additions to the group that created the Section included: J. W. Gary of Corpus Christi, Tanner Hunt of Beaumont, Bob Cox of Odessa, Rick Peebles of Baytown, Bill Bingham and Bill Bednar of Austin, Jim Deatherage of Irving, Paul Lyle of Plainview, Don Dean of Amarillo, Sam Sparks (now a U.S. District judge), and Bud Null of Victoria.

In 1974 and 1977, the School Law Section hosted receptions for the attorneys attending the National School Boards Association's Council of School Attorneys annual seminars in Houston. In 1978, attorneys representing school districts created the Council of School Attorneys, which was affiliated with the Texas Association of School Boards and the National School Boards Association.

The establishment of the Council of School Attorneys as a school boards' advocacy organization could have spelled the end of the School Law Section, but it did not. Jim Deatherage of Irving, Bill Bednar of Austin, and I led an effort to ensure the continued viability of the Section by recruiting lawyers for Section membership who did not represent school districts but instead represented plaintiffs and employee organizations. As these new members became actively involved in the Section's leadership, the Section's future as a non-advocacy information sharing and networking organization on the model of the National Organization on Legal Problems of Education (now the Education Law Association) was solidified. Jay Brim of Austin, Neal Adams of Bedford, Karen Johnson, Jeri Stone and Lonnie Hollingsworth of Austin, were early leaders from the non-school-district school practice. The Section is now a vehicle through which lawyers who represent diverse and different interests find common ground to discuss education law issues.

In the late to mid-1980s, probably 1985 or 1986, at a State Bar of Texas annual meeting in Dallas, Section Chair Charles Thompson from Atlanta, pointed out that the Section had a lot of money in the bank and was not doing anything with it. Jay Brim, Janet Horton, Rick Peebles, Karen Johnson, Tom Garner, Merri Schneider-Vogel and others suggested that the Section might consider a summer retreat at a resort location and invite families. The proposal developed legs, and the first School Law Section retreat was held at Tapatio Springs, west of San Antonio near Boerne. The retreat featured a Friday and Saturday morning seminar for continuing legal education purposes, with a golf tournament on Friday afternoon. Friday night included a communal dinner of lawyers and their families. The Section picked up the common costs and the attendees paid for their travel, housing, greens fees, and incidental expenses. The event was an instant success, and it has been the centerpiece for the development of camaraderie among practitioners from all sectors of education law for which the Section is recognized.

University of Texas graduate Tom Garner and Texas A&M former student Neal Adams had a contentious case in Port Lavaca which initially did little for building their personal relationship. With a little outside mediation I provided at Tom's request, and their diligence to serve their respective clients, the matter was resolved and the two became great friends. (I grew up in Lolita, a community about 18 miles from Port Lavaca.) Although I knew Tom well, my involvement in the mediation was my first meeting with Neal. As the years passed, both Tom and Neal served as chairs of the School Law Section, and each thought he was the better golfer. With Tom's death, the section's golf tournament was named the Tom Garner Memorial Golf Tournament.

In 2012, Neal Adams and Janet Horton put forth a proposal to recognize school law practitioners for their lifetime achievement. The first was given in 2012, and with humility it was dubbed the "Kelly Frels Lifetime Achievement Award." Jay Brim, Dorcas Green, Bill Bednar, Neal Adams, Janet Horton, Jim Walsh, and David Thompson have received the award. The Dean of the School Law Section, Cecil Morgan, and past chair, Tom Garner, have been given the Lifetime Achievement Award posthumously.

The School Law Section now has over 600 members and is governed by an executive committee whose membership represents all areas of the state and reflects the practice diversity of the section's membership. The section continues to conduct its annual seminar retreat each summer at resort locations in San Antonio, Austin and Galveston where families are welcome. The Section also publishes a newsletter and periodically sponsors other seminars. Besides my serving as chair of the School Law Section in 1980-82, Bracewell partners Jeff Horner, Janet Horton, Lisa Brown, Merri Schneider-Vogel and Lynn Rossi Scott have served in that role. Bracewell's former associate Elneita Hutchins-Taylor, now general counsel at HISD, has also served as chair.

The National School Boards Association's Council of School Attorneys

The National School Boards Association ("NSBA") and American Association of School Administration ("AASA") convention was in Houston in 1974; along with the school board members and administrators came their lawyers. The School Law Section of the State Bar leaders decided we needed to give our fellow school district lawyers a Texas welcome with a cocktail party at the Whitehall Hotel. Grant Cook was the chair of the Section, and he appointed me, the secretary and treasurer, to raise the money and organize the cocktail party. A number of firms contributed up to $50 each, and for $500+ we had a great cocktail reception at the seminar—complete with a piano player.

In the process of orchestrating the cocktail reception, I became acquainted with Tom Shannon, the founder of the Council of School Attorneys ("COSA") in 1967. Shannon liked the party we threw and asked me if he could submit my name to the COSA Nominating Committee to become an officer. I told Tom I was not a member of COSA and was only a fourth-year lawyer. He said they needed young blood willing to work. I became the second vice-chair of COSA at the ripe old age of 30. Being in the right spot at the right time and doing grunt work paid off again.

What I remember most about COSA are the annual seminars and the mid-year advocacy workshops we developed. I chaired the first advocacy workshop on Captiva Island, Florida, with the centerpiece being "how to try a civil rights lawsuit" (which few lawyers had actually done, especially to a jury). I became frustrated with the lack of school-related trial material available nationally, so we used mostly what we had developed at Bracewell. A subsequent seminar in Snowmass, Colorado, featured the preparation of a trial notebook.

These seminars were intertwined with cutting-edge legal issues supported with advocacy tips. They attracted real trial lawyers who became the core of COSA's membership for years to come. These early participants included: Ed Bittle of Iowa, Dean Jollay and Bob Baker of Ohio, John Ward of Louisiana, Chuck Wade and Larry French of Oklahoma, Ken Childs of South Carolina, Irving Evers of New Jersey, Fred Rausch of Kansas, Chuck Keller of Michigan, John MacDonald of Arizona, Carmella Bowns of Washington, James Deatherage, Rick Peebles and Bill Bednar of Texas, Jim Clark and Warren Kreunen of Wisconsin, Dick Bump, Jerry Caplan and Ben Craig of Colorado, Peter Popovich of Minnesota, Freeman Leverett of Georgia, and Ralph Stern of California (also a past president of NOLPE in 1983).

Other COSA workshops were held in Cozumel, Puerto Rico, Beaver Creek, and other beach and ski resorts. The NSBA's general counsel, Gus Steinhilber, and his assistant general counsel, Gwen Gregory, were very supportive of COSA's role in the NSBA and contributed significantly to COSA's development. Gus served a term as NOLPE's president in 1977 and Gwen was responsible for the NSBA's Washington lobby work and advocacy efforts. Gwen annually presented her "Supreme Court Review" at the COSA and ELA conventions. Gus and Gwen retired, with Gus and Dolores living in Maryland and Gwen and Dick splitting time between Virginia and Cozumel. Gus died in 2011. Dick was a school administrator who later did legislative work in D.C. Susan Butler, who assisted Gus and Gwen, took responsibility for COSA's operation, and she retired somewhere around 2010.

COSA provided opportunities for me and others to speak and write, and the need was certainly there as basic information was needed by all lawyers to effectively represent school districts. A common need—the effective representation of school clients—brought and held us together. Except for one early chair of COSA who unsuccessfully attempted to use his position with COSA to enhance his practice, competition for clients was never the reason lawyers wrote or spoke at these seminars. A list of the past chairs of COSA is attached as Appendix-D.

The Texas Association of School Boards Council of School Attorneys

The Texas Association of School Boards ("TASB"), a state affiliate of the National School Boards Association ("NSBA"), is mentioned in many of these reflections. The TASB was created in 1951 and has been consistently present in Texas education and in the development of the school law practice. Even though the TASB was not directly involved in the early development years of school law, its executive director of the 1970s, Cecil Rusk, invited me to the TASB San Antonio fall conventions to speak on numerous occasions.

I met Cecil through Ruby Clifton, Assistant Superintendent for Board Services of the HISD, and my speeches to the Gulf Coast Area Association of School Boards. Cecil even tried to get me to move to Austin and become TASB's lawyer. (Ruby Clifton served the HISD as board secretary for many years. She treated all board members alike and, at age 95, went to her grave in 2005 never having written about her experiences.) Orbry Holden succeeded Cecil Rusk as Executive Director, who was followed by Billy D. Walker in 1991. James B. ("Jim") Crow has been Executor Director since Billy Walker's death.

Joe Hairston and Tom Doyal joined Cecil as TASB's first in-house lawyers, and they were always open to including other lawyers in programs and other activities in the organization. After all, we school lawyers were in this together to help school districts. After finishing law school at The University of Texas in 1978, David Thompson joined TASB as a lobbyist. It was with Joe and Tom in charge that we developed the TASB policies that are now used by most Texas school districts and colleges. The original guide for these TASB model policies were those we developed for the HISD in 1970-72. I recall the many meetings we had on policy development at the TASB 11th Street office near the Capitol. Ironically, the HISD was one of the last school districts to use the TASB policy service.

In 1978, the Texas school district lawyers became a state affiliate of the NSBA's Council of School Attorneys. Texas school district lawyers needed an advocacy group, and the State Bar of Texas School Law Section's membership was, of course, open to any Texas lawyer regardless of whom the lawyer represented. Jim Deatherage was asked to serve as chair of TASB's COSA, largely because of his experience as a NSBA/COSA board member for six years. I served as chair after Jim and have been joined over the years by my fellow, now former, Bracewell partners Janet Horton, Jeff Horner, Merri Schneider-Vogel, Lisa Brown, and Lynn Rossi Scott. Former Bracewell associate, Elneita Hutchins-Taylor, now general counsel for the Houston Independent School District, has also served as chair. A complete list of the past chairs of TASB's COSA is attached as Appendix-E.

The Texas Association of School Administrators ("TASA") works closely with the TASB, and the two organizations host an annual meeting in September of the combined groups. TASB's COSA provides an advocacy seminar for school districts on the Sunday of the TASB/TASA convention.

Tom Doyal and Joe Hairston left TASB to start their own Austin school law firm and were soon joined by Jim Walsh, who began his practice with my UT Law School classmate Jerry Saegert. The firm is now Walsh, Gallegos, Trevino, Russo & Kyle P.C. After Tom and Joe departed the TASB, the lawyers' relationship with TASB began to change. TASB moved to north Austin and began to offer a host of services to school districts, including insurance such as workers compensation and officers and director's liability insurance. One reason the TASB got into "sponsoring" insurance was to make it more readily available in a tightly controlled market.

Once the TASB was in the extended service business, the organization had to staff up, and this included its own legal staff. Ray Morrison, a former HISD Board member, became TASB's general counsel, and other lawyers were hired to provide advice to school districts. When Ray came to power at TASB, Bracewell and I did not fare well at the TASB, even to the point that TASB appointed lawyers from other firms to represent HISD and other Bracewell school district clients who had TASB insurance coverage when the districts were sued. These events, especially the administration of the insurance program, ushered in a changed relationship with Bracewell and many other school district lawyers. Fortunately, TASB today has a different direction and has again become much more inclusive of all school lawyers under the leadership of Joy Baskin, the current TASB general counsel.

TASA's longtime Executive Director Johnny Veselka (who retired in 2018) and Bracewell's former partner, David Thompson, have had many joint experiences, and Neal Adams has been TASA's long-term lawyer. Philip Fraissinet, formerly a Bracewell partner and now Managing Partner of Thompson & Horton, was a law student intern at TASA while in his third year of law school.

The University of Texas School Law Conference – UT School of Law

Sometime in 1985 I was approached by Donna Passons, the Continuing Legal Education Director for The University of Texas School of Law, who asked me to chair a committee to organize and produce a school law seminar for the Law School. I contacted several lawyers, including Bill Bingham and Bill Bednar in Austin, Rick Peebles of Baytown, Karen Johnson and Jay Brim of Austin, plus several others, probably including Joe Hairston of Austin.

The first seminar was staged on March 6 and 7, 1986, in one of the Law School's largest lecture classrooms. The conference grew over the years because we had high-quality speakers, relevant topics, and the seminar was held at the right time of the year (late February or early March, when there were no other education law meetings with which to compete). The Law School also secured continuing education credit for school board members and school administration training, as well as for lawyers. An increasing number of attendees in succeeding years exceeded the Law School's physical capacity, so the seminar was moved to the main ballrooms of various hotels. The conference is now held at The University of Texas AT&T Conference Center, where attendance has leveled off at about 400.

The head of the annual planning committee is now the chair of the State Bar's School Law Section. Lawyers from the state's professional educational organizations are included, along with school district in-house counsel and private practice lawyers who represent clients on all sides of the docket. The program is nonpartisan and non-advocacy. Its program content is fashioned after the inclusive agenda of the Education Law Association. The University of Texas School Law Seminar has probably become the premier Texas school law seminar.

Hearings Before the Commissioner of Education and the State Board of Education

When I began practicing school law in 1970, Section 11.13[26] of the then recently codified Texas Education Code provided for education matters in dispute at local school districts to be appealed for a hearing before the Commissioner of Education who, at that time, was Dr. J. W. Edgar. A state Board of Education rule, *Procedures on Hearings and Appeals* (amended 1972),[27] required school districts to afford a due process hearing on matters of dispute before an appeal could be taken to the Commissioner. Article 5154(c),[28] the state's right-to-work statute, provided for local school board hearings on employees' grievances, so school district patrons and employees could ask the school board to hear just about any school-related complaint they had.

The hearings of local complaints were usually pretty informal, including "hearing of citizen" type proceedings where those involved had a couple of minutes to address any concern. Terminations and serious grievances were generally more formal proceedings because more was at stake. The Fifth Circuit's *Ferguson v. Thomas*,[29] and the Supreme Court's *Board of Regents v. Roth* and *Perry v. Sindermann*[30] made any hearing involving the proposed deprival of property rights under a contract subject to more significant due process requirements.[31]

Bill Wilde and I participated in a number of local hearings and in the appeal hearings before the Commissioner of Education. The hearings before the Commissioner were conducted under the Texas Rules of Evidence, so they were much like trials in district court. We would travel to Austin the day before and participate in the hearing at the old TEA building on 11th Street. Sometimes the hearings would extend to a second or third day, and we would stay at the Downtowner Hotel, a couple of blocks away.

The Commissioner's decisions were seldom appealed, but when they were, Bill and I would return to Austin for the monthly Saturday meeting of the State Board of Education. A hearing before the State Board was on the record developed in the Commissioner's hearing. Joe Kelly Butler, a former HISD school board member and president, served as the long-term chair of the State Board of Education. Few decisions of the Commissioner of Education that were affirmed by the State Board of Education were ever appealed to a state district court, so the Commissioner's decisions had virtual precedential value. Beginning in 1995, all disputes appealed to the Commissioner were heard on the record developed before the local school board, so de novo hearings are no longer conducted before the Commissioner. Paul Lyle of Plainview performed a great service when he compiled and indexed all the Commissioners' opinions for everyone's use.

William C. "Bill" Bednar, one of my UT law school classmates who had served as an assistant attorney general on school matters, succeeded Chester Ollison as general counsel of the TEA. Chester served as Commissioner Edgars' lawyer and as TEA's general counsel from 1950 to 1976. Upon Chester's retirement, Bill Bednar served in that role until mid-1979. Bill was followed by David Ryan (1979-1982), Richard Arnett (1982-1985), David Thompson (1985-1990) and Kevin O'Hanlon (1990-1993). David Anderson was TEA's general counsel from 1990 through 2016, when he retired. Von Byer is TEA's current general counsel. All the former general counsels, except for Chester Ollison, David Thompson, and David Anderson, have become lawyers in the private practice of school law in Austin. David, of course, is a partner of Thompson & Horton in Houston.

Dealing with the HEW

School desegregation activities accelerated following the passage of the 1964 Civil Rights Act, and school districts faced losing their federal funds if they did not desegregate. Some districts had one or more black schools, so when forced to integrate, most school boards simply closed the black schools and fired many, if not all, of the black teachers. The Brazosport ISD, the Sweeney ISD, the Somerville ISD, plus many others fired virtually all of their black teachers. Years later, the Office for Civil Rights ("OCR") of the Department of Health, Education and Welfare ("HEW"), filed an administrative action to cut off Brazosport's federal funds because of the terminations. (Federal education matters are now under the jurisdiction of the Department of Education.)

The OCR was serious about securing extensive money damages for all the fired teachers, to the point that payment of money damages was unrealistic even for a property-wealthy district like Brazosport. We grew frustrated with how the Dallas Regional Office OCR attorneys treated us, so Brazosport Superintendent Kenneth Wilson and I sought an audience with HEW officials in Washington, DC. I got a seat on a Texas International Airlines flight near the front of the plane for the trip to Washington, and Kenneth Wilson, a smoker, got in the last row of the smoking section.

It was a cold day in Washington, with snow on the ground. When we arrived and cleared security at the office building, we were met by HEW officials and those same Dallas office OCR lawyers, who by that time had fully briefed their Washington brethren. Wilson and I got "talked down to" in a manner I have never forgotten. We pushed back, but the government was full of bullies who were fed by the fervor of the overwhelming support of Congress, the Executive Office, and the courts to correct historical wrongs and to protect civil rights. The best I can say for the day is that we all had to stand in the snow together when the HEW building was evacuated because someone called in a bomb threat. The Vietnam War and its fallout created an uneasy atmosphere in Washington and across the nation, so bomb threats were not unusual.

I valued my health, so on the flight back to Houston I again got as close to the front of the plane as possible, but I visited Wilson in the smoking area. I asked him what he took away from the meeting. His reply was, "I learned how not to treat people who come to you with issues, and I'll always be receptive and polite to patrons and staff who have problems. I never want to treat anyone like we were treated today." I suppose the OCR lawyers learned that Brazosport would simply not fold, so the matter settled with reasonable, yet fair, payments to the fired teachers and the development and implementation of my first affirmative action recruitment plan. A similar proceeding against the Somerville ISD was likewise resolved.

School Finance – The Unending Saga

As noted earlier in the discussion of the State Bar's School Law Section, one of the first significant school finance cases was the one filed in the Ft. Worth federal court in the 1960s by the major urban districts over how assessed property values were used to distribute state funds. The lawsuit was dismissed with the adoption of the statewide ad valorem appraisal system based upon county appraisal districts overseen by the State Properties Tax Board.

The really significant challenge to the state's overall system of funding public schools was brought by private plaintiffs through the Mexican-American Legal Education Fund in the Edgewood ISD in San Antonio. The United States Supreme Court, in *San Antonio ISD v. Rodriguez*,[32] held that because the state undertook to provide public schools, the issue of inequality in funding property-poor districts was a matter of state law that did not implicate the Equal Protection or Due Process clauses of the United States Constitution.

After the Supreme Courts' *Rodriguez* decision, the battles over financing public schools have been waged in the state court systems. *Serrano v. Priest*[33] in California led the way to contest the distribution of state funds based upon the state constitution. The various Texas school finance systems have been before the Texas Supreme Court seven times over twenty-seven years,[34] with the latest decision coming on May 13, 2016. Unlike the six prior occasions, the court in *Morath v. Texas Taxpayers and Student Fairness Coalition, et al.*,[35] found that the Texas school finance scheme met the minimum constitutional standards of Article VII § 1 of the Texas Constitution.[36] The court somehow avoided holding that the recapture provisions of the finance system was a state property tax that would violate the Texas Constitution.[37]

While the 2016 Supreme Court called the Texas school finance system "Byzantine," it went to great lengths to distinguish the 2016 facts from the facts involved in the holdings of the six preceding cases. In what some have described as judicial inactivism and virtually an inexplicable deference to the legislature, then-Justice Don Willett, writing for the court, liberally cited the Coleman Report,[38] a 1966 study that concluded that the socioeconomic status of a child's parents is the best indicator of that child's education success. The more affluent a child's parents are, the better the child will achieve. Justice Willett adopted the conclusion of some commentators who believe there is only a weak correlation between public school funding and educational achievement. He stated there was no evidence of any education programs that could close the achievement gap between children from low socioeconomic families and children from more affluent families.

The Coleman Report was prepared in 1966, two years after the passage of the Civil Right Act of 1964 and only one year after the Elementary and Secondary School Act of 1965 (ESEA),[39] which began to flow federal funds to states and schools to fund remedial programs to help close the achievement gap between children from poverty and the more affluent. How the court could give a 1966 study such weight fifty years later, in 2016, seems illogical. There are numerous studies—many of which made their way into the trial court record, but ignored by Justice Willett and his brethren on the Texas Supreme Court—of successful educational interventions that have narrowed the achievement gap, notably early intervention through pre-K and other early childhood development programs.

At least for the foreseeable future, public school funding in Texas will rest with the legislature with one factual certainty: too little is being provided by the state to fund necessary programs and properly pay and train teachers. Our state leaders and the legislature have been disinclined to put more money into public education. Back in the 1950s, the state provided about 75% of the cost of operating our public schools whose curriculum was almost exclusively focused on reading, writing, and arithmetic. In the 2010s, the state of Texas pays only about 38% of the overall cost of operating Texas public schools whose curriculum is responsible for responding to the knowledge base that has been significantly expanded by advances, primarily in science, mathematics, and technology. The remainder of the cost is paid for by local property taxes, plus some federal and miscellaneous funds.

School districts like the HISD, the Spring Branch ISD, and the La Porte ISD get no net state funding. In school year 2018-2019, the state of Texas provided zero% of HISD's, Spring Branch ISD's, and La Porte ISD's costs. HISD taxpayers, through local property taxes, paid all the costs of school operation except for the 9.55% from federal funds and 2.17% from donations, gate receipts, etc. Additionally, HISD sent approximately $272 million in local property taxes to the state's general fund (which is $96 million net after subtracting state funds received) and Spring Branch ISD sent $88 million of local property taxes to the state's general fund (which is $62 million net after subtracting state funds received). These payments of local taxes to the state is through a process called recapture. In 2019, 217 of the approximately 1200 Texas school districts sent $2.6 billion of local property tax money to the state treasury.

The picture is just as stark for Texas colleges and universities, where the percentage provided by the state is as low as 14% for The University of Texas and Texas A&M. Our public universities could probably now be called "state sponsored" rather than "state supported," At the same time, legislative efforts are under way to further reduce school districts' ability to raise local property tax money, some of which is needed to pay for unfunded mandates by the legislature. The 2016 court certainly did not show any inclination to become involved—even where property-rich school districts are required to send local tax money to the state, where it is placed in the general fund and the funds can be used for any state purpose. Why this recapture of local districts' ad valorem tax money is not an unconstitutional state property tax defies logic. Hopefully the Court will overrule that holding if presented the opportunity.

In discussions with fiscal conservatives who support public school education, one comment permeates. "I don't favor just throwing money at public schools, but I would favor spending money for programs that 'work'." In my *Houston Chronicle* op-ed piece, "To Rebuild Our Schools, We Must Do More than Paint the Façade," I identified two fundamentals that must be adequately funded for our schools to work: (1) an emphasis on parenting, coupled with early childhood education; and (2) preparing, hiring, and retaining quality teachers. These factors, plus others, are addressed in more detail in these reflections.[40]

Identifying school programs and practices that "work" has always been somewhat elusive because judging the quality of programs has been evaluated subjectively. With test data now readily available, it is becoming easier to analyze programs more objectively. We may even get back to using student test data for the purpose it was historically intended—to compare student performance with the curriculum and teaching techniques, and then make changes and adjustments to improve student performance. While school districts must be held accountable using test data, I believe student testing has been overemphasized. It is easy for test data to become a punitive tool to punish teachers and schools.

A next step in data analysis is collecting test results and other reliable data and subjecting them to critical analysis to determine what programs and strategies work. Once a successful strategy, program, or process is identified, it can be evaluated for possible application by others. This application of best practices in education holds great promise for several reasons. Being data-driven, the results are more objective and reliable. Teachers and administrators will be less likely to dismiss or criticize the findings, so they should be more accepting of the findings and more willing to replicate the practice in their schools. Changing the culture of some schools from criticizing the success of others to one of embracing and emulating a successful program would be a major accomplishment.

As discussed in the reflection "Schools in Economically Diminished Areas," the Greater Houston Partnership (GHP) led a Houston area collaborative effort of school districts, many organizations, and individuals to enhance and further early childhood education. Similar early childhood focuses are under way in Dallas and San Antonio. The goal is to have all Houston-area children reading at grade level by the end of third grade. A natural extension of this effort called Good Reason Houston has been launched in conjunction with the Dallas-area organization Commit, which is the GHP's and coalition members' deep dive into student records and other data. The goal is to determine what programs and approaches work to improve student performance, and then to identify successful programs and approaches that can be replicated to improve student achievement. An overriding goal of this data-driven effort is to identify the programs that work to share with leery legislators and the fiscally conservative. Hopefully, these legislators and individuals will then support the necessary funding for their replication, the recruitment and training of quality teachers, and the other costs of school operation.

Dress Codes, Hair Regulations, and Student Walkouts

A common legal issue involving public schools in the late 1960s and early 1970s was the authority of school boards to regulate the dress and grooming of students. Cases were filed all over the country, and the results varied from court to court. Two 1972 Fifth Circuit opinions clarified the issue for Texas' public schools and colleges. *Lansdale v. Tyler Junior College*[41] invalidated unreasonable regulations of college students' hairstyles, but the court in *Karr v. Schmidt*[42] found that high school students have no constitutional right to wear their hair in a length or style that suits the wearer. *Handler v. San Jacinto College District*[43] followed by holding that colleges could not regulate the facial hair of college faculty members.

The evolution of these hair and grooming cases was reflective of the federal courts upholding more stringent regulations regarding younger students in the public school setting, while recognizing that the advanced maturity level of college students and the more open setting of colleges lessened colleges' authority to regulate dress and behavior. I have always likened these holdings by describing them as a giant pyramid, with younger children at the base and graduate school students at the apex. The schools have more responsibility for the care and safety of young children, so stricter rules and regulations are needed. The justification for regulations diminishes as the students mature and the educational environment offers more freedom and openness. This is the current legally correct expression of the age-old principle that, depending on the maturity level of a student, a school stands in loco parentis (in the place of the parent) to a child.

Once *Karr v. Schmidt* closed the federal courthouse to lawsuits contesting hair and dress regulations, students and parents focused on lobbying school boards for less-restrictive regulations. While many of the lobby efforts were successful, some students felt constrained by the regulations and literally took their complaints to the streets by walking out of school. My first experience with a walkout was at Mayde Creek High School in the Katy ISD in the 1980s, with a second major walkout at Reagan High School in the HISD during the early 1990s. Interestingly, both of these walkouts occurred during the spring, which convinced me that "in the spring, sap rises in trees and adolescents alike."[44]

In each situation, we advised the school authorities to warn the students in advance of the walkout that "walking out" was a violation of the student code of conduct and to inform them of the penalties. Once the walkout began, the school administrators used the technique we had used so successfully with the HISD teacher strike in 1971—they stood at the exits and videotaped the students who walked out. They then took roll in each class to see who was present. Those who weren't in class, but had previously been in attendance that day, were presumed to have walked out. It was pretty difficult for a student or a parent at a discipline hearing to deny participation in the walkout when the student was on the walkout video and not in a subsequent class.

Reagan High School's principal warned students that walking out was a code violation, and school administrators took videos of those walking out. Some of the Reagan students who planned to walk out apparently engaged lawyers before doing so. Many of the students demanded hearings, so the school's administration set up a number of rooms staffed by administrative hearing officers from other schools. We provided the hearing officers scripts to follow to ensure that due process was afforded each student. A number of different lawyers represented students, so we provided an equal number of school lawyers to represent the school administration. The hearings went well, with the videos and class attendance records being the primary evidence. The punishments were lenient, and the students and their lawyers seemed satisfied with the final resolution. In fact, several of the students' lawyers and I have maintained cordial professional contacts ever since.

"I Don't Like to Lose" – Dr. Tom Spencer

San Jacinto College had lost several groundbreaking lawsuits. The first was *Handler v. San Jacinto College District*,[45] a case discussed earlier that held a college could not dictate the hairstyles of faculty members. The second, *Goss v. San Jacinto College District*,[46] held that a faculty member could not be denied a contract renewal when a jury found that a substantial motivating factor in the nonrenewal was the faculty member's exercise of her First Amendment rights. Both cases were brought by attorney Larry Watts. (Larry proved to be a regular generator of business for Bracewell's school practice.)

I answered the phone one afternoon in late 1979 or early 1980, and this strong voice addressed me, "Mr. Frels, this is Dr. Tom Spencer. I have been involved in some lawsuits which we have lost. I don't like to lose, and I understand you might be able to help me." Dr. Spencer, Dr. Tom Sewell, Dr. Monte Blue, Dr. Ron Rucker and I met the next week in one of our conference rooms to explore what could be done to cut San Jacinto College's loses. Thus, began my long and rewarding relationship with San Jacinto College.

We completely rewrote the college's policies, making them specific and understandable. No one on the drafting team wanted a lot of extra words that might obscure the meaning of the policies. The board and upper-level staff were brought into the later stages of the drafting process, so everyone could have input and there would be no surprises with the final product. After the policies were adopted by the board, I conducted seminars with small groups of administration at each of the three campuses, Central, North, and South. The administrators became knowledgeable of the policies and the law related to them. They also developed a confidence in knowing what to do when a situation arose involving the application of a specific policy. We next in-serviced the faculty, so they would know what the policies covered and hopefully feel that the college wanted them to be a part of the process.

The lawsuits against San Jacinto College ceased and Dr. Spencer retired without losing another case. The college continues to include sexual harassment and other current legal issues in their administrative and staff in-services. And, of course, the administration and board continue to update the policies.

Here Is the File – *Green v. Houston Baptist University*

On a Friday afternoon in 1982, Searcy Bracewell called to tell me the board members of Houston Baptist University ("HBU") wanted me to represent them in their individual capacities in a suit by a former music professor named Green. These board members were prominent men, and they had been sued individually. They wanted someone independent of the university and the administration to protect their interests. "Here is the file, and by the way," Searcy said, "The case is set for a jury trial on Monday."

I called Jeff Davis, the lawyer for HBU, and I spent the rest of Friday afternoon preparing for meetings with the board members over the weekend. After the meetings and further reviewing the files, I felt as prepared as possible for the jury trial in Judge Ruby Sondock's district court. Actually, the Monday trial was the best of all worlds. It was a jury trial on tenure issues representing defendants who were not directly involved in the discipline resulting from the incidents that led to Professor Green's firing. I had not been troubled with conducting discovery and I knew the law, so I took the case as I found it.

The jury panel voir dire was the most fascinating I ever experienced. When Judge Sondock asked if anyone had a problem with rendering a verdict against HBU or any of the defendants, several hands shot up. One said that she was a very religious person and another that he had graduated from HBU. A man in the last row, whom I shall never forget, raised his hand and excitedly blurted out, "I could not render a verdict against God." This was a foreshadowing of how well the case would go. Why the plaintiff's lawyer did not ask to disqualify the panel is beyond me.

Green's tenure expert from the University of Houston couldn't testify without reading from his notes, and the plaintiff's lawyer could hardly ask a question that was not objectionable as being leading. The twenty-year plaintiff's lawyer proved to be a lawyer who had apparently practiced one year twenty times. It did not take the jury long to return a defense verdict.

Being Trumped by John Lewis

John Lewis, the Cleveland managing partner of Squire, Sanders & Dempsey, and I dined at the Legal Seafood Restaurant one evening during a NOLPE meeting in Boston in the early 1980s. John followed me by six years as president of NOLPE. We had a great meal and I pulled out my "new" American Express Gold Card, over which John proudly placed his "new" American Express Platinum Card. Both cards were keystones of American Express' newest initiative to offer an upgrade to the green card. "Guess I trumped you, Kelly." John got to pay for the meal.

Immigration – Undocumented Aliens

The late 1970s and early 1980s presented the first substantial wave of undocumented Mexican immigrants to Texas and the United States. Former State Bar President Orrin Johnson, who represented the Harlingen Independent

School District, approached me about a developing issue Harlingen and the other Rio Grande Valley districts faced. Mexican women were coming across the United States-Mexico border to have children who, upon birth, would be U.S. citizens. While we determined that the practice was a United States constitutional issue by virtue of the Fourteenth Amendment, we might do something about the non-U.S. citizen children who came across the border to attend Texas schools. Legislation was drafted that added "legally admitted aliens" to the Texas law for those entitled to attend the free public school of Texas, and the legislature approved the change in 1975.[47] Thus, the concept that "illegal aliens" (now, the accepted designation is "undocumented immigrants" or "undocumented aliens") were not entitled to attend Texas public schools without payment of a fee was put into play.

These undocumented immigrants began attempting to enroll in schools despite the state law that provided free access only to "legally admitted" aliens. Several cases were filed in Houston's state and federal courts, and we always got them dismissed or we won summary judgments.[48] In 1979, cases filed in the federal courts all over the state—except for the Tyler ISD case, which was a class action in Judge William Wayne Justice's United States District Court in the Eastern District of Texas—were consolidated for trial in United States District Judge Woodrow Seals' court by the Judicial Panel on Multidistrict Litigation. Among the school district lawyers with me representing school district defendants in Judge Seals' court were Jack Tidwell of Odessa, Stanley Baskin of Pasadena, and Rick Peebles of Baytown. The Texas Attorney General sent Assistant Attorney General Susan Dasher to represent the state of Texas in Judge Seals' court and the one case in Judge Justice's court.

Once the state of Texas showed up in Judge Seals' court, all the school districts told the school district lawyers to withdraw and leave it to the Attorney General's Office and Susan Dasher. Dasher was tight with the plaintiffs, and she did little to present any compelling evidence of the state's interest in the law she was defending. She also was defending a statute which prior Attorney General John Hill had opined would be unconstitutional if enacted by the Legislature.

At the only hearing in Houston we all attended, Judge Seals made several statements of interest. He began by telling the assembled group what a great school lawyer I was and they should all pay attention to what I said. I had had numerous cases in Judge Seals' court and had successfully supported him on appeal when he ruled correctly and reversed him when he ruled the wrong way. We personally liked each other, despite his first comment about me to Bill Wilde in chambers on my first case, *Kitchen v. HISD*—"Wilde, who is he? He looks like a John Bircher." I leaned over to Tidwell and said, "Jack, he usually doesn't make those complimentary comments unless he is going to rule against my client."

Judge Seals' other comment during the case, to plaintiff's lawyer Isaias Torres, is burned in my memory. It was something to the effect of, "Mr. Torres, I know what you folks want, you want to reclaim Texas and have the United States border at the Red River." Later in the trial, a newspaper reported that Judge Seals said something like, "I don't know of anything important written in Spanish." I knew what the result of the case would be; Judge Seals would rule for the plaintiffs. Needless to say, the plaintiffs prevailed before Judge Seals.[49] Judge Justice ruled in the Tyler ISD case that prohibiting undocumented children from Texas public schools without paying tuition violated the Constitution, and the Fifth Circuit affirmed his decision.[50] The United States Supreme Court consolidated the decisions of Judges Justice and Seals for briefing and argument under the style of the Tyler ISD case, *Plyler v. Doe*. The Supreme Court ruled that illegal aliens were persons for Equal Protection analysis under the Fourteenth Amendment, and that the enforcement of the nation's immigration laws is a matter solely for Congress.[51] Undocumented children were entitled to attend Texas public schools without the payment of tuition.

It is interesting to examine this case in the context of discussions in the twenty-first century on immigration and the effect of illegal immigration on our schools, our health care system, business, and life in general. Although Congress enacted a comprehensive immigration law in 1986, the executive branch, Democrats and Republicans alike, never really enforced it. Congress did not appropriate sufficient funds for presidents to do so. The immigration courts continue to be inadequately staffed and funded to promptly process cases, with the result being gridlock. This collective inaction has resulted in a substantial number of undocumented immigrants entering the United States, having children who are U.S. citizens, and otherwise establishing their lives in America. Many children were brought to the United States from other countries, were educated in our schools and many are now adults. As a consequence, we must have another comprehensive round of legislation similar to 1986, but this time the immigrant laws must be enforced. Congress' current inability to enact a comprehensive immigration law is clearly having an impact on schools, health care, businesses, and especially the lives of the undocumented immigrants who live in the shadows of our society.

A second case involving undocumented immigrants involved custodial employees of the Pasadena ISD who used the social security numbers of U.S. citizens for employment. When the Pasadena ISD found out that the custodians had lied about the social security numbers, they fired the "at will" custodians for lying and using others' social security numbers. In what I feel is one of the most outrageous decisions by a federal judge, United States District Court Judge Gabrielle McDonald enjoined the Pasadena ISD from firing the custodians. It was only after sufficient public outrage and the criticism of her decision by legal commentators that she finally reversed herself after the trial on the merits.[52] A significant reason she changed her position, in my opinion, was the exceptional brief, only ten pages long, written by Bracewell associate Arturo Michel, who became Houston's city attorney in 2004. Arturo is now a partner with Thompson & Horton.

Sovereign Immunity and Student Injuries

Through the years, a frequent legal claim against school districts has been for injuries to the person or property of students, teachers, and others. The most common claims I encountered as an associate in the 1970s were for damages caused by the operation of vehicles, and the second most common were for student injuries in classes or in sports. Under Bill Wilde's direction, I always filed a plea to the jurisdiction based upon the school district having no liability under the doctrine of sovereign immunity; i.e., the English law doctrine that "the king can do no wrong." This was a clearly established legal principle in Texas that was confirmed by the Texas Supreme Court in *Barr v. Bernard*.[53] Some judges required that we file a motion for summary judgment, but the cases always got dismissed.

In 1985, the Texas Legislature enacted the Texas Tort Claims Act.[54] School districts and community college's sovereign immunity was legislatively waived, but only for injuries sustained by school employees negligently operating motor-driven vehicles in the course of their employment. The school districts bought liability insurance to cover these claims, which were handled by insurance defense lawyers.

After being shut out of Texas courts for student injuries, plaintiffs' lawyers, especially the ever-creative Larry Watts, resorted to the federal courts, attempting to create a constitutional tort for student injuries. One of the first cases I handled was *Vorhies v. Conroe Independent School District*,[55] where a student cut off his hand using a circular saw in a shop class. The United States District Court dismissed the case, refusing to find that there was a cause of action arising under the United States Constitution. Similar student injury cases met the same fate.

The United States Supreme Court opened the federal courthouse door slightly to egregious negligent acts in *Monell v. Department of Social Services of the City of New York*[56] and *Parratt v. Taylor*.[57] The holdings in these cases are so narrow that virtually no plaintiffs can slip through the small crack. Also, except for injuries caused by the negligent operation of motor vehicles, Texas school districts remain immune from student injury suits.

Open Meetings, Open Records, and Privacy

The 63rd Texas Legislature of 1973 was reform-minded in the wake of the Sharpstown scandal that occurred after the adoption of certain banking legislation in the 1969 legislative session. The Texas Open Meetings Act[58] and the Texas Open Records Act[59] provided substantial transparency into the operations of Texas' governmental entities. The effects of these laws on school districts and community college operations provided an immediate and lasting focus for school lawyers.

The Open Meetings Act

Prior to 1973, public school districts and community colleges conducted most of their business at public meetings. The HISD, and perhaps other school districts, often used a process to vote on issues without calling a meeting. This process, called "polling the board," involved the board president or a school board staff member calling each board member with a proposal to be voted on, whereupon the board members would verbally vote yes, no, or abstain. There was no formal meeting of the board when a polling occurred, so these proposals were not discussed publicly. The results of these polls would then become the action of the board, and the votes taken by the polling would be included in the board minutes. Boards could discuss virtually any issue in a closed or executive session.

With the passage of the 1973 Open Meetings Act ("OMA"), calling and conducting board meetings changed. The OMA prescribed how the meetings of public bodies in Texas must be noticed and conducted. The date, time and place of any meeting of a quorum of the board members had to be posted in a place accessible to the public. The requirement that the agenda items to be considered at any meeting had to be listed in the public notice and the requirement that items to be discussed in closed or executive sessions had to be listed were huge changes from the way things had been done for years. Warren Whitham of Dallas, the chair of the State Bar's School Law Section, developed a set of sample public meeting notices for use by school boards. Versions of Warren's sample notices continue in use today.

The OMA provided criminal penalties for certain violations, and action taken on matters that were not sufficiently noticed could be voided by a court. Needless to say, school administrators and school trustees wanted school lawyers to provide counsel and help insure that they did not run afoul of the OMA. School lawyers were called upon to attend board meetings more regularly, especially during the initial implementation of the OMA.

To help insure that our client districts complied with the OMA, we developed a handbook for their boards and administrators. This handbook included the language of the OMA, our legal and practical advice on how to comply, and sample notices for regular and special meetings. We also prepared a script of how the meeting should be run, especially for that portion of the meeting when a board would adjourn to closed or executive sessions and then reconvene in open session to vote on any items discussed in the closed session. As the caselaw of the OMA developed, the Texas Attorney General developed a handbook to guide public officials to use for compliance training. This material has pretty much replaced our handbooks, except for the scripts and sample notices. The Attorney General's handbook is periodically updated and is available online.[60]

The Open Records Act

The Texas Open Records Act, which is now referred to as the Public Information Act ("PIA"),[61] opened most governmental records to the public. The PIA provided a system for requesting access to public records from the custodian of the records and prescribed how and when the requestor could access the records, as well as how copies could be made and at what cost to the person requesting. Certain records held by a school district or other public body were made confidential by the PIA and not subject to release to the public. Examples of confidential records are employee social security numbers, trade secrets of companies doing business with a district, and most personally identifiable information of students.

Unlike the OMA, where the Attorney General's role is limited to offering non-binding opinions, the PIA requires that a governmental entity, upon receipt of a request for information the entity feels is confidential under the Act, must seek an opinion from the Attorney General on whether the record must be released. If the school district or the requestor disagrees with the open records decision of the Attorney General, the opinion may be contested by filing suit in district court.

The Family Education Rights and Privacy Act

As Texas and other states enacted open meeting and open record laws, parental concerns that student and family records and information might be released emerged. In order to have consistent treatment nationwide of student and family information held by schools that received federal funds, Congress in 1974 passed the Family Educational Rights and Privacy Act (FERPA).[62]

FERPA was designed to help ensure that student records maintained by school districts and institutions of higher education were accurate, and that the privacy of the information contained in student records was effectively protected from disclosure to third parties and internally kept from those persons without a legitimate educational interest in them. As with all laws, FERPA included a list of exceptions of records that could be released without the consent of the parents. These exceptions primarily relate to safety and health. Parents, and students who have attained 18 years of age may, of course, consent to the release of their personally identifiable data to others.

As one might imagine, the OMA, the PIA, and FERPA changed how school districts, community colleges, and four-year universities conducted business. The School Law Section of the State Bar of Texas, the National School Boards Association, Council of School Attorneys, and the National Organization on the Legal Problems of Education (ELA) held special seminars on FERPA, and most of these organizations placed FERPA on their annual meeting agendas. I spoke on FERPA at many of these seminars and wrote several articles on access to student records.

Our client's districts were frantic for advice on how to comply with FERPA, and they expected immediate guidance. As soon as we figured out how the PIA and FERPA worked together, we conducted in-services, and just as we did for the Open Meetings Act, we developed a handbook with sample forms to facilitate compliance with the new laws. As we learned more, we revised the handbook. The Texas Attorney General has now prepared a Public Information Act Handbook containing most of this information, and it is available online.[63]

All of these transparency and privacy laws have provided considerable work for school and other government entity lawyers. The area has been so active that specific lawyers within firms and school district and higher education general counsel offices have specialized in it, and some lawyers' practices are substantially or wholly focused on this area. Likewise, school districts and other educational institutions have administrative and staff specialists who work with the governmental body's custodian of records, whose duties involve reviewing and responding to requests for information.

Student Discipline – Suspensions, Corporal Punishment, and Search and Seizure

Throughout these reflections, I have written about student behavior and school discipline. In fact, my first case as a lawyer involved the distribution of literature and student Paul Kitchen's subsequent suspension. School campuses are the scenes of student fights, walkouts, theft, and the possession and use of knives, guns, alcohol, and drugs. As school lawyers, we got involved in these student behavior issues, and student discipline became a staple in the school law practice. School lawyers' involvement in these incidents of misbehavior increased as the law concerning the handling of student discipline evolved in the federal courts, and as more of society's misbehavior issues and lawlessness flowed onto our school campuses. After all, our schools are a reflection of our society.

Student Suspensions and Expulsions

In the early days of my school law practice, Texas vested the control of student behavior in the school board, which was authorized to adopt rules for student conduct.[64] Trustees were allowed to "suspend from the privileges of the school any pupil found guilty of incorrigible conduct."[65] Any real legal debate in those days generally centered on the meaning of what was "incorrigible" conduct. Students involved in serious misconduct were often suspended for the remainder of the school year, never to return to school again. Students could be summarily suspended without notice of the reasons and with no due process hearing.

Other common forms of punishment for misbehavior were detentions and paddling (corporal punishment). Fights that occurred on school grounds were generally handled by detentions, paddling, or short suspensions. Occasionally a coach would give feuding boys boxing gloves and have them get after it until the fire between them flamed out. In the early 1970s, students in rural school districts were probably the only students who had guns on campus, and those guns were displayed in open sight on racks in their family pickups. One never knew when a rattlesnake or cottonmouth moccasin might appear, or a game bird might be found—in hunting season, of course.

The HISD, the state's largest school district, was the first Texas district to be required to give a student notice of the reasons for a proposed suspension and the opportunity for a hearing to determine if the allegations were true, and, if true, what punishment was appropriate. This came about through a lawsuit brought by attorney Robert E. "Bob" Hall of the labor law firm, Dixie Wolf & Hall. Bob sued on behalf of Dan Sullivan and Mike Fisher, who were suspended when they published and distributed a student newspaper, *Pflashlyte*, critical of school officials at Sharpstown High School. United States District Judge Woodrow Seals found that the students' First Amendment rights had been violated and they had been denied constitutionally required due process in their suspensions.[66]

The HISD Board, under the control of the recently elected Citizens for Good Schools (CGS) slate, established a student, faculty, and community committee to draft student discipline rules regarding the distribution of literature and procedures that would be followed in student suspensions. The effort was led by young attorneys Jonathan Day, Bill Coats, David Redford, Travis Broesche, and Marc Grossberg, all of whom have remained active in school, college, and other community affairs throughout their legal careers and in retirement. These newly adopted student discipline policies were in effect and were followed in the distribution of literature and student suspension case involving Paul Kitchen, whose suspension was upheld by the Fifth Circuit.[67] HISD's successful use of a community committee to recommend "reasonable rules" for student conduct offered a valuable lesson in school district policy making that I employed with clients throughout my career.

The Fifth Circuit, and finally the Supreme Court in *Goss v. Lopez*,[68] weighed in on the procedural due process required before a student could be suspended for a substantial time or expelled from school under the Due Process Clause of the Fourteenth Amendment. The legally required due process for a student expulsion was similar to the due process required to terminate teachers under contracts—one cannot have a right to a state-provided education taken away without due process of law. I was called upon numerous times to make presentations to school administrators and lawyer groups on student suspensions and expulsions, and many of these presentations later became articles.

As with all major issues involving procedures and process, we developed a manual for our school clients to use in student suspension hearings. These manuals included sample letters and a script for hearing officers to follow. When the student had a lawyer at a hearing, we generally appeared to provide counsel to the school administrator proposing the suspension. Some of the administrators conducting hearings became so adept at conducting hearings, they did not need any school district lawyers to attend.

Corporal Punishment

Corporal punishment (paddling or hitting the body) was commonly used as a disciplinary tool prior to and during the 1970s. Corporal punishment was authorized for use by persons in parental control and educations as an exception to the lawful violence statute of the Texas Penal Code.[69]

If a parent felt a child was injured as a result of corporal punishment, or the student had been the subject of "excessive" corporal punishment, the avenue of "relief" was to make a complaint with the school administration against the educator who administered the paddling, normally an administrator or coach. Occasionally the excessive administrations of corporal punishment, which usually caused severe bruising, resulted in parents filing criminal complaints against the school employees who delivered the licks, generally with a specially designed board kept in the principal's or coach's office. I recall looking at some pretty gruesome pictures of bruised children who had been paddled. Since criminal complaints were filed against individuals, we referred the employees to criminal law specialists. The school district, of course, paid the criminal lawyer's fees, since the paddling was done in the course of employment.

After the comprehensive desegregation of the HISD in 1970, and several years later when more students with special needs were being educated in the schools, parents and advocacy groups against corporal punishment became more forceful in their opposition. Hardly an HISD school board meeting passed without someone speaking against the use of corporal punishment during the hearing of citizens part of the meeting. The first modification of the HISD corporal punishment policy was that a parent could notify a child's school in writing that the child not be paddled. The next step in policy development limiting corporal punishment was that a parent had to agree that corporal punishment could be used, and finally, corporal punishment was abolished. Today, Chapter 37 of the Texas Education Code allows a school district to use corporal punishment unless a parent annually objects to its use in writing. I understand that fifteen states, mainly in the South, continue to use corporal punishment as a disciplinary tool.

Search of Lockers, Students and Cars

Student discipline many times involves school authorities searching students' lockers, cars, backpacks, and person for weapons, drugs, or other contraband. Before the United States Constitution came to campus, schools historically operated on the concept that school officials stood *in loco parentis* (in the place of the parents) while a student was at school. When the Supreme Court applied the First Amendment to student speech on school campuses through the Fourteenth Amendment in 1969, via *Tinker*, *in loco parentis* changed through a series of student discipline cases that wound their way through the appellate courts.

Faced with the question of whether the Fourth Amendment (prohibition of unreasonable search or seizure) would be applied to the search of students and their lockers and cars, and if so under what standard, I set about an extensive research effort to see if *in loco parentis* any longer had applicability to student searches. I found very little in the caselaw and decided to write an article for the *Houston Law Review* to provide a survey of existing cases and to project what I thought the courts would eventually decide.[70] This was the most difficult article I ever attempted, in large part because there was so little law. I got up early each morning before going to the office to work on it.

In the article, I projected that the Supreme Court would apply the Fourth Amendment in the school setting to personal searches, but that the court would recognize the uniqueness of the school environment and approve the less-onerous reasonable suspicion standard for school discipline purposes. I felt that the Fourth Amendment would not be applied to student lockers, especially if schools told students that lockers were school property and students should not expect that the lockers were private. Lawyer friends expressed their appreciation for my having conducted the review and for my suggestions of what the courts might ultimately decide. As it turned out, my prognostication was correct. Another positive to writing the article was that the University of Houston Law Review editor, Sherry Radack, who is now the Chief Justice of Houston's First Court of Appeals, became a Bracewell lawyer.

Years passed and the drug use epidemic that has permeated American society came to schools. Canines were used to sniff out drugs at airports and workplaces, so why not use them in schools? Fellow Texas attorney Rick Peebles had the seminal dog search case of *Horton et al v. Goose Creek*

Independent School District,[71] which applied the reasonable suspicion standard to canine searches of students where the dog's alert provided individualized suspicion. The court found that the alert from a "reliable" drug-sniffing dog was appropriate to determine individualized suspicion. The use of canines to search lockers and cars on school campuses was not a search because the Fourth Amendment protects people, not places. The lockers were school property, and students voluntarily chose to park their cars on campus. Needless to say, we all had fun speculating about how to determine whether a particular dog was "reliable."

Numerous cases on various aspects of student searches have been decided. All courts seem to recognize and respect that school campuses are different from our general society, and that student safety is an all-important consideration when guns, knives, and drugs are likely to be present in the schools. It is acknowledged that guns, knives, and drugs are brought onto our nation's school grounds regularly by students. The mass shootings of students and teachers—at Columbine High School in Jefferson County, Colorado on April 20, 1999; Sandy Hook Elementary in Newtown, Connecticut on December 14, 2012; Stoneman Douglas High School in Parkland, Broward County, Florida on February 14, 2018; and Santa Fe High School in Texas on May 18, 2018—underscore the need to keep our schools safe for the children who are required by our state laws to attend.

Student Discipline Codes

Texas student discipline laws began very simply, with Section 21.301 of the Education Code permitting trustees to provide for the suspension of students guilty of "incorrigible" behavior. Today, the entire Chapter 37 of the Education Code[72] is devoted to the subject. Between the 1960s and today, numerous judicial decisions and legislative acts have added to the development of student disciplinary law. Texas laws now require that a student continue to receive educational services during the time the student is removed from attending regular classes. (This concern was always at the front of Judge Seals' consideration in the early student suspension cases.)

Texas even adopted zero-tolerance student discipline laws, some of which remain in force, that criminalized some disciplinary matters that historically had been handled internally by school officials. I believe there must be a balance struck between the serious lawless acts of students that should be handled by law enforcement and the more juvenile acts of misbehavior that should legitimately be handled in school. Young people do not need to be saddled for life with a criminal conviction for minor acts of misconduct. I acknowledge that where to draw that line can be problematic; student safety and preserving a learning environment are the deciding factors. No matter how that balance is struck, the safety of students has to be the most important consideration. When administrators are invested with discretion in punishment, their decisions must be consistent and evenhanded to avoid discriminatory treatment

The 1969 court order in *Sullivan v. HISD* resulted in the HISD developing a written student discipline code. That student, faculty and community committee recommended a code that gave students notice of what constituted a disciplinary infraction, the potential punishment for violating any of the provisions and laid out a procedure for determining if an infraction did, in fact, take place. Chapter 37 of the Texas Education Code requires that all Texas public schools have a code of student conduct and prescribes what must be included. Much has changed in the last almost fifty years from the simple statutes permitting school boards to expel students guilty of "incorrigible" behavior.

Greg Kite and the University Interscholastic League

The University Interscholastic League ("UIL") is a state organization based at The University of Texas Austin that regulates athletics and other extracurricular events in Texas schools. In the 1970s, the UIL was controlled by middle-aged and older men who had been around athletics all their lives. The separate Prairie View Interscholastic League (PVIL) for black schools that existed during the dual-school days of Texas was combined with the larger UIL in 1970.

The UIL in 1978 had a rule that prohibited high school students from attending summer basketball camps. Many other states did not prohibit such attendance, and talented high school basketball players were beginning to attend summer camps to showcase their skills for college scouts. Greg Kite was an outstanding Westbury High School (HISD) player who felt not attending summer camp disadvantaged him with out-of-state players in his competitive quest for a college scholarship, so his parents sued the UIL in the summer of 1978. The case was assigned to United States District Judge Finis Cowan, a man who loved basketball.

Pat Fry, a summer associate who would later join Bracewell and become a partner, was working with me as a summer clerk. (Pat later went to Bracewell's Washington, D.C. office, then left the firm and eventually married Bracewell's Washington partner, Gene Godley. She continues to practice law in D.C.) I had a teacher dismissal hearing on the evening before the preliminary injunction hearing on the Kite matter before Judge Cowan. The Texas Attorney General did not have a lawyer available on short notice to prepare the UIL witnesses, and the UIL had no independent counsel at that time. The burden fell to us to prepare these witnesses. With no associate help available at the time, I sent Pat to meet with the UIL officials to prepare them for the hearing. I felt badly for sending Pat to deal with UIL Executive Director V. Bailey Marshall and his cadre of older male coaches. Upon arriving, Pat said she explained to V.

Bailey and the others who she was, and to my pleasant surprise, Pat apparently secured the confidence of the whole bunch. The UIL witnesses came to the hearing better prepared than if I had done it myself. I later learned that Pat, who had played varsity volleyball at Trinity University in San Antonio, could really do jock talk.

With Judge Cowan's permission, Pat sat with me at counsel table and, with Judge Cowan's permission, actually participated in the trial. Judge Cowan conducted the hearing, but it became clear early on that he had made up his mind—Kite was going to summer camp. The court reporter included Pat as an attorney, and she was included with the list of lawyers when Judge Cowan's opinion was printed in the Federal Supplement.[73] Greg Kite went to camp, got a college scholarship, and played with the NBA's Boston Celtics. The UIL amended its rule to allow camp attendance.

The Advent of the Fax Machine and More Technology

When I began my practice in 1970, some senior lawyers were still dictating to secretaries who took shorthand then converted the words on a manual typewriter. If a mistake was made in typing on the manual typewriters, the page had to be started over. There were no copy machines, so copies were made using carbon paper and onionskin paper. Most of the lawyers at Bracewell were more into the technology of the day and had begun using Dictaphones, where the dictation was recorded on a belt which was then played on a machine by the secretary. The manual typewriters were replaced by the IBM Selectric, which used a memory card, so carbon paper and onionskin soon disappeared from the firm's supply cabinet. The dictation machines and the Selectric typewriters enhanced the efficiency of the practice and made the sharing of secretaries by attorneys more realistic.

One of the biggest changes in the practice of law was the advent of the fax machine. Before the fax, questions of clients were generally asked by telephone, but relevant documents had to be hand-delivered or mailed. This time lag gave lawyers an opportunity to think before having to give more than a gut reaction to a question. With the arrival of the fax machine, documents might come with the question or even before the client's telephone call. The speed of the practice of law accelerated. About this time, Federal Express emerged with its local overnight and expedited long distance delivery services. FedEx was soon joined by UPS and other companies offering similar services, so even the lengthy documents or bulky materials arrived faster.

Cellular telephones and the desktop computer were the next technological steps toward lawyers losing the ability to realistically control their lives. These technological advancements have been a blessing and a curse. The huge Motorola cell phone I bought in the 1980s allowed me to coach my son Jonathan's baseball team and still give input at a school board meeting without being present. It meant I was always "on call"—but, interestingly, I never received a client call during a practice or a game.

The computer marked the beginning of what has become online research and the filing of pleadings and other documents with courts and agencies. The computer assures us of instant and wide email communication, but we are always thumbing our BlackBerries, iPads, smartphones, etc., to see if someone says we are needed—even when they really do not. (Clients surely don't want lawyers to use these devices in their presence, especially since they are paying for the lawyers' time.) Even the fax machine, which started it all, is being replaced by the computer's ability to scan documents in color and send them as an email on the internet; however, faxing material, rather than emailing it, is still a more secure practice.

Cell phones and computers have made the practice of law more efficient, but it seems we have largely sacrificed personal relationships and contacts with our clients and other lawyers. Communications through emails and texts may be fast, but listening to one another in conversations is conducive to achieving understanding. I ask, "Have we done a proper job of controlling our use of technology, or does it now control us?"

House Bill 72 and Teacher Testing Cases

House Bill 72,[74] enacted by the Texas Legislature in 1984 at the urging of Governor Mark White, was the state's first real "school reform legislation." H.B. 72 covered many areas of school operations, from the date of trustee elections through student discipline. It affected teacher compensation, vocational education, extracurricular participation, and many other areas. In fact, H.B. 72 addressed what I feel is one of the central issues still faced today, teacher compensation, by adding $4 billion primarily for salaries and retirement benefits. A part of these additional funds paid for reducing class sizes in the lower grades. In some areas, H.B. 72 focused on procedures rather than on substantive issues, probably a result of lawyer-drafters based on the assumption that if you follow a procedure, you will get a good result.

H.B. 72's implementation took much energy and attention of school administrators and lawyers. Many of its provisions spawned lawsuits, and we school lawyers dubbed it the "Lawyers Relief Act of 1984." In reality, H.B. 72 probably did more to promote the development of school lawyering than any single event beyond *Brown v. Board of Education,* the civil rights legislation and the litigation of constitutional and statutory issues.

H.B. 72 instituted a basic skills test for teachers (the TECAT) as a condition of teachers being licensed to teach. Needless to say, a number of teachers in the HISD and elsewhere did not pass the TECAT, even after a couple of tries. Since these teachers could no longer be certified, they could not be paid to teach. Because the state laws were so clear, the HISD held a mass hearing where any teacher the HISD understood had failed the TECAT could present evidence that he or she had in fact passed the TECAT. None of the teachers did at the hearing, and all were fired. Chris Tritico, a very capable plaintiffs' lawyer, represented the mass of newly uncertified teachers in a suit that landed in Judge Lewis Moore's state district court.

Judge Moore apparently had a difficult time with the case, because we had hearing after hearing. I don't think Judge Moore wanted to hurt the teachers, and he certainly wanted to treat them fairly. The plaintiffs were not working, so they had nothing to do during the day, and they packed the courtroom for every hearing. Judge Moore had to look at their faces all the time while we lawyers sat with our backs to the gallery. The Texas Commissioner of Education, Bill Kirby, testified one day that the law was the law and he had no leeway in denying the teachers continued certification. Finally, we had a trial on the merits, after which Judge Moore ruled that the plaintiffs could not teach because they were no longer certified. There was no appeal.

Another contest by a teacher fired for failing the TECAT, *Lass v. HISD*, was filed before the TEA by attorney Robert E. "Bob" Hall. The HISD prevailed before the Commissioner of Education, and Hall appealed it to district court in Travis County. Janet Horton, who worked with me on the case as a recent Bracewell associate, was well into her years as a partner when the case was finally dismissed. *Lass* was the case that wouldn't die, even though it couldn't breathe.

As a postscript, one of the teachers who failed the TECAT was Jackie Carr, the famous head basketball coach who led Wheatley High School to several state championships. Jackie later passed the test, was rehired by the HISD, and returned to Wheatley. Later assigned to Del Mar Stadium to assist in mentoring new basketball coaches, Carr sued over his assignment in Judge Mark Davidson's state district court, and, after mediation, was paid a settlement sum that resulted in his resignation. (Judge Davidson, like Judge Finis Cowan, loved basketball. Is there something about judges and basketball?) Carr's case was my last active case before my 2006 sabbatical. (Jackie, at age 74, was to have coached Houston's new American Basketball League team in 2008, but the league never got off the ground.)

No Pass, No Play – An H.B. 72 Issue

Probably the most controversial provision of H.B. 72 provided that if a student did not pass his or her coursework, the student could not participate in extracurricular activities. Translation in Texas: he couldn't play football if he did not pass. Suits were filed against a number of school districts, including Houston and Spring Branch. Jeff Horner of Bracewell represented Houston, and Jeff Davis did the honors for Spring Branch.

The case was tried by State District Judge Marsha Anthony who had been elected in the 1984 Republican landslide (straight-ticket voting) which unseated all the Democrat judges in Harris County who were up for election. (A Democratic Party landslide in 2018 unseated all the Republican Party judges up for election in Harris County.) Judge Anthony had little experience as a trial lawyer. I spent one afternoon observing the proceeding and decided one day was enough. Ultimately, the Texas Supreme Court upheld no-pass, no-play in *Stamos v. Spring Branch ISD, et al.*[75]

The Career Ladder Debacle – Merit Pay

HISD's desegregation efforts of the 1970s and 1980s were significantly built on the district's comprehensive magnet school plan; however, providing quality, integrated education at all schools was based on an educational enhancement program called the Houston Education Excellence Plan (HEEP). The plan was the brainchild of Superintendent Billy Reagan, who developed HEEP with the active support of the philanthropic community and some core supporters of public education.

HEEP had many facets emphasizing what has historically proven to be important to student learning: recruiting and retaining a stable teaching corps, engaging parents in their children's education, creating and furthering effective administrative leadership, and improving student attendance. HEEP also focused on effectively utilizing the financial resources available. I was very involved in the development and implementation of one part of the program, the Second Mile Plan, a teacher and staff merit pay plan based upon improving student performance. The Second Mile Plan financially rewarded the teachers, administrators, and staff at schools that experienced certain levels of student growth measured by all students' performance on the Iowa Test of Basic Skills, a nationally normed reference test. The Second Mile Plan was beginning to produce substantial results, when along came H.B. 72 in 1984.

The legislature through H.B. 72 attempted to take HISD's team-focused merit pay plan from the concept of rewarding all teachers and staff at a school for overall student improvement to making payments based on an individual teacher's ability to teach through the ill-fated "career ladder plan." The career ladder merit pay plan, based upon observable evaluations, was a disaster from the start; state funding ultimately dried up, as did the plan. The career ladder spawned many TEA hearings and lawsuits. This merit pay plan was a central cause of H.B. 72 becoming known as the "Lawyers' Relief Act of 1984." Without using longitudinal student test data to judge an individual teacher's performance, merit pay works better when a team effort is rewarded. Merit pay not based on longitudinal test data is even more contentious and divisive when some individuals receive substantially greater monetary rewards than others.

Objecting to Judge DeAnda's Questions and Arguing the First Amendment with Judge Justice

A city of McAllen employment case brought by police officer Neubauer could not be settled, so it was tried to a six-person jury, with no member having been educated beyond high school. The case was before United States District Court Judge James DeAnda in Brownsville. Judge DeAnda, a former plaintiff and civil rights lawyer who had represented a Mexican-American defendant from Edna, Texas, in the renowned *Hernandez* criminal case before the United States Supreme Court, had just been appointed to the federal bench. Preston Hendrickson of Edinburg represented Neubauer. Janet Horton, in her first jury trial, assisted me.

Preston Hendrickson was presenting officer Neubauer on direct examination, and I successfully objected to just about every question. Finally, Judge DeAnda commenced asking Neubauer the same questions he had excluded when Hendrickson was propounding them. The judge was killing us with the jury, so I rose and asked to approach the bench with the court reporter in tow, whereupon I told Judge DeAnda I had to object to his questions. He said he could ask questions, and I agreed, but I said it didn't seem fair or proper that he was asking the same questions that he would not permit Preston to ask. I told him I felt it necessary to object to protect the record and my client's interests. He looked at me and said, "You know, I think you are right." He asked no more objectionable questions.

The charge session with Judge DeAnda was a lesson in trying jury cases. Judge DeAnda did not like our submissions, but he liked Hendrickson's. I objected on every basis I could conjure up at a time in legal history when the central issues of free speech and association jurisprudence were being developed in the appellate courts. As it turned out, the jury popped the city of McAllen with a substantial verdict. The city wanted someone else to handle the appeal, but with our help. We suggested that the city hire Eduardo Rodriguez of Brownsville. (Eduardo later followed me as president of the State Bar of Texas in 2005-2006.) Janet Horton wrote most of the brief, and the appeal was successful. To my great relief, the Fifth Circuit found I had sufficiently objected to testimony and to the charge to preserve errors.

Judge DeAnda and I became personal friends over the years, especially after he moved to Houston, where he ultimately became the Chief Judge of the Southern District of Texas. We always joked about my objections to his questions—it was a first, and maybe a last, for both of us. Judge DeAnda retired and became an effective mediator who helped resolve several of our cases. He died of prostate cancer in 2006. I will always remember the Texas A&M University Singing Cadets performing the stirring and passionate first verse of the Aggie War Hymn (not the one you hear at football games) as his casket left St. Michael Catholic Church.

Another memorable federal judge moment came when I was presenting a motion for summary judgment argument to United States District Judge William Wayne Justice in Tyler late one afternoon. The motion was on behalf of the Westwood ISD, s small school district located just west of Palestine in East Texas. Westwood had been sued by attorney Larry Daves of Tyler. Westwood had nonrenewed an African-American coach who had uttered a four-letter word when his team fumbled on the opponent's one-yard line. Although there was a racial discrimination claim in the case, the main issue was freedom of speech.

After I presented my argument, and maybe after a short presentation by attorney Daves, Judge Justice took up the plaintiff's First Amendment argument. Judge Justice and I had at least a half-hour argument with give-and-take on the application of the First Amendment in the school setting. It was among the most stimulating arguments of my career, and I thoroughly enjoyed it—even though I realized that my client was going to come out on the short end. Apparently Judge Justice also appreciated the level of the argument. After we both exhausted the arguments supporting our positions, Judge Justice said, "Mr. Frels, I enjoyed this discussion. I will take your motion under advisement. In the meantime, I assume you will settle this case." The case settled soon thereafter on reasonable terms to Westwood ISD.

In years thereafter at state bar meetings, I would often find Judge Justice having early morning coffee, generally sitting alone. We would sometimes talk about that day in his courtroom, but we would always find other interesting topics to discuss. He ultimately moved to Austin, where he lived out his years on senior status.

Introduction to Due Process Hearings in Special Education

The issue was simple, but important: Should students with intellectual or physical disabilities be allowed to attend school and receive an education that takes into account the student's disability? Several courts said yes. Many state legislatures, including Texas, also said yes, and in 1975, Congress passed a comprehensive law requiring educational services for those with handicaps, P.L. 94-142, the Education for All Handicapped Children Act (EAHCA).[76]

After various reauthorizations by Congress, this law is now known as the Individuals with Disabilities Education Act (IDEA).[77]

This area of the law has become a cottage industry, and it has catapulted many women administrators with special education experience into principalships and superintendencies. Patricia Shell of HISD, who became the Brazosport ISD superintendent, is a prime example. Among the initial issues was what process should be followed in determining if a child is qualified for special educational services, and if so, what services should be provided? La Porte ISD happened to have the first such case in the state.

Bill Bednar was the TEA's general counsel when the La Porte case arose in 1976. Bill and I had read everything we could find on the subject and, without written rules, we decided that there had to be a hearing of record (with a court reporter), and the hearing officer needed to be someone independent of the school district. It was also decided that the hearing should not take place in school facilities. The result was that attorney Mike Driscoll, a La Porte native (who later served as Harris County Attorney), was employed as the hearing officer. The hearing was held at the old La Porte City Hall, and it was recorded by a court reporter.

A student in the La Porte middle school was intellectually disabled, and her mother felt she should be a scholar. (The accepted terminology at the time was "mentally retarded." The accepted terminology now is "intellectually disabled.") It was a stressful hearing because the mother apparently did not like lawyers, and she either could not find one to take her case or she could not afford one. It may have been for all these reasons. The La Porte superintendent just wanted it over—the mother was a constant presence at school presenting her demands. The district eventually agreed to provide some services, and I frankly don't remember if Mike Driscoll ever had to render a decision. I do know that the next La Porte superintendent, Robert Williams, engaged the child's mother in school activities, so peace prevailed at the school district.[78]

As the demand for special education hearings grew, I found myself unable to meet my commitments to clients on existing matters and work on special education issues. Jean Bilger Arnold, who assisted me on the special education hearings I had conducted, was pressed into service, and she became a special education specialist. Jean moved to Virginia and later became the chair of the National School Board's Council of School Attorneys. She and her husband Harold Dodge, a former superintendent, now live in Mobile, Alabama.

Janet Horton picked up the special education mantle when she joined Bracewell, after Jean left Texas, and has become one of the state's foremost experts in the education of students with disabilities. Jim Walsh of Austin, another leader in school district special services, also known as "Law Dawg", is a lively and interesting speaker. Jim is one of those speakers, like professor and lawyer Robert Phay of the University of North Carolina, whom one goes to hear because you always learn something of value. James Holtz served as a TEA hearing officer in special education due process hearings for many years before becoming an attorney for parents.

Chris Borreca, who was the director of education for Houston's Center for the Retarded, now simply known as "the Center," was a natural for the work when he joined Bracewell's School Law Section, and Chris has become a practice leader. Former Bracewell partners Merri Schneider-Vogel and David Hodgins have taken a particular interest in special education. Chris and Janet played a huge role for Texas schools and those nationally in the last congressional reauthorization of IDEA in 2004. At their urging, many changes were made in Congress to make IDEA more balanced and user-friendly to school districts, while protecting the rights of parents and children.

There is much that could be written about providing education to those with special needs. Patricia Shell and her HISD staff were especially effective in the implementation of special education, and there were very few requests for hearings during her tenure. The IDEA is a funding statute that promises some federal funds to school districts that comply with its requirement for the education of students with disabilities. Congress also passed the Rehabilitation Act of 1973 that includes Section 504,[79] a civil rights law that protects persons with disabilities, including students, from discrimination in programs that receive federal financial assistance. This is an entire area of the law that would consume many pages when written by someone with real knowledge. Since my actual practice was limited to special education's beginning, I can write only about that which I know.

Introduction to AIDS

Schools were introduced to AIDS through the life and death of Ryan White, a student who was diagnosed with AIDS following a blood transfusion. Because the HIV virus was known to be highly transmittable, the question was "Should Ryan be allowed to attend public school?" The school said "no," and the court said "yes." How was this to be accomplished when the medical experts could not agree on how the HIV virus was transmitted? The doctors did agree that the HIV virus could be transmitted through exchanges of blood and sexual intercourse, but how about through saliva, vomit, and other bodily fluids?

The National School Boards Association, through its Council of School Attorneys, sponsored a forum on AIDS in Washington where all related issues were thoroughly discussed to the extent the medical experts had at the time. Everyone was fearful because so little was known about something so deadly.

AIDS, to the extent it had surfaced, had been an issue only really known in the gay community and through exchange of needles during drug use. Now Ryan White had introduced the AIDS issue to the general public. The one standard that emerged from the Washington meeting was to treat all blood and other bodily excretions as HIV-infected. As a result, rubber gloves became the standard in handling blood, along with a 10% bleach solution to clean up spills. School personnel are now trained on these universal precautions, and they are routinely incorporated into school policies and protocols.

Two of the cases we first dealt with were at the community college level and involved students who were HIV-positive in a nurse training program and the culinary program. Education of college staff about the disease was critical in resolving the cases. Medical science has made huge advancements in the treatment of persons living with HIV, and much has been devoted to the spread of the HIV virus. Despite these advances, school personnel consider and implement accommodations for employees and students diagnosed with AIDS or who are HIV-positive. Lawyers who have developed expertise in the area of disability law like Janet Horton, Chris Borreca, Merri Schneider-Vogel, David Hodgins, and Jim Walsh continue to advise their school clients on employment and educational service issues related to individuals living with HIV. All school personnel are now trained on all aspects of HIV and AIDS prevention protocol and care.

Home School Lawsuit

Texas has long had a compulsory attendance law, Texas Education Code, Section 25.085 which requires children ages 6-18 to attend public school unless exempted by Texas Education Code, Section 25.085, which lists attending an "appropriate school." Until the home school movement came about in the mid-1980s, it is doubtful anyone thought the home schooling of children qualified as attendance at a private school. That, however, was the result in *Texas Education Agency v. Leeper*.[80] Janet Horton represented the Katy ISD in the case, and Tony Safi represented the El Paso ISD, two individually named districts, along with Michael Bucek, who represented the Arlington ISD.

The number of Texas children being home schooled has increased, and it has spawned another cottage industry with online and commercial curriculum supported by a home school association. Home-schooled students are tested through standardized tests and may participate in the co-curricular activities of the school district in which they reside. Since home-schooled children are considered by Texas law to be private-schooled, would their parents be entitled to receive state-financed vouchers, should vouchers ever be approved by the Texas Legislature?

Exhaustion of Administrative Remedies – *Houston Federation of Teachers v. HISD*

One of the first principles of school law Bill Wilde taught me was that a lawsuit was premature and should be dismissed if the plaintiff has not first exhausted his or her administrative remedies. The idea behind exhaustion of administrative remedies is to give the political body or official responsible for the policy issue an opportunity to resolve the issue and make a decision before a court gets involved. Depending upon the type of case, abstention is raised in state courts by a plea to the jurisdiction or a plea in abatement. In federal court, exhaustion is raised through a Rule 12(b) motion. My first law review article in the *NOLPE School Law Journal*[81] focused on applying the abstention doctrine in federal court during the early 1970s, a time in history when school boards exercised absolute authority and when some federal courts wanted to be super school boards in applying the evolving civil rights laws to school districts. Courts should abstain from acting until the school district's final authority, the school board, has had the opportunity to act.

A court test of abstention in Texas came about when, under Billy Reagan's leadership in the early 1980s, HISD developed the "Second Mile Plan," a creative approach to improving student performance through monetary incentives for all teachers at schools who raised student achievement above predictable levels. The plan also offered rewards for student and teacher attendance, with restrictions on teacher and student absences. For example, students with perfect attendance got a ticket to the amusement park, AstroWorld, at the end of the school year. The result was more student time on task and greater accountability, as measured by standardized tests overall and in specific subjects at the secondary level. Student attendance improved, so more money came from the state for improved average daily attendance. The overall rewards for teachers were based upon the performance at a school, so that teams, rather than just individuals, were rewarded.

Some teachers did not approve of requirements made on them regarding attendance and duties, especially attendance at before- and after-school events, so they sued in state court based on not having duties beyond the school day as defined in school board policy. The Houston Federation of Teachers (HFT) suit, brought by attorney Chris Tritico, was assigned to visiting Judge Joe Kelly of Victoria, who always came to Houston and sat as a visiting judge preceding the week of the Houston Bar Association's November Harvest Party.

Judge Kelly would have nothing to do with applying the concept of abstaining or waiting to rule until the HISD Board had considered the teachers' complaint. He entered an injunction preventing the enforcement of the order on teacher attendance at these events, so we appealed. We won at the Court of Appeals, but we then encountered the "liberal" Texas Supreme Court which was then dominated by the plaintiff trial lawyers' faction. The Supreme Court reversed by a 5-4 margin.[82] The HFT case limited abstention, but the facts of the case are so narrow the ruling has had little or no impact.

Larry Watts Stories

No reflections on school law in twentieth-century Texas would be complete without something about plaintiffs' lawyer Larry Watts. Larry was representing teachers and other employees in Houston when I arrived in 1970, and he continues to do so. Larry approaches client representation with a flair for the dramatic. Never to be underestimated, he was and continues to be a formidable opponent. My experiences confronting Larry's creativity and challenging style over many years certainly helped make me a better lawyer. His aunt, Annie Watts, worked for Fentress Bracewell at our firm. Here are a couple of Larry stories—there are many more:

We were hired by the City of McAllen to defend it in a series of civil rights suits, including the Neubauer case mentioned earlier. One group of actions brought by Texas Rural Legal Aid lawyer Jim Harrington stemmed from the McAllen police abusing prisoners, especially at their bookings. The city videotaped the bookings of prisoners by the police, and the tapes showed police striking the handcuffed prisoners. The power of the tapes was illustrated by one where one officer booked a person and grabbed him by the hair and pounded his head on the table. Carol Vance, the long-term Harris County District Attorney, then an active Bracewell partner, represented the city in effectively settling these cases. The second batch of cases were employment and union representation cases brought by Larry Watts and Rio Grande Valley lawyers Preston Hendrickson and Bobby Garcia. The city of McAllen people had never encountered anyone like Larry before. They needed a neutralizer who could get on a plane and leave town, and I was believed to be that person.

Othal Brand, who had developed a successful produce company in the Valley with a sugar beet operation in Hereford, Texas, was the long-term mayor of McAllen. Othal was a person people tended to either love or hate. Some of the city's police and firefighters did not like the mayor or those on his team. Mayor Brand was an imposing figure with black-rimmed glasses who had dropped out of school, joined the Navy, and become a champion boxer. At age 70, he was playing racquetball daily and punching a bag which had cement at its center.

Politically, Mayor Brand was a Ronald Reagan Republican, possibly before Ronald Reagan knew what being one was. Brand quietly helped community people pay bills and send kids to college. If you were down on your luck without it being your fault, the mayor was the one to see. Some McAllen people considered him a patrón.

The reason for this introduction to Mayor Brand is to get back to Larry Watts, who was deposing the mayor in Preston Hendrickson's office in Edinburg one fall morning. Tension gripped the room as Larry took successive demeaning shots at the mayor. I had been in the hall several times, calming the mayor, and we had already called the federal judge once for a ruling on how the deposition was to be conducted. Preston Hendrickson's dad, a lawyer from the school of treating your foes with dignity, arrived to show off his dressed ducks he had shot that morning. Upon the showing of the ducks, Larry began walking around the room comparing the mayor to a duck. The mayor had enough and announced that he was leaving, whereupon Larry challenged him to a fight. I had a choice: I could break it up by stepping between them, or I could let Mayor Brand punch Watts out. At my peril, I stepped in and separated them. (Several years later, I had to step between Larry and Joe Hairston at a termination hearing at Montgomery ISD.)

About the time I was assuming the managing partner role at Bracewell, Larry again entered my life with a racially charged political case in Texarkana involving my old friend and Texarkana superintendent, Gary Collins. Collins had the courage to reassign a local icon from the principalship of a school where student achievement had hit an all-time low. The Texarkana ISD Board was to consider her grievance, and Larry was representing her. Like so many before them, the Texarkana administration and board seemed perplexed with how to avoid the hearing becoming a community and media event. Gary called me in early December, and I agreed to help with the pre-Christmas hearing. We set the grievance hearing for one hour per side, with the local lawyer for the Texarkana Board presiding. I represented the administration.

I spent the entire day of the hearing with Gary and his staff preparing for the hearing. To gain entry to the hearing that evening, each person had to pass through a metal detector—the first time I had the experience at a school board meeting. Gary told me it was a volatile environment. When Larry saw me at the table, he had a strange look. He took more than half of his allotted time objecting to the process, whereupon the presiding officer finally told him to proceed with evidence because he was using his allotted time complaining. The board ultimately voted to approve the transfer and denied the grievance.

As we left the hearing for Gary's house to meet with his staff, he said, "Well, guess I can take off this bullet-proof vest. I've had death threats, and I have a note in a safety deposit box to open if I'm killed." My reply was, "I was sitting next to you all day and night, and angry people are not very good shots."

Larry Watts appealed the denial of the Texarkana administrator's grievance to the Commissioner of Education, and I understand that the ten-hour grievance hearing is the longest de novo hearing in TEA history. Chris Gilbert, a new Bracewell associate who was assisting me on the appeal, received his litigation baptism in the matter with Larry Watts' usual First Amendment and due process issues. The proceeding at the TEA included a complex legal issue that arose when, late on a Friday afternoon of the hearing, Larry attempted to impeach a Texarkana school district administrator witness whom Larry had previously represented. We stopped the hearing and were able to secure Bill Bednar to represent the witness individually. When testimony resumed on Saturday morning with Bill Bednar present, Larry abandoned his attempted impeachment.

Because the hearing dragged on over time, several different hearing officers were involved in the resolution of the matter. Proposed decisions were written, objections made, proposals withdrawn, and proposals reissued. Finally, the hearing officer and the Commissioner dismissed the appeal. The issues in the appeal also became the subject of a lawsuit in federal court in Texarkana, which Chris Gilbert handled through trial and the Fifth Circuit. Chris is now a seasoned trial lawyer who has authored a book on the First Amendment. There is little doubt that this case was as significant to Chris' development as a lawyer as the Paul Kitchen case, discussed earlier, was for me. Incidentally, Chris and Larry today continue to tangle in courtrooms on similar issues.

More on the McAllen Lawsuits

Issues from the lawsuits for the City of McAllen are mentioned frequently in these reflections. Although the lawsuits representing the city were not school cases, they were First Amendment employment cases, and I had probably had more experience defending them than anyone else at the time. Besides that, I was not from the Valley and could get on a plane and leave. No Valley lawyer would touch them, and if the city lost the cases, the officials could blame that "out-of-town lawyer."

The McAllen airport was small and did not have advanced communication capability in the early 1980s. Texas International (then Continental, now United) was the only way to get to McAllen when the cases began. Toward the end of the cases, Southwest Airlines began flights from Houston using Harlingen's old Air Force base. One foggy day, the pilot missed the air field at McAllen on his first pass—he would have landed in an onion field had he not pulled up. As he made his second pass, I was anxious, and Janet Horton, who was sitting next to me, had her eyes shut and the arm rests tightly gripped. That landing gave meaning to the term "while knuckles."

I always had a set of headlights following me when I was in McAllen at night, and the same occurred even in Brownsville when I was at the Federal courthouse. The McAllen city manager was our client individually and in his official capacity. I learned only after the cases were all resolved that he was not real careful about what he said publicly regarding the issues in the lawsuit and our strategy. He would dine with me at restaurants where I now understand that people associated with the other side were conveniently seated so they could hear what we were talking about. Fortunately, there were few real strategic issues for us to discuss. My communications with the city manager were more about keeping him informed of the cases' status and to see if he had learned anything helpful.

Carmela, Jonathan, and Catherine went with me by car on one trip to McAllen in 1982. We checked into the La Posada Hotel late in the evening when a male clerk was at the desk. The hotel had only a small room left, so the next morning, Carmela went to the front desk to see about getting a larger one. The woman working the desk, without any introduction, called her by name, "Hello, Mrs. Frels." Much later, after the cases were concluded, I was told that the hotel clerk was a relative of someone involved in the lawsuits. I had always assumed that it was more secure for me to make phone calls from pay phones with a credit card rather than from my hotel room. No cell phones were available in the early 1980s.

Tim Cooper Selected Tales

No rendition of the early days of the school practice at Bracewell would be complete without including a few of Tim Cooper's adventures. Tim remains a truly great friend who was a unique school lawyer at Bracewell from 1979 to 1985.

The State Bar of Texas annual meetings of the 1970s and early 1980s were places where lawyers should be—after all, that is where the judges were—and virtually all Texas lawyers of that time claimed to be trial lawyers. At a time when the state had 25,000 lawyers, these annual meetings would draw thousands of lawyers and judges. Beginning in 1972, the School Law Section of the State Bar conducted a well-attended seminar at each annual meeting.

One year, the State Bar of Texas meeting was held in Houston at the Shamrock Hilton, the lavish hotel at Main and Holcombe built by oil wildcatter Glen McCarthy. The hotel pool was large enough to have speedboats pulling skiers, and it was here that Cooper accepted the dare of Jim Deatherage of Irving, and some other lawyers, to "dive"—actually jump off the high board—fully clothed in a suit and tie. As he was about to climb the ladder, Carmela was able to extract his wallet and shoes so they would not get ruined. Well, Cooper did it in front of everyone, gaining the admiration of his fellow school lawyers, though I'm not sure about the others who witnessed the feat. Cooper reported that the suit and tie dry-cleaned nicely.

The annual TASB/TASA convention was historically held in San Antonio each September. The Texas Council of School Attorneys, formed in 1978, presented a seminar on Sunday morning. Cooper regularly entertained the crowd on Saturday night at Dirty Nelly's, an Irish bar on the Riverwalk level of the Hilton Palacio del Rio Hotel. Tim grew up singing all the old songs that the bar had on its song sheets, so he would help lead the singing. He was the life of the party, and it seemed everyone knew him. Every year, he would dance a strip tease (he kept his pants on, thank God) to the music of *New York, New York*. One night, two female board members (somewhat rare during this era) from the panhandle community of White Deer (great class A football teams) who knew of Tim's performances stopped me on a sidewalk to find out when Tim would be at Dirty Nelly's.

One TASB/TASA convention night in 1985 I had attended to some organizational duties, so I was late in getting to Dirty Nelly's. Before I got to the Hilton Hotel where Dirty Nelly's was located, two different groups stopped me to ask if I heard what had happened to Cooper. They all said he was dancing, actually doing an above-the-waist strip, when he looped his tie over a woman's head who was joining the fun. Her boyfriend had experienced a tour in Vietnam (remember that San Antonio is a military town), and he looked like an aging Popeye the Sailor Man. He took umbrage with Cooper's messing with her and cold-cocked him. Cooper apparently went sprawling on the floor across the room as if the wall sucked him in.

When I arrived, I found Cooper and many of the HISD Board members and spouses having a great, singing time. It seems this guy had a Vietnam flashback and saw Tim as the aggressor and popped him. It was at that time that Marquis Alexander (the husband of HISD Board member Blue Alexander), who stood about 6' 6" and 250 pounds, and Tim's friend and Bracewell associate Steve Braun, who also stood 6' 6" or better, arose and told the soldier, "You just hit our friend and you need to apologize." Good judgment apparently prevailed. Before Dirty Nelly's closed, Cooper and Popeye the Sailor Man were cutting up on the dance floor. Superintendent Al Hook of Alief ISD and Bracewell partner Jeff Horner were still laughing from the scene an hour after it happened.

The National School Boards Association held its convention in Houston and Tim (a Harvard law graduate) had become a fixture at Bracewell. Tim, an entertainer himself, was in charge of social activities for the lawyer part of the convention, and he chose a forty-mile road trip to the Simonton Rodeo via a bus fully equipped with beer and chips.

The Simonton Rodeo provided the full venue of rodeo events, with an added event for children to get into the rodeo arena and take a $10 bill off a goat's ear and an adult event that involved taking a $100 bill off a bull's horn. Cooper was like the Pied Piper in getting some of the out-of-state lawyers into the arena for the $100 bull's horn event. Richard Schwartz of Raleigh, North Carolina, who had been a wrestler at Duke, led the way into the arena. After a few minutes, Cooper was sitting atop the arena fence cheering everyone on.

Richard was also being cheered on by a group of high school girls chanting "Rocky"—from the movie, of course.

The bull apparently grew tired of being chased. He charged Richard, knocking him down, goring him slightly, and stepped on his chest. Richard "Rocky" Schwartz struggled out of the arena and iced his chest and rib cage all the way back to the Hyatt Hotel in downtown Houston.

Rocky appeared the next day with bruises on his chest and rib cage that looked like a bull's hoofs. He told this story to the nurse at the doctor's office upon his return to Raleigh, and when the doctor came into the room with the file, he said, "You did what? You were gored and stepped on by a what?" Richard had broken several ribs and has forever been known by his Texas friends as "Rocky." The rodeo trip was not repeated with other out-of-town groups.

One December Monday morning, the lawyers of the firm were meeting when we were greeted with sleigh bells and "ho-ho-hos" from Cooper (dressed in an elf costume) and associate Bob Parsley (dressed as Santa). They handed out candy and gave a few gag gifts. The Bracewell Santa and Elf tradition was born. After Parsley left to do commercial real estate, I became the Santa. When Cooper left the firm for New York, Jeff Horner became the Elf. Both of us retired from the roles in 2004, after twenty years of spreading holiday cheer.

Cooper was unique, and he could never be replicated. His personality facilitated his telling off-color jokes to virtually anyone, and the person would laugh. If anyone else had tried it, the recipient would have been insulted.

The Plane Ride to Eagle Pass

One late spring evening when I was at a La Porte ISD board meeting, Eagle Pass ISD Superintendent Dr. Gonzalo Garza called. He and his board determined they had four trustees whose relatives were school employees, and they needed immediate help to resolve their nepotism issues. Could I come to an emergency board meeting the next night?

The only way to get to Eagle Pass for a meeting the next day was to fly through San Antonio. Tim Cooper and I flew Southwest Airlines to San Antonio's airport where we met our transportation to Eagle Pass—a single-engine, double-wing, three-seat aircraft. The flight to San Antonio itself was a white-knuckle experience, as the plane tossed and vibrated as it flew over a spring thunderstorm. If weather conditions were not better in San Antonio, we weren't getting on any single-engine, open-cockpit plane. Clear skies appeared in San Antonio, so Tim and I took off for Eagle Pass, located to San

Antonio's west on the U.S./Texas-Mexico border. As we flew away from the airport, I remarked to the pilot that he did not have instrumentation. He replied that he would simply follow Interstate 10 and other highways to Eagle Pass. Fortunately, it was clear and early in the afternoon, so we had sunlight and he could see the highway.

There was no airport in Eagle Pass, so we landed in a pasture where we were met by Dr. Garza in a pickup. At the board meeting, we worked out a legally acceptable plan for resolving the nepotism issues through a series of resignations and the appointment of successor trustees. After a late dinner preceded by imported Mexican beer and frozen margaritas, we retired to what was then probably the only motel in Eagle Pass.

The return flight was much less stressful; having flown once in the single-engine, open-cockpit plane, the second time around was less intimidating. Regardless, it was great to board a Southwest Airlines flight in San Antonio with clear skies for our ultimate return to Houston. One travel principle that was reinforced by this trip is that it is better to fly or drive west in the morning and east in the afternoon, with the sun at your back.

The "Heart Attack" – Texas Southmost College

Sometime in 1985, I received a call from two board members of the Texas Southmost College Board of Trustees. They said they had heard me speak and hoped I could help them with a leadership change at the college. They were calling as individuals and not on behalf of the entire board. I agreed to meet with them without charge in our Houston office, where we developed a plan for them to proceed.

The first step was for the college board to hire Bracewell as special counsel, which the board accomplished in short order. As it turned out, all of the board members felt the college president had to go. Subsequent negotiations with him to resign and walk away failed, so a proposal to terminate his employment with supporting reasons was prepared and presented to him.

Tim Cooper represented the board of trustees in the termination of the president, who was represented by Larry Watts. Tim called at about 11:00 p.m. on the night of the hearing and said he was examining the president on the stand, and the president passed out with an apparent heart attack. Cooper worried that he had killed him. I responded, "Cooper, considering all the circumstances, I think this is more of a show than an illness, and the worst that will happen is the settlement amount will go up." The president "recovered" the next day.

The president, in fact, did not have a heart attack, but the hearing was never resumed. A resignation and settlement were worked out, at an amount above what I had originally anticipated. Dr. Juliet Garcia was employed as the new president, and she later became president of The University of Texas-Brownsville. UT-Brownsville and UT-Pan American were combined by the Texas Legislature in 2015 to become The University of Texas-Rio Grande Valley.

It was not long after the "heart attack" incident that Tim Cooper came to me and said he no longer wanted to be a lawyer. Tim went to New York, where he pursued acting and later became a small group travel consultant. I will always believe that this incident sent Cooper over the edge and convinced him that being a lawyer was not his true calling.

Green Tee Terrace Goes to Pearland ISD

Green Tee Terrace is a golf course subdivision in Pearland, Texas that at one time was in the Clear Creek ISD. Green Tee students had to travel up to ten miles to attend the Clear Creek middle and high schools, when the Pearland ISD schools were but a mile or so away. Lawyer friend Jerry Kacal and his wife Linda were Green Tee residents, and they came to me sometime in the mid-1980s to see if I could help them and their neighbors in Green Tee become a part of the Pearland District. I had never represented a parent group before, much less one that wanted to detach territory from one school district and add it to another. Our firm had never been adverse to a school district in any matter.

The reasons supporting the detachment and annexation were compelling. In addition to the long travel time over high-traffic roads on buses for middle and high schools, the elementary children from Green Tee had to attend the elementary school next to the abandoned hazardous waste site of the Brio Refinery. I agreed, and with the assistance of associate Steve Braun, we set the process in motion. Naturally, this effort irritated the Clear Creek trustees and administration, who enlisted the legal assistance of legendary trial lawyer Rayborne Thompson, of Vinson & Elkins.

Pearland ISD, Clear Creek ISD, and Green Tee were collectively in three Texas counties – Galveston, Brazoria, and Harris. To secure detachment, Green Tee proponents had to secure the approval of the commissioner's court in all three counties. Clear Creek had the political clout with the Galveston County judge and two commissioners, so we lost on a 3-2 vote. The Clear Creek trustees were pretty smug after the Galveston County commissioner's vote. Green Tee appealed to the Texas Commissioner of Education, who saw the indisputable educational justification for the detachment from Clear Creek and the attachment to Pearland, so he approved the detachment. Clear Creek appealed to the state district court in Austin.

Rayborne Thompson was assisted by a young associate who was taking a deposition in the case. I objected to one of his questions. This apparently irritated the young associate, because he called me a four-letter name. I responded "You called me a what?" Rayborne indicated both amusement and concern with the conduct of the associate and suggested that the associate move along to another subject. Being called a name in that deposition was my only experience of that nature in all my years of practice.

We went to trial on the record developed before the Commissioner of Education before the state district judge in Austin. The Clear Creek trustees and administrators present were pretty cocky in the Austin courtroom the morning of the trial. I wondered if they had this step wired like they did in Galveston. Judge Paul Davis walked in and took his seat on the bench. "Good morning ladies and gentlemen. Kelly, I haven't seen you since law school." The expression on the faces of the Clear Creek folks changed dramatically. Green Tee had the commissioner's decision and the merits of the case on its side, so we prevailed before Judge Davis, and Green Tee became a part of the Pearland District.

While we never received anywhere near full payment for our legal work, despite several fundraisers which Steve Braun and I attended, I felt justice was served. Needless to say, my relationship with Clear Creek was cold until years later, after those trustees and administrators left the board and the administration. But, the children of Green Tee finally received the education they deserved and in their hometown of Pearland. Clear Creek closed the elementary school next to the hazardous waste site and built a new high school on the west side of Interstate 45, nearer to Pearland.

Steve Braun – The Law or Professional Basketball

Steve Braun had an outstanding college basketball career at Houston Baptist University before deciding on law school. Steve joined Bracewell, where he and Jeff Horner recruited enough ringers to win lawyer league championships for the firm. One night on a road trip to the K-8 school district, Damon ISD, Steve sheepishly told me he was offered the chance to play professionally in the European League for a German team (every European team was allowed one American). Steve was probably taken aback when I said he could be a lawyer all his life, but age and physical conditions would one day limit his ability to play basketball at that level.

Steve played for the Germans and was in Berlin on that amazing evening of November 9, 1989, when the Berlin Wall came down. I cherish the piece of the Berlin Wall Steve retrieved for me that evening. Steve came back to

Bracewell to help in the firm's school asbestos cases, and he is now a legal recruiter and hearing officer.

Cars Driven by Superintendents and School Lawyers

A superintendent in the early 1970s told me he never drove a car that was considered more expensive than the cars driven by a majority of his school board members. Driving a foreign car like a Mercedes or BMW was out of the question. A high-end Buick, Ford, or Oldsmobile was acceptable, but a Cadillac or Lincoln was not. From the tone of his remark, I understood he was telling me the same standards applied to cars driven by the school district's lawyers.

One superintendent came to a Houston area school district from out of state in the early 1980s driving a BMW. I related my story to him and suggested that driving a BMW in his district might not be such a good idea. Sure enough, his BMW became a topic of conversation, and for many reasons in addition to his BMW, he did not last long in that superintendency.

I followed the superintendent's advice throughout my practice years. One night I was interviewing to represent a rural East Texas school district in a lawsuit. I was asked if I had some written information concerning our firm. I was able to say, "It's in my truck (Suburban) outside." We got hired—hopefully for more substantial reasons.

As board members upgraded their cars, I finally bought a Cadillac in the 1980s. After that car was used up, I reverted to the Chevy Tahoe, which has been my staple ever since. Now trustees drive a variety of cars and trucks, so little attention is paid to the private vehicles of superintendents and school lawyers. A school superintendent might even get by with a BMW today.

Title IX, Education Amendments of 1972 – Gender Equality

Title IX of the 1972 Education Amendments to the Elementary and Secondary Education Act[83] had a somewhat gradual, but ultimately a significant impact on public schools, colleges, and universities that received federal funding. Title IX prohibits gender (sexual) discrimination in programs that range from college admission and participation in programs to the award of scholarships and fellowships. The most obvious impact of Title IX has been on the participation of women in athletic programs.

Title IX caused the most concern among male school administrators and largely male school board members when it came to women's participation in high school athletics. Do we have to have women's teams, and do the facilities for females have to be equal to those of males? And, are female coaches supposed to be paid the same as male coaches? These and many other questions were asked, and, over time, answered.

The most interesting discussions of gender equality I recall occurred when male school board members who had athletic daughters raised questions and pushed for schools to expand athletic team offerings and facilities for women that were equal to those of men. Money was certainly a consideration, as was the timing of the transition. The transition to offer more women's sports and the acquisition of equal facilities has taken time, but schools now have softball as well as baseball fields, and women's basketball facilities are becoming more equal to the men's facilities. This transition to more equal facilities is especially evident in districts with new middle and senior high schools, and in those districts that have recently remodeled their facilities.

Aside from athletics, Title IX has influenced the academic side of education. More females are taking courses like advanced math and science that were historically male-dominated. Attitudes about gender inclusion have gradually changed, especially with more women serving on school boards and in administrative positions. I remember that while my first female superintendent was a novelty, today women superintendents are commonplace.

Title IX has had a strong influence in bringing about greater gender equality in higher education and professional schools. There were thirteen women in my first-year law school class of 500 in 1967, and today law school classes are pretty much equal percentages of male and female. The same is true of medical schools. In the 2012 and 2016 Summer Olympics, the U.S. women's teams bought home more medals than the men's team. There are certainly more women teaching in college, and business is seeing an ever-increasing number involved at all levels. More women will surely become involved in business leadership positions, just like what has occurred in education. While change has been measured, it has occurred, and it will continue.

Litigation will ultimately determine whether Title IX applies to transgender individuals. Unfortunately, the issue will probably be decided on the issue of the use of restrooms, where schools and their lawyers are again on the cutting edge of societal issues. After all, which societal issues don't find their way to our public schools?

Emergence of Women in the Law

While there were only thirteen women in my 1970 graduating class at The University of Texas School of Law, the percentage of women lawyers began to rise in the late 1970s and early 1980s. It was a natural for women to represent school districts where females were rising to prominence as administrators and being elected to school boards. The women who were administrative pioneers, like Brazosport Superintendent Patricia Shell, came primarily through their responsibilities and leadership in special education.

Jean Harshbarger Bilger came to Bracewell from the University of Virginia Law School in time to hit the incoming tide of special education matters and become an expert in the area. Her initial exposure was to assist me in the state's first special education hearing in La Porte ISD. Having taught in the Houston public schools for several years before attending The University of Texas School of Law, Janet Horton was a natural fit for education law upon graduation in 1980. She jumped in and inherited the *Leeper* home-schooling case in state court in Austin.

Janet also became immediately involved in the McAllen cases. As evident by the stories in these reflections, McAllen was an experience for all of us. It was there that Janet experienced the indignity of being denied service at the McAllen's La Posada Hotel bar because she was a single woman, until I arrived, after passing by the Houston Oilers cheerleaders' lingerie show downstairs. Times have changed! Another memorable McAllen moment was the behavior of a firefighter captain Janet was deposing one morning. (I broke in Janet and all lawyers with responsibility early.) The firefighter kept taking out his lighter and burning loose threads on his clothes. That tactic did not distract Janet, so he started pulling out his chest hairs and torching them. If it affected Janet, I couldn't tell it. He eventually stopped the show—maybe for fear that he would start a forest fire on his chest.

One night Janet and I were eating a northern Mexican dinner at the La Cucaracha Restaurant in Reynosa, Mexico, where I saw a friend and bridge club member of Carmela's. I told Janet we needed to go over and talk to her and those with her. Janet was curious why, and I responded, "Nancy sees me with this good-looking young woman in Mexico—she will call Carmela tonight." As it turned out, Nancy's aunt from McAllen, who was with her, had been following our cases in *The McAllen Monitor* and on television. The aunt recognized us. Nancy did call Carmela that night, but not before I did.

Janet was the first woman attorney to have a child while practicing law at Bracewell. Megan is now a speech pathologist in Shreveport, Louisiana. Janet helped fashion the firm's maternity leave program (now including paternity leave), which has served the firm and its attorneys well. Janet also served as Bracewell's first woman section head when she led the firm's School Law Section in the late 1990s. She was the first woman to chair the State Bar School Law Section, and she is a named partner in Thompson & Horton.

In the 1970s and 1980s, many male lawyers were reluctant to include women lawyers in lunches and events for fear of what people would think. I frequently took women lawyers and clients to lunch at the Houston Club and other restaurants. At the Houston Club or at a restaurant, I always asked to be seated near the front where I could introduce my female guest to those I knew as they entered the room. Some men today, Vice President Pence among them, will not travel or dine with a woman unless his wife is present. I could never have developed the women lawyers to become successful and equal to men without including them in the same activities as male lawyers, including lunches and car trips, and putting them on the front line.

I consider it an accomplishment that the commitment to hire and promote women and minorities in Bracewell's school practice was successful. At the time Thompson & Horton was formed by former Bracewell lawyers, Bracewell's public law practice group had 38% women partners and 70% women associates. We also had 15% minority partners and 50% minority associates.

Over the years, the percentage of women superintendents, college presidents, and board members has significantly increased. Our firm's commitment to hire, train, and promote women across the board, especially as lawyers, has served us well.

David, Would You Consider Coming to Houston?

Tim Cooper left in 1985 saying, "I don't want to be a lawyer any more. Maybe a bartender or actor, but not a lawyer." We needed a senior lawyer to join our section. I had met Jim Nelson, a lawyer and school board member through the Ector County (Odessa) ISD desegregation case. He had a great practice at the Shafer firm in Odessa, and his wife Karen had just started a business, so our offer of a move to Houston at the time was out of the question. (Ultimately, Jim became the Texas Commissioner of Education; the superintendent in Richardson, Texas; an executive for an education software company in San Diego; then of counsel in Thompson & Horton's Austin office, before returning to Odessa).

While at the Texas Association of School Boards, from 1978-1985, David Thompson had become a leader in school law issues. David began serving as general counsel for the TEA in 1985. While at the TEA, David had been co-counsel for the State of Texas in the public school finance case and knew the legislative process by virtue of having been the chief lobbyist for the TASB. He and his wife Tamara loved Austin, and I thought there was no way they would move to Houston.

After getting approval from the firm's Advisory Committee, I called David in early 1990 and asked him, "David, would you consider coming to Houston to practice law?" David replied, "Kelly, people in Austin don't talk about moving to Houston. People in Houston talk about moving to Austin." Surprisingly, he did not say no, and after several visits to Houston, David became a partner in Bracewell in May 1990. David is the acknowledged leader in public school finance, and he knows how to get things done in the Texas Legislature. David is now a named partner in Thompson & Horton.

The Lopez Connection – David and Vianei

David Lopez was elected to the HISD Board of Education in 1973 as an at-large candidate. A native of Laredo and a newspaper reporter in Corpus Christi before attending law school, David was the HISD's first Hispanic board member. Hispanics had always been considered white in the HISD's dual-school system. After Hispanics were recognized as a separate ethnic minority by the Supreme Court in *Keyes v. School District No. 1, Denver, Colorado* in 1973,[84] David persuaded the HISD Board to recognize Hispanics as a separate minority for remedial purposes under the desegregation order. There has never been a court finding that the HISD discriminated against Hispanics, but Hispanics were thereafter considered a separate ethnic group for desegregation remedy purposes.

David and his wife Romelia's daughter, Vianei, graduated from Kinkaid at 16 and Princeton at 19. She took a clock apart and reassembled it when she was about four years old. I told David and Romelia at that time if Vianei became a lawyer, we wanted a shot at getting her to work at Bracewell. Vianei clerked for us when she was too young to legally drink and joined the firm's school practice after law school at The University of Texas. After five years, she moved to Abilene, where she practiced law. Vianei also served as a director on the State Bar of Texas Board during my president-elect year. She and her husband now practice law in Fort Worth.

David and I handled a number of cases and disputes for our respective clients. In one memorable one, *Lozano v. HISD*, David and I were in Judge Seals' court. In an in-chamber conference, Judge Seals said, "Frels, this case is going to be settled, and you are in charge of getting it done." I called Superintendent Billy Reagan with the news from the judge's chambers. As we left, I told David, "David, Judge Seals said I had to settle it, but he means that you have to meet me halfway." The case settled halfway. Over the years I have referred many people with school problems in districts we do not represent to David.

Cheerleader Cases

Every school lawyer gets a cheerleader case sooner or later. I can't even remember my first or last one, but they usually involved the selection process, or a cheerleader's drinking alcohol or similar misbehavior. Former Bracewell partner Merri Schneider-Vogel seemed to have had more than her fair share of these cases over the years. There was even the infamous "Cheerleader Mom

Case" where a Houston area mother hired a hit man to knock off her daughter's cheerleader rival. That occurred in a school district we did not represent.

High School Graduation – To Walk or Not?

In the spring, sap rises in the trees and in adolescents. Even kids who have exhibited model behavior are prone to skip school or engage in over-the-line pranks in the spring of their senior year. As the end of the school year approaches, administrators have few disciplinary tools available to dissuade seniors from doing stupid things, except for the threat of not permitting misbehaving seniors from participating in the graduation ceremony. To everyone, graduation is the celebration of a milestone, and some seniors are the first in the family to graduate from high school. Many seniors have family members from out-of-town who make the trip to celebrate the accomplishment and see the senior walk across the stage.

Graduation ceremonies are held near Memorial Day, and I remember many years when judges would enter a temporary restraining order (TRO) without a hearing against a school district to allow a senior to participate in the graduation ceremony. I vividly recall being contacted while in Galveston on a Memorial Day Saturday to go to Montgomery County to represent a district on a TRO issue. TRO's can be issued ex parte, without notice to the school district or a hearing. After the graduation ceremony, the TRO is moot, and the issue simply goes away.

To combat ex parte TRO's, we began sending written notice to the Harris County's ancillary clerk well before graduation season every year listing the school districts in Harris County we represented. We asked to be notified of any TRO request against any of our client school districts so our clients could have a hearing. We gave the ancillary clerk the office, home and cell numbers of a number of our school lawyers. Giving notice to the district clerk worked well, because the ancillary clerks would tell TRO-seeking lawyers that Bracewell was the lawyer for the school district and that we asked to be notified of any TRO request so we could have a hearing before a TRO was issued. The practice of lawyers securing ex parte TRO's to allow seniors to walk across the stage dried up.

School District and College Police Departments

When I began my school law practice in 1970, then-Houston Police Chief Herman Short told HISD officials that his police officers were not coming on HISD campuses. (This was around the time of the highly publicized police intervention at Texas Southern University.) His comments also came about the time the HISD was implementing the comprehensive court-ordered desegregation plan after the August 25, 1970, Fifth Circuit decision—a time of change and uncertainty.

The HISD began to search for a solution to the refusal of Chief Short to allow officers on duty to enter Houston's public schools. Some relief was found by hiring off-duty peace officers, but that was only a partial solution. There was no statutory authority to create an HISD police force, so "brown shirt" security guards who did not carry weapons were hired, and former coach Les Burton became their leader. Ultimately, the legislature authorized public schools to create their own police departments staffed by certified law enforcement officers. These peace officers now actively coordinate and work with Houston city police, those from the Harris County Sheriff's Office, and the numerous other police forces in the Houston area.

The concept of educational institutions having police departments has spread to community colleges, universities, and special districts. Much of this push has been to have a police force responsible for the institution, but another motivation has been economics. The city and county resources for policing have been spread pretty thinly, and those entities are hard-pressed to raise taxes to provide the sometimes unique police coverage needed by school districts, colleges, and other entities.

There were growing pains with school districts' and community colleges' conversion to a certified police department—a paramilitary organization run by a police chief and a hierarchy of officers. I recall one situation where I needed the testimony of a police officer in a civil lawsuit. The officer refused to cooperate because "I am not responsible to the college." When asked to whom he was responsible, he replied, "the police chief." After he admitted he was paid by the college, and after my discussion with the police chief, the officer finally cooperated.

The Media – Friend or Foe?

Working with the media has been constant and significant in school practice. In the early days, when the courtroom was shaping education policy, school district lawyers were placed on center stage. Superintendents and board members wanted the lawyer to do the explaining and take the heat of the television lights. Speaking from the front of the HISD Administration Building, I appeared live on the ABC national morning news show during the metropolitan part of the HISD desegregation case. Bracewell partner Jennifer Weston appeared live on the "Today Show" to talk about sexual harassment in schools. I was on television and radio so often during the Westheimer controversy in the mid- and late 1970s that people would stop me on the street, or at ballgames and events, to ask, "Haven't I seen you on TV?"

It seemed that the media followed me everywhere. During the middle of the proposed Westheimer school case, I flew good old Texas International to Little Rock one night to make a speech to the Arkansas school lawyers' organization. The pilot could not verify that the landing gear was engaged, so a member of the crew pulled up the carpet by my seat and shined a flashlight into the interior of the plane to determine whether the wheels were locked for landing. The runway in Little Rock was lined with emergency vehicles with red lights blinking when we landed. After getting to the hotel, I switched on the news, and it was covering our landing. Arkansas Governor Orville Faubus was on the flight, and the television showed me deplaning immediately after him. There I was, again, on television, but in Arkansas. I called Carmela with the story by land line, using a credit card. We had a good laugh about the media seeming to follow me.

Interesting people have reported the education news in Houston. In the 1970s, when women were really breaking into the media, the HISD beat attracted some memorable folks. Jessica Savich, of national network fame before her tragic death, started in Houston before heading to New York. DeDe Feldman, who now lives in Austin with her retired Vinson & Elkins husband, Joe Bill Watkins, was the constant voice of KTRH 740. Bill Hensel of the *Houston Chronicle*, who is now with the Houston Port Authority, started on the education beat. Susan Bischoff, who became the business editor at the *Houston Chronicle*, started on the HISD beat where she met her husband, Jim Barlow, the spokesperson for the HISD. Wayne Dolcefino of Channel 13 followed Marvin Zindler as an investigative reporter. Wayne appeared at virtually all school districts to pursue his hard-hitting investigative reporting on school-related cases. Bill Broyles, an early editor of *Texas Monthly*, started as the HISD spokesperson during the Citizens for Good Schools and Superintendent George Garver era.

One school client was experiencing significant difficulty in dealing with, much less working with, Wayne Dolcefino. I finally had to take the client's upper-level administration for media training by Dan Ammerman, a retired Channel 11 TV anchor. We role-played, and the staff learned how to prepare for and respond to reporters' questions. The sessions apparently worked because Wayne started getting answers from a confident staff, and his presence at the institution waned.

I have found that the media will generally treat you fairly if you follow a few basic rules. While it is always best to call the client before talking with the reporter, the reporter's call should be returned ASAP because of news deadlines. The client's side of the issue cannot be reported if you do not beat that deadline. "No comment" should never be the response to a question. I simply explain why I cannot answer a question. If a lawyer cannot talk about something because of the attorney/client privilege, tell the reporter that you wish you could talk about the issue, but it would be professionally inappropriate for you to talk about something within the attorney/client privilege. Most reporters understand privilege.

It is helpful to think through and define the message you want to send in an interview. Thoughts should be broken into short segments for television or radio. Sometimes making notes about the message and standing when talking on the telephone are helpful—I tend to think and talk more fluently when standing (the old trial lawyer in me). If possible, I ask the reporter before the interview what he or she wants to know so I can help achieve the reporter's objective and yet protect the client's interest. Many times reporters have helpful knowledge which they will share, so I never hesitate to ask a reporter questions about what he or she knows.

I have come to believe that an active media acting under the freedom of the First Amendment is essential to the maintenance of our freedom and our representative democracy. Yes, reporters and editors may get it wrong from time to time and inaccurately report facts, but those errors generally get corrected when there is a free flow of information. Advertisers and sponsors help police media abuses by withdrawing advertising when a media representative gets too far out of line. Far more challenging is the flow of "facts" and opinions from blogs and social media where an erroneous fact can be repeated without any limits. If something erroneous is said enough times without correction, people believe it is a "fact."

Teacher Termination Issues – A Constant Throughout

Teacher termination issues are a constant in school law practice. Numerous specific teacher cases have been mentioned in these stories, and there have been many more that have influenced the development of my practice and the school practice generally. Many of the early teacher cases in federal court involved whether procedural due process was required to terminate or to reassign a teacher, and if so, what procedures must be followed. These uncertainties caused school administrators and school boards to fear making recommendations to terminate an employee.

Cases such as *Ferguson v. Thomas*, *Roth v. Board of Regents*, and *Perry v. Sindermann*[85] helped fashion the legal framework for teacher and other employee discipline and dismissal matters. With these cases, it became clear that state laws and employment contracts actually established the property interest to which procedural due process requirements are to be applied. In the early years of my practice, state statutes, rules of the State Board of Education, and school board policies provided employees with hearing opportunities directly before the school board. These hearings lasted for hours, and school board members often were sucked into getting personally involved. It was not unusual for hearings to last six to ten hours, with school board members spending the night at hearings. Some hearings extended over several nights.

One of the most challenging aspects of putting on the administration's case for termination was to get the witnesses to avoid talking "educationese" and keeping the issues simple and focused. One especially challenging reassignment hearing involved a member of the HISD special education administrative team led by Dr. Charles Meisgeier and Dr. Barry Dollar. These child psychologists were brilliant academics, but experienced real difficulty simplifying why the person needed to be moved or terminated. It took me two full afternoons of coaching to get them to a vocabulary level so others could easily understand what they were saying. Fortunately, they finally succeeded, and the board voted to reassign the employee.

In another hearing, I was cross-examining an English teacher represented by Chris Tritico in his first teacher termination case, using one of her letters to her principal—a letter filled with grammatical mistakes. After about ten minutes, HISD Board member and lawyer, Ron Franklin asked, "Counsel, how much more of this are you going to do? We get the point." I passed the witness, and the board voted unanimously to terminate the teacher.

Board members became weary of these long hearings. What superintendent would want to put his or her administrators and board members through such hearings on a regular basis? Board members also feared that they would get sued and might lose any wealth they had accumulated. Fewer people became board candidates, and administrators backed off from trying to fire teachers.

To help counteract the laboriousness of hearings and to streamline them, we developed sample notice letters for administrators to use when communicating with teachers, as well as scripts for the board president to follow at hearings to ensure that the hearings were properly conducted. While these materials helped add order, hearings remained time-consuming and unpopular. We also helped the administrators prepare their cases through better documentation and more effective counseling. (From these efforts came the Education Law Association monograph, *A Documentation System for Teacher Improvement or Termination*, now in its seventh edition and still selling well.)

Even using this process, the hearing to terminate the principal at an elementary school in the HISD for cheating on student test scores for the Second Mile stipend took eighty hours. This case was extremely complex, and I had to hire a psychiatrist to help me analyze a hostile teacher witness who had been manipulated by the principal. The teacher ultimately turned out to be a very helpful witness, just as the psychiatrist said she would if I was sensitive to her position. (She was apparently looking for an opportunity to clear her name.) The HISD Board voted 5-4 to terminate the principal.

As the legal standards became better defined, the Texas Legislature began to enact statutes that changed the hearing process and redefined the basic teacher contract laws. Districts that had adopted probationary and continuing contracts (tenure) have been permitted to move away from continuing contracts and are now permitted to give term contracts to teachers after a probationary period. A statewide system of independent hearing officers who hear the evidence and recommend decisions to the board of trustees for teacher dismissals is now in place. School boards now vote on terminations after hearing oral arguments on the record, developed before the hearing officer with the aid of the hearing officer's recommendation. Order with fairness has finally come to this part of the school law practice.

Teacher dismissal cases have also provided a regular group of lawyers who represent them. It was in the HISD's *Wright & Meyers v. HISD*[86] that I first encountered Larry Watts. Robert E. "Bob" Hall was the lawyer for the Houston Teachers Association and various individual teachers. Dick Strahan, now deceased, represented the Houston Principals Association and a number of individual HISD administrators. Chris Tritico has represented numerous teachers, as well as the Houston Federation of Teachers in the HISD. David Lopez has been a regular representing teachers and administrations since he left the HISD Board. Before Chris Tritico, George Kirk and the husband and wife team of Stuart and Carol Nelkin represented numerous teachers very effectively. Larry Daves of Tyler had a brief tenure as a teacher lawyer in several of my East Texas school cases. Occasionally, Jay Brim, Rick Arnett, or Mark Robinett of Austin ventured to the Houston area to represent a teacher or administrator. Neal Adams of Bedford, a former Hurst-Euless-Bedford ISD trustee and a former member of the Texas College Coordinating Board, has represented administrators through the TASA. We have worked out a number of superintendent departures with Neal Adams and Vidal Martinez of Houston. The administration of justice is clearly better served when quality lawyers represent each side of a dispute. I have been fortunate to have had, with very few exceptions, good lawyers on the other side.

The Gordon Cotton Principalship – An Example of School Leadership

I became acquainted with Gordon Cotton, the principal of HISD's Waltrip High School, through my first lawsuit as a lawyer in 1970 and the *Paul Kitchen* case, discussed earlier. Waltrip High School is located in the middle-class Oak Forest neighborhood off Loop 610 and Ella Boulevard, in northwest Houston.

While other schools were experiencing teacher unrest and significant teacher turnover in the early 1970s, Waltrip, under Gordon Cotton's leadership, was a relative sea of calm. A few teachers came and went at Waltrip, but all who left Waltrip quietly resigned. Most teachers who taught at Waltrip were long-termers, and, upon close examination, administrative leadership emerged as the primary reason. Teachers and other staff knew the standards they were expected to achieve and maintain. If a teacher failed to perform to standard, Principal Cotton or his assistants would identify the teacher's primary problems and offer help. The teachers who failed to achieve acceptable performance after opportunities to improve seemed to recognize their failures; rather than blaming someone, they resigned and went on to do something else. Compassionate but firm leadership from the top created an environment for learning to take place. This atmosphere extended to the entire school, including the support staff, the students, and their parents.

I have used Gordon Cotton's leadership as the example of how an effective principal can play a primary role in fashioning a successful school. Houston and Texas public schools have many such leaders who work collaboratively with teachers, staff, and parents to define the school's goal, set standards, and maintain those standards. These leaders share and reward success, all the while treating people fairly.

Here Comes the City – Changes in Small-town Districts

Life in Texas' small towns in the 1960s and 1970s was culturally and politically different from life in the cities in many ways. Residents of small-town school districts knew each other, and the schools and churches were clearly the centers of their communities' activities. This unique culture began to feel the impact of the city culture with the suburban growth that accelerated in the late 1970s, a growth that continues today.

As a high school student at Industrial ISD in Jackson County in 1958-62, our teams played football, basketball, etc. against Pearland ISD in District 28-A. (My graduating class in 1962 had 44 students.) Today, Pearland ISD, which borders the Houston ISD on the south, has two 6A high schools. The Katy ISD, located to Houston ISD's west, had one high school located in the city of Katy when I began representing the district in the 1980s. Katy ISD now has seven 6A high schools, and the district continues to grow. The Conroe ISD in Montgomery County, located to Houston's north, had one high school in the city of Conroe until George Mitchell developed the Woodlands, which spurred growth south of the San Jacinto River, a historic dividing line between north and south Montgomery County. Conroe ISD now has six high schools, and residential growth continues. Tomball and Sugar Land, other former small towns in the Houston area, have experienced similar growth.

Other major Texas cities like Dallas, Austin, Fort Worth, and San Antonio have seen the same suburban growth as Houston, and their surrounding small towns with independent school districts have been similarly impacted. Suburban growth adjacent to smaller cities like Waco, Lubbock, and El Paso has resulted in the growth of surrounding small-town school districts.

Before the arrival of the suburbanites, incumbents on school boards in small towns rarely experienced a contested race. As the cities grew out to these small towns, the school districts saw the newcomers running against incumbent trustees, with many getting elected. In some districts, factions developed, pairing "old town" candidates against the "newcomers," or the "city people."

Many of the small-town districts went through a period of adjustment to these demographic changes with one faction prevailing in one election and with another faction winning in a subsequent contest. Some sitting superintendents in these growing districts retired or were replaced during the changing times. Some of the superintendents who replaced long-term superintendents became "change agents," who themselves were replaced when political equilibrium was achieved on the school board. Most of the district leadership changes were smooth, but some were more contentious.

Changing Superintendents – "Neal, Wait Until After Midnight"

In addition to teacher terminations, boards have regularly wanted to change leadership at the superintendency. I developed a reputation as a lawyer who could help school districts make a smooth transition from one superintendent to another. We actually began representing a number of school districts by helping the board successfully have the superintendent peacefully resign. A majority of the situations were pretty simple, because the superintendents knew things weren't going well and realized it was time to move on. Some separations were, however, contested, and some even became contentious. Several of the memorable superintendent changes are referenced throughout these reflections.

One early summer night in a growing suburban Houston school district, Neal Adams was representing a change agent superintendent whom the board wanted to replace. We engaged in hours of back-and-forth offers and counteroffers, a process that I have never found especially productive. Finally, Neal and I came to an amount of money with terms we both felt were fair to our respective clients, but my client board had one member holding out for a lesser amount. About 11:30, I told Neal, "Let's keep going past midnight because that's when the air conditioning goes off. After it gets hot, I think the matter will settle for the amount we feel is fair." About 12:45 we had a deal, and the board voted unanimously, then adjourned.

The Santa Fe ISD Prayer Case – How We Were Hired

While president of the Houston Bar Association in 1995, I was on my way to a live broadcast at a Christian radio station when I got a call from David

Hodgins, a new lateral associate in the firm's School Law Section. David was apparently the next most senior lawyer in the office when Lisa Brown received a call from an insurance company to represent the Santa Fe ISD in a case in Galveston federal court where Judge Sam Kent had already issued an injunction preventing the district from distributing copies of the Bible, having a baccalaureate service, and from saying prayers at football games. A school board meeting was being held that night to discuss the case and to hire lawyers. Lisa had committed to attend another board meeting that evening. David was willing to go solo to Santa Fe, but I told him to pick me up in the parking lot of the radio station.

David drove and I reviewed the meager file we had been faxed. The hiring of lawyers was posted for open session, and a discussion of the case with counsel was posted for closed session. Since Bracewell had not been hired by the Santa Fe Board, any discussion of our experiences and how we would handle the case prior to our being hired had to be done in open session. A majority of the board members were pleased to have us, but some ultra-right conservatives felt we were too biased in favor of following the established law, and they were committed to change the law to allow prayer at football games. On a split vote, we were hired and proceeded to consult with the board in closed session.

After the closed session, which lasted well into the night, we drove back to Houston. The rest is, as they say, history. Bracewell partner Lisa Brown, with the help of associate Reagan Pratt, a former law clerk of Judge Sam Kent and associate Philip Fraissinet, finished representing the school district through the opinion by the Fifth Circuit. We helped develop a policy which was as close to being constitutionally acceptable under the First Amendment as the ultra-conservatives on the board would accept. Ultimately, a religious advocacy legal group headed by Jay Sekulow, who became one of President Trump's lawyers, offered to represent the school district before the United States Supreme Court without charge—but only after Lisa got the Supreme Court to accept the case on certiorari.[87]

Sexual Harassment and Sexual Misconduct

In the late 1980s, sexual harassment was emerging as an employment issue of the future. Complaints filed with the Equal Employment Opportunities Commission under Title VII were increasing, and cases were being filed and opinions written. I developed materials on the subject and began to include the prevention of employee sexual harassment in client seminars.

I was spread about as thin as possible when a long-term client, San Jacinto College, asked me to do a series of in-services on sexual harassment for their classified staff. I told associate Lisa Brown that sexual harassment was an area

I did not have time to develop, and the subject was an opportunity for her to become an expert. She participated with me at the in-services and began her journey to becoming the go-to sexual harassment lawyer. Lisa and I wrote articles on sexual harassment for the National School Board's Council of School Attorneys' publication, and she began making speeches on the subject. Needless to say, she has become a nationally recognized sexual harassment expert. Lisa has expanded the practice, with sexual harassment and sexual assaults becoming prominent issues in higher education under Title IX.

Prior to the 1995 enactment of Chapter 261 of the Texas Family Code,[88] reports of school employees allegedly sexually harassing students, or reports of school employees being engaged in inappropriate sexual conduct with students, were usually made to the building principal or other administrators. We were generally brought in to investigate the allegations. It was in these investigations that we first utilized written questions that required employees to answer them under oath.

Once the Texas mandatory reporting law for suspected child abuse or neglect became effective, anyone who had reasonable cause to believe abuse or neglect occurred was required to report to law enforcement or Children's Protective Service. It took time for everyone involved in the reporting and investigating process to understand their duties and roles. Once that occurred, school lawyers' role became providing advice on the reporting process and on any resulting employment issues.

Transgender Issues

Our first experience with transgender issues and clients was at a local community college in the late 1980s. A biological man who was beginning gender reassignment wanted to use the women's dressing room at the campus exercise facility. This resulted in an aggressive, negative reaction from the women patrons. I gave my gut level advice to the college and turned the matter over to our newly minted sexual harassment expert, Lisa Brown. "Lisa, you're the sex expert, here is a chance to broaden your practice." Lisa and college officials worked out a neutral or unisex location that solved this particular issue. There were no cases on the issue, so the practical, gut reaction advice was about as good as the client was going to get; that advice, along with the administrators' reasonableness, resolved the issue.

A subsequent and even more interesting matter presented itself at another Houston-area education institution. A longtime professor, previously married with two middle school-aged children, was undergoing gender reassignment. The professor had begun hormone treatments and was beyond the basic psychological decision to transition, and had begun wearing feminine clothing on weekends. The educational institution was located in a politically conservative area, but the professor was uniformly supported by his colleagues in this transition, and a unisex restroom was found for her use during the transition. The only legal issue we ultimately assisted with was to facilitate her name change and help give notice of that change to other governmental agencies.

It is regrettable that the transgender bathroom issue on public school and college campuses has been politicized by all sides of the issue. My experience over the years has been that schools are staffed with practical and sensitive people who find a way to "work things out" for everyone concerned.

Pro Se Plaintiffs

Pro se plaintiffs—those individuals who represent themselves without the aid of a lawyer—are a trial lawyer's nightmare, especially in the public setting of educational institutions where lawyers are the face of the institution they represent. Judges also want to be certain pro se plaintiffs get a fair shake because judges and lawyers believe the courts need to be open to all. Several specific instances of pro se plaintiffs come to mind.

The first, and by far the most interesting, involved a former HISD employee whose pro se suit landed in United States District Judge Woodrow Seals' court. This woman was really confused. At a hearing on her request to reinstate her dismissed case, she brought a silver-plated shovel in a big bag. She accused Bill Wilde and me of using the shovel to dig in her yard and plant something evil. This display was too much for Judge Seals, who denied her motion to reinstate her case and banned her from the 11th floor of the federal courthouse. He called a United States marshal to escort her out of the building. That was the last we heard of her.

One pro se case in state district court resulted in the judge asking us as HISD attorneys to help the pro se with discovery and filings. We actually sent the plaintiff a full set of interrogatories, made sure he didn't miss deadlines, and gave him all the information we had. We eventually got a summary judgment; interestingly, the pro se apparently felt he had been treated fairly by the judge and our client. Some pro se plaintiffs I encountered over the years probably had some legal training or had researched courthouse files to the extent they did a fairly decent job—several even better than a couple of lawyers I encountered.

Asbestos – What a Challenge

At some point in the 1970s or early 1980s, medical experts began to link exposure to asbestos fibers with asbestosis and lung cancer. The asbestos-related diseases manifested themselves years, often decades, after exposure, making establishing cause-and-effect difficult. The early focus of the asbestos-related lawsuits was on behalf of those who worked in shipyards and in construction with asbestos products. The health and safety concerns about exposure to asbestos ultimately shifted to protecting schoolchildren, who were more vulnerable to the asbestos fibers than adults. (Asbestos-related diseases began to appear in family members of asbestos industry-related workers whose work clothing contained the fibers.)

Martin Dies, of Orange, Texas, had represented East Texas school districts for years on faulty roof design cases. Bracewell actually referred a roof case to Martin because we did not sue businesses. (The line in those days between doing plaintiff and defense work was much brighter than it is today.) Martin's father, a state senator who then became Texas Attorney General, had been a close friend of Searcy Bracewell, the sole state senator from Harris County until redistricting after *Baker v. Carr*.[89] Martin liked Searcy and respected our firm, especially our school practice.

Martin and I made our first contact regarding asbestos in the schools sometime in the early 1980s. He had initiated a suit in Beaumont federal court on behalf of several of the East Texas school districts seeking the cost of removing the asbestos from ceilings where it had been installed, ostensibly as a fire retardant. We were interested in helping our school clients recover the cost of removing the asbestos from the asbestos product manufacturers. It was becoming clearer that schools would ultimately be required by law or government regulations, at great cost, to remove or encase "friable" asbestos.

David Thompson, who at the time was the chief lobbyist for the TASB, agreed to reserve a meeting room at the TASB/TASA convention in San Antonio for lawyers to meet with school districts who wanted to know more about joining the asbestos cases in Beaumont or a national class action. The national class action on behalf of school districts seeking recovery for asbestos abatement had been filed by Ron Motley, a mass tort attorney from South Carolina. The argument was advanced at the San Antonio meeting by some local lawyers working with Motley that the real benefit of being a part of the national class action would reduce the districts' financial exposure because school districts would not be required to contribute up-front expense money, but those districts in our case would. (Bracewell and Martin Dies actually up-fronted most of the money for our clients' case.) Ultimately, most larger districts joined the HISD in our case, as did the City of Houston, the DFW Airport Authority, and Harris County.

I remained involved with the policy side of the case and, to a much lesser extent, the day-to-day work. Partners Robert Watts and Ron Scott coordinated the case for Bracewell. Washington Bracewell partner Luis Nido and his team prosecuted an asbestos removal case for Mercer University. Along the way,

Martin associated his current partner Dickie Hile, then of Jasper, as co-counsel. Martin ultimately married our D.C. partner Darci Rock, who worked on the Virginia and Texas asbestos cases. Dickie, Martin, and Darcie now live and practice in Austin. Dickie has been very active in professional issues with the State Bar of Texas and certain administrative issues of the Texas Supreme Court.

The lawyers for one manufacturing defendant, Andrews Kurth in Houston, were aggressive. During the early discovery part of the case, Andrews Kurth noticed numerous depositions of school administrators and board members all over the state to commence on the same day. Bracewell had about 200 lawyers in Houston at the time, and we mobilized a contingent of forty-plus trial, labor, and school lawyers to defend at the depositions. We prepared a deposition notebook and briefed all these trial lawyers, plus many of our local counsel, who then briefed the school officials on what to expect at deposition. We did not file motions to quash the massive simultaneous deposition movement; we simply out-prepared Andrews Kurth and spread out all over the state. I recall being with the Midland ISD officials for their depositions. After two days using this approach, Andrews Kurth abandoned the tactic, and our clients did not receive further deposition notices. We had beaten the defense team at its own game.

We pressed our discovery of the defendant companies—where we were greeted by many "Here is the warehouse" responses—but we continued to dig. Martin employed an engineer as an expert who developed a scientifically based system that could match the ceiling samples found in a school with each company's asbestos ceiling texture formula, so it became easier to prove which company's asbestos product was used in a school. The digging into boxes in an East Coast warehouse finally bore fruit, with the discovery by one of our paralegals of documents which forced settlement.

The settlement money came in over the years, but the most significant settlements were paid in 1988 and 1993, times of a depressed economy in Texas. Our clients were pleased because they received almost full value for the actual costs of asbestos removal, less the legal fees and any special costs. Sixty-five of Bracewell's 200-plus lawyers at the time worked on some aspect of one of the asbestos cases, so asbestos was truly a firm endeavor. We were also able to settle a multiple school district asbestos case in Colorado, where we worked with Boulder lawyer Dick Bump and his firm. The national class action produced virtually no recovery for the school districts that choose to stay in that case. By settlement time, OSHA and other regulations were in place that dictated how the asbestos abatement was to be accomplished. These regulations also extended to asbestos in pipe installation and floor tiles.

Joan Raymond – Trying Times

In 1986, HISD's Board hired a unique person to be superintendent: Joan Raymond, who was the superintendent in Yonkers, New York. I first met her when the board hired her to succeed Billy Reagan. I told her I would prepare her contract, and she told me it must include a Lincoln Town Car and a driver. (The Lincoln Town Car was a high-end car like the other superintendent's BMW referred to earlier. The Lincoln later became a community issue, and its required identification as an HISD vehicle resulted from state legislation.)

Dr. Raymond changed the board's outside auditors and the financial advisors. She also shuffled the administration in a way to remove as much of Billy Reagan's past as possible. She apparently wanted to change anything that people could use to compare Billy Reagan with her. She never talked with Billy Reagan during her superintendency.

Dick Johnson, the publisher of the *Houston Chronicle*, and Tony Pederson, the *Chronicle* editor, apparently were not fans of Raymond. The superintendent was very sensitive about anyone having access to her college transcript. Others told me she changed her surname to Raymond about the time she received her doctorate so it would be more compatible with the title "Dr."

When a question arose about the legitimacy of university degrees and the certification credentials of HISD administrators, the *Houston Chronicle* sought copies of all administrators' transcripts, including Dr. Raymond's. Naturally, the HISD refused to release these transcripts. The lawsuit that ensued, *Houston Chronicle* cases collectively,[90] was a real legal ride involving statutory and constitutional issues. Bill Ogden and Joel White represented the *Chronicle*, and Arturo Michel and I represented the HISD. Since Bracewell also did environmental and labor work for the *Chronicle*, we had a business conflict. We asked the *Chronicle* to delay a temporary injunction hearing so the HISD could get different counsel. The *Chronicle* refused, so under the State Bar Disciplinary Rules, Bill Wilde and I concluded that we had to protect the HISD's interests by representing it, regardless of our business conflicts. We did not have a legal conflict.

The *Houston Chronicle* sought a mandamus before the Texas Supreme Court to force the state district judge to rule while we secured help from the legislature. Even though we got the legislative help protecting college transcripts from public disclosure (including the *Chronicle*), issues of common law and the constitutional right of privacy remained for trial. In the early morning hours on the eve of trial, Arturo Michel was the victim of a head-on collision on Allen Parkway when a kid who had stolen a car hit him. Arturo was going home from the office when this wreck happened. Even though he was badly injured, Arturo's call to me from Ben Taub Hospital was, "The brief and documents are on my ledge." Graciously, Bill Ogden agreed to a continuance of the trial, and he sent Arturo flowers. We eventually won the case after a trial before state district Judge Dan Downey, who still talks about the fun he had dealing with the lawyers and the complex constitutional, statutory, and common law legal issues involved. Bill Ogden and I developed a friendship that continues today.

Dr. Raymond never did like me much, especially after I represented the board in the renegotiation of her employment contract. She was represented in the negotiations by a National Football League Players' Union lawyer from Chicago. I stood up for the board's positions in the negotiations, and my doing so apparently did not please Dr. Raymond. Her dislike for me seemed to intensify.

One day, Dr. Raymond called me and asked me to do something that I told her my ethical duty to the board would not permit me to do. She cursed a bit and told me that she would get the board to hire her own lawyer, and I assured her that lawyer would feel like I did on the issue. I also told her that when she was gone, I would still be there.

She got the HISD Board to allow her to have an in-house counsel and, I am certain that if ever asked, he told her the same thing about her request. Needless to say, my relationship with her continued to worsen, even to the point that I was prepared to resign as counsel if the relationship with her became more contentious. Interestingly, her relationship with the board was apparently not any better than hers with me.

Thus, Dr. Raymond ran her course with the board and the Houston business community. She moved on with her golden parachute she had negotiated with the board using her NFL players' lawyer, but she and the Lincoln Town Car were history. Some complained that she was paid too much to leave, but I maintain that the money was well spent.

Frank Petruzielo, Rod Paige, and Kaye Stripling

While these reflections are not intended to be an HISD history, the HISD was been a constant in my life since I arrived at Bracewell in August 1970. Several events surrounding these HISD superintendents are worthy of note.

Frank Petruzielo followed Joan Raymond. His first responsibility was to repair relationships. Second, he proceeded to address the next big movement in national school reform, which was to return the primary responsibility of running a campus to the principal, teachers, and community. In the 1960s and 1970s, when the Constitution came to campus through the application of free speech, due process and desegregation, the most effective way to ensure compliance with these laws was to centralize the functions, so school campuses were stripped of much of their independence. Site-based management was designed to restore a large share of that campus independence, but on the basis of shared responsibility.

Frank's Achilles heel was a deputy superintendent who apparently followed Frank from school district to school district. This fellow acted as Frank's hatchet man, a job at which he seemed to excel. After creating much turmoil and consternation in the HISD, he finally moved on.

When Frank left to pursue other opportunities in 1994, further school reform was heavy in the air and the HISD Board was ready to move on it. (Frank was, in reality, a change agent for HISD.) To the surprise of many, the board chose one of its own members, Dr. Rod Paige, Dean of the Education Department at Texas Southern University, as the new superintendent. Dr. Paige had to resign from the board before his selection as superintendent, and once approved as superintendent, he then had to secure state certification as a superintendent. It was a time of political and legal maneuvering that again took us into the federal and state courts.

The first suit in state court by Mexican-American Bar Association affiliated lawyers challenged the location where the meeting notice for the board meeting at which Dr. Paige was hired was posted. After a court challenge to the posting location was filed, we took the conservative route and posted another meeting notice on the glass door of the administration building, and the board conducted another meeting. The board again selected Dr. Paige. The group opposed Dr. Paige because its members stated they wanted an Hispanic for superintendent. They then sued in federal court using civil rights claims to complain that trustees had violated the Open Meetings Act by talking with each other in numbers less than a quorum. We were able to prevail in the suit through a well-reasoned opinion by United States District Judge Lynn Hughes.

With Dr. Paige's leadership and a reform-minded HISD Board, the board's strategic plan, "Beliefs and Visions," was implemented. The community bought into "Beliefs and Visions," which were simply stated and easily understood, along with many programs that Governor George W. Bush used to fashion his version of school reform for the state of Texas. I successfully used the process and concepts of "Beliefs and Visions" with several organizations in which I was involved. The Texas reforms then became the blueprint for the "No Child Left Behind Act" that President Bush persuaded Congress to adopt in 2001. By then, Dr. Paige was President Bush's Secretary of Education.

HISD administrative veteran Dr. Kaye Stripling followed Dr. Paige and served as superintendent for several years, until her retirement. By that time, I had begun the process of having the next generation of Bracewell lawyers represent the District. David Thompson took over the outside general counsel role of the HISD representation during the superintendency of Dr. Abelando "Abe" Saavedra. David and his firm, Thompson & Horton, continue to provide HISD's outside counsel representation.

Lawsuits, and Avoiding Them

School lawyers represent clients mainly in matters of constitutional and civil rights, plus issues of policy. Most school cases involve cutting-edge constitutional issues, and many involve the application of policy, so money is normally not much of an issue—except for termination cases and attorney fees. While our clients have prevailed in most of the litigated matters, we have lost a few along the way. Disputes that were based only on state statutes or school district policies were filed with the Commissioner of Education for his review. Disputes on the application of school laws and policy had to be heard by the Commissioner before a suit could be filed in state district court. This was especially true in the 1970s and 1980s, when a significant number of school law issues were being decided. Cases involving the application of the Constitution or congressional acts were filed in federal court. Appendix-F includes a listing of all the reported cases in which I was the lead co-counsel or amicus curiae with another member of Bracewell. There were, of course, many cases we tried that did not result in published opinions.

Many school district disputes were, and continue to be, a result of teachers, parents, employees, and lawyers not communicating with the right person at the school district. I fielded many calls from lawyers representing clients with disputes whom I asked, "Has your client talked with the teacher, principal, etc. to see if this can be resolved?" Many times they had not, so I directed them to the proper administrator at the school district. "If your client cannot resolve the problem, please call me back, and we will see if someone else might help." Very few lawyers ever called me back, and when they did, we usually were able to find the right administrator to resolve the issue.

The same was true of many lawsuits that were filed by lawyers unfamiliar with informal dispute resolution in a school system. Before or immediately after the filing of a lawsuit, I made it a practice to call the lawyer and discuss his or her client's grievance. Some matters were quickly resolved, while others took more time and more discussions to reach an amicable resolution. I have always felt I mediated and resolved many school clients' cases before mediation was formally introduced as a means of dispute resolution. Lawsuits filed by employee organizations or political advocacy groups were not as easily resolved because most of the issues in dispute were political. Some cases, of course, were filed by lawyers who were either looking to make their mark, or who were just "tough" advocates to whom winning seemed to be everything, regardless of their client's interests.

The key to school districts being able to avoid lawsuits is to have administrators versed in the law who are willing to talk with anxious and even angry people about resolving their problems. Early on in my career, I conducted in-services with small groups of HISD's school principals, assistant principals, and other administrators on the law applicable to school districts, injunctions to which the HISD was subject, and strategies for resolving problems. No question was off-limits, so I found I could not answer many of the questions. When I could not provide an answer, I would admit I did not know the answer, and I would research it and then share my answer at a subsequent session. The administrators many times presented practical solutions to resolve issues. These sessions gave the administrators the knowledge and confidence they needed to work through parent, employee, and patron concerns. An administrator who knows the legal framework and has discussed how problems can be resolved with others develops a confidence to communicate, so problems can be resolved before people feel like they have to get a lawyer and sue.

The small group learning sessions were ultimately changed to larger groups where the presentations were more lecture, with less of the give-and-take that characterized the smaller group meetings. Other districts saw the value of the small group sessions, especially on communication with employees and the documentation of their performance.

Sessions devoted to employee communication and documentation were held at many school districts and in seminar venues. The process of communicating with teachers and other employees and documenting those communications that we developed became a NOLPE (ELA) monograph, *A Documentation System for Teacher Improvement or Termination*, which is in its seventh edition and is available in print through the ELA Bookstore (www.educationlaw.org) or digital version through Amazon.

One Friday, I got a call from a Beaumont lawyer who said he was on the way to Harris County to file an injunction action against the HISD in a student injury case. By talking with him, I learned he had been a lawyer for a short time and that he was clueless about governmental immunity. I asked him to hold up filing a lawsuit pending my faxing him some case citations and a motion for summary judgment I had filed on another case on a student injury issue. Later, he called back and thanked me, and he told me he would

Sixth and seventh editions of the ELA monograph, *A Documentation System for Teacher Improvement or Termination*

By Kelly Frels

not be filing the lawsuit. In my retirement, lawyers often approach me at bar meetings and around town and say something like, "You don't remember me, but I represented a client in a matter with HISD, and you helped me resolve it. Thank you." Those stories and "thank yous" have been the best rewards possible for my working with people to resolve their clients' problems.

Road Trips with Associates

It was always an adventure to take associates to evening school board meetings. First, attending night meetings is an acid test for whether a lawyer is serious about representing school districts and colleges. To be an effective school lawyer, one must attend board meetings at all hours of the day and night. Secondly, riding in the confines of a car for several hours is a great learning time where seemingly "dumb" questions can be asked and experiences about being a lawyer can be shared. Road trips afford the chance to talk philosophy, ideas, practice concepts, and time to just tell stories. (Family trips with children serve the same purpose.)

Normally road trips involved me driving my car, because I generally knew where I was going. On two memorable occasions, my car was in the shop, so we went in the associates' cars. One afternoon Steve Braun drove me to Tomball ISD in his "hippie van," an old Volkswagen van that was not air-conditioned. Although I liked the old van, the long, dusty drive with the windows down prompted me to comment to Steve that I thought we paid him enough to get an air-conditioned vehicle. Likewise, on a 100-degree summer afternoon, I had to change a tire on Lisa Brown's law school-vintage car on the side of IH-10 near Katy. I was sweaty when we arrived at the Katy ISD board meeting. The trustees had a good laugh. Lisa ultimately traded for a newer model car with better tires.

Now retired, I no longer have an active role with associates. Also, today, there is so much emphasis on billing hours that such trips are more difficult when both the partner and associate must account for hours. Technology has also impacted travel—personally being in attendance at all meetings is not needed as much as it once was. However, my experiences suggest that face time and personal interaction with clients at board meetings and elsewhere is still important in developing and maintaining relationships. Billing pressures and technology advances have really changed the mentoring process!

Other Desegregation Cases

Removal of the state-mandated, dual-school system in Texas and those systems in the southern states has been a central focus of school lawyers. The HISD's journey from a dual-school system to unitary status is reviewed in some detail earlier in these reflections. Representing the HISD in its desegregation case gave several of our lawyers the opportunity to become engaged in other districts' desegregation cases, a few of which were filed by individual plaintiffs before the 1964 Civil Rights Act. Most desegregation cases were filed by the U.S. Department of Justice in 1969 and 1970, when the Justice Department was funded and staffed to undertake these cases. The state's overall desegregation case, *U.S. v. Texas*,[91] was filed in Judge William Wayne Justice's court in the Eastern District, Tyler Division. Judge Justice was known to be plaintiff-friendly in civil rights matters, so many of the state's civil rights-related cases were filed in his court. The statewide desegregation case, and virtually all individual school district desegregation cases in Texas and elsewhere across the South, have now been dismissed.

I was involved in the Ector County ISD (Odessa) desegregation case through local lawyers Bob Cox and Jack Tidwell.[92] While in Odessa, Bob Cox introduced me to my first West Texas breakfast of biscuits and gravy at his favorite café, and Jack Tidwell did the same with his love of single malt Scotch. Ector County ISD was home to Permian High School, which at the time was consistently producing Class 5A state football champions. One Friday, Jack Tidwell and I were driving about a half mile from Permian High School when I heard a loud and booming chant of, "Mo-Jo", "Mo-Jo", the Permian yell. It was from the Permian pep rally.

Friday Night Lights,[93] the first non-legal book I read after law school, was based upon Permian's football team. *Friday Night Lights* also became a television series. The oil-based economy was booming when I arrived in 1982, and it was a bust by the time we finished the case in 1984. In 2019, the Permian Basin is again the Texas center of oil production—this time using fracking. When I first arrived in Odessa and began preparation for trial, I received well-prepared maps, charts and outlines of the issues prepared by several bright and creative school administrators. One night during trial, there was a fire alarm at the Midland Hilton where I was staying. I had to decide what to take as I made my way down the stairs. I grabbed the trial notebooks which contained much of this material.

Jeff Horner and I represented Galena Park ISD, Crosby ISD and Katy ISD in cases which were filed by the U.S. Department of Justice in 1970. All these districts had individual black schools at the time suits were filed in 1970, and, while the districts quickly desegregated, the cases remained on the court dockets for years. All have now been dismissed.

The Aldine ISD desegregation case was filed in 1956, the same year as the Houston ISD case, and by the same lawyers, Weldon Berry and Francis Williams. Like the other districts, Aldine adopted an effective desegregation plan, but the case remained on the court's docket. I was asked by lawyer Jeff Davis and the Aldine superintendent and board to help get the case dismissed in the 1990s. Jeff Davis was a partner of Reynolds Allen & Cook, Aldine's original lawyers. Community activist Roy Malonson of Acres Homes opposed the dismissal for the same reason the Houston ISD and Jefferson County, Louisiana plaintiffs objected—they wanted the security blanket of a court order and the continued presence of a United States District Judge. Aldine's students, although largely from low-socioeconomic families, scored well on achievement tests. The Aldine school board and professional employees were racially and ethnically diverse. After reviewing the test scores and visiting the Aldine ISD several times, the U.S. Justice Department lawyer agreed that Aldine was unitary, and the case was dismissed.

One of the interesting aspects of these long-lived desegregation cases is that the cases either outlived the original plaintiffs, lawyers, and the school district lawyers, or the lawyers handling the cases retired. Having started my desegregation work as a first-year lawyer, I am one of a few veterans of the desegregation cases who remained available. During my phase-down years as a Bracewell partner, I served as a "monitor" for United States District Judge Kirk Englehardt in the Jefferson Parish, Louisiana School District case. After fifty-five years of off-and-on litigation, the Jefferson Parish case finally settled in 2011. After my retirement, I served as a mediator in a dispute that arose among the Jefferson County settling parties. The settlement agreement in the Jefferson Parish case would have ended in 2014, but it has been extended by the agreement of the parties.

Value of Humor

Being a pretty matter-of-fact person, my using humor has always been risky. In several memorable instances, I saw humor used with great effectiveness by masters of the art. The first was by Joel Coolidge, a lawyer and spokesperson for the proposed WISD. When interviewed by the media, Joel always had one-liners that made his point so well. I had to admire him, even though I thought his positions were often preposterous. Perhaps the most humorous lawyer around is Joe Hairston of Austin, who is so good he also does enjoyable after-dinner speeches. Jim Walsh of Austin likewise uses humor effectively.

Another dry humorist was Jack Tidwell, a great trial lawyer in Odessa. I assisted Jack and his partner Bob Cox in the Ector County (Odessa) desegregation case. At one tense time in the Odessa case's trial, United States District Judge Fred Shannon asked how far a building was to a school attendance boundary line. Jack jumped up and said, "About a good nine-iron shot, Your Honor," and the courtroom erupted. Judge Shannon laughed and told him thanks. I've tried to use humor since then, usually in a self-deprecating manner, and it has worked. Humor must be used with care and only in appropriate circumstances.

Lawyers Working Together

Throughout these reflections, I have mentioned many school district lawyers with whom I have worked in representing clients. There are others whose stories have not been included, but who deserve mention. I am certain I will miss some of the many school lawyers who should be named, so I ask forgiveness in advance for any omissions.

John Hardy, of Tyler, was a briefing clerk for me at Bracewell while he was attending law school at the University of Houston. When John moved to Tyler, he became the Tyler ISD lawyer and eventually the lawyer for other school districts. I represented some of John's clients when he had conflicts, and he served as our go-to lawyer for securing waivers from the enforcement of reversionary clauses in deeds from Judge William Wayne Justice under the statewide desegregation order. John Hardy III, who went to Camp Longhorn with our son, Jonathan, now practices with his father and represents clients on school matters.

I had some matters involving Bob Sanders of Amarillo, and Bob and I consulted many times on issues related to Amarillo College. I've had the same relationship with Wayne Haglund of Lufkin and Bill Bednar of Austin. Jim Deatherage of Irving, Tony Safi of El Paso, Tanner Hunt of Beaumont, Mike Atkins of Odessa, and Tom Carr of Fort Worth have all been active in school lawyer organizations. Jim Walsh and members of his firm, Walsh, Gallegos, Treviño, Russo & Kyle, have been active participants in school law organizations and in representing school districts throughout the state.

Rick Peebles of Baytown, as well as Jeff Davis (deceased) and Richard Hightower of Houston, have served as hearing officers for our clients, and I have served as a hearing officer for clients of Joe Hairston of Austin and Tom Garner (deceased) of Port Lavaca. We have also assisted Rick Peebles on some special issues for his clients. Don Byrnes, who was general counsel of Houston Baptist University for many years, has retired, but he served as a mediator in one of our cases. David Feldman, who also served as the City Attorney for the city of Houston, has been active in representing Houston-area school districts. Although I never worked with Paul Lyle of Plainview on a legal matter, Paul made a positive contribution to the school practice with his compilation of the Texas Commission of Education decisions.

In-house general counsel have increased over the years, with my initial contact being with Robert Young of the Dallas Community College System. Don Boehm and Kaye DeWalt have served the HISD, and former Bracewell lawyer Elneita Hutchins-Taylor is now HISD's general counsel, after serving for years as Cypress-Fairbanks ISD's general counsel. Kaye DeWalt, following the retirement of long-time lawyer Jonathan Handke, is now general counsel in the

Aldine ISD. Former Bracewell lawyer Marney Collins Sims serves as general counsel at Cypress-Fairbanks ISD. Susan Bohn, also a former Bracewell lawyer who was general counsel for Lake Travis ISD, is now superintendent of Aledo ISD. Former Bracewell associates Randy Gunter, Kim Brooks James, and Harry Wright serve as general counsel in the Liberty ISD, Beaumont ISD and Bryan ISD, respectively.

My focus in these reflections has been on the early days of the school law practice, especially from 1970 through 2008, and I have written quite a bit about several of my former Bracewell partners. Unfortunately, I just do not have space to tell additional tales involving more current school practice issues. As a result, my former Bracewell partners Merri Schneider-Vogel, Lisa Brown, Chris Gilbert, Chris Borreca, Philip Fraissinet, and David Hodgins, who are all now partners in Thompson & Horton, have been shortchanged. Jennifer Weston is now Bracewell's general counsel. All are first-class lawyers who have represented education clients in a wide variety of matters. I am sure more of their stories will be told later by others.

Jarvis Hollingsworth and I first met through the Houston Bar Association when he was an associate with Fulbright & Jaworski. He took a short detour through a California-based firm's Austin office, then returned to Houston where he joined Bracewell's public law practice. Lynn Rossi Scott has been a pioneer of sorts in the Dallas and Fort Worth school practice because she is a long-practicing Dallas-area school lawyer who did not collect delinquent ad valorem taxes. Lynn was a partner in Bracewell's Dallas office for many years before joining her present firm, Brackett & Ellis, in Fort Worth. Brackett & Ellis represents a wide range of school districts in the Fort Worth/Dallas area.

Without these partners, associates, and others about whom I have written, Bracewell would never have been able to develop the breadth of expertise in education law and provide the client services we have. I am most grateful to the former and present lawyers of the Bracewell team.

School Lawyers Must Be Astute Politicians and Must Avoid Partisan Politics

I always shared one important principle with new school lawyers. A school lawyer must be such a good politician that the lawyer must not let his or her personal political feelings influence the legal advice given. A school lawyer—any lawyer for that matter—must leave partisan politics at home when working with public clients. Although school board members are chosen through nonpartisan elections, they are politicians who are policy makers. Ideally, a school lawyer should be such a good politician that the clients don't know the lawyer's politics. I have been so dedicated to this principle that I have become a true independent—so much so that some Democrats think I am a Republican, and some Republicans think I am a Democrat.

This proposition has been tested time and time again over the years. Most school boards want the lawyer to give them the options on policy matters, along with the legal risks, and the board members will make the policy decision. Some boards want the lawyer to tell the board what to do. These boards often want to tell others, "We decided based on the advice of counsel," or, to cover themselves even more, "That is what the lawyer told us to do." Other boards simply and honestly do not know what to do and are looking for guidance.

I was faced with this last example in an executive session in a Houston area district at 1:00 a.m. After disclaiming several ways that what I was going to say was not legal advice and that I was not elected to make these decisions, I told the board members what I would do. A board member promptly said that sounded good. They went into open session, and the motion to do what I said promptly passed unanimously. So much for my wanting to avoid becoming involved in policy decisions!

Speaking and Writing

The first speech I ever made on a legal topic to a school group was in 1971, when Ruby Clifton, long-time HISD Assistant Superintendent to the HISD Board, asked me to speak to the Gulf Coast Area Association of School Boards on continuing contracts. Ruby was the leader of the Gulf Coast group of school trustees and superintendents that met several times a year. (The Gulf Coast Area School Boards' Association was created before Texas had Regional Education Service Centers.) Only Houston, La Porte, Deer Park, and Spring Branch had adopted continuing contracts at the time, and I think Ruby wanted me to demonstrate the difficulty in terminating a continuing contract or "tenured" teacher so other districts would stay with their term contracts. It is unclear if my presentation had any effect, but the other districts stayed with their term contracts.

After that evening of public speaking initiation, I was asked back to the Gulf Coast Area School Boards' Association several times to speak on corporal punishment, student discipline, search and seizure, and other legal issues of the day. These opportunities were a great introduction to speaking, and virtually each speech, based on practical experience and legal research, was then converted to an article that professional magazines of the day were eager to publish. Some of the articles, in turn, became monographs published by NOLPE/ELA and the NSBA's Council of School Attorneys (COSA).

The most renowned of these monographs has been *A Documentation System for Teacher Improvement or Termination*, which I was encouraged to write by leaders of NOLPE (ELA) who heard me address the topic during a speaking tour which included Penn State University and the University of Pittsburgh. These NOLPE leaders complimented some of the sample memoranda we had utilized in the HISD. The documentation system was actually developed at the urging of HISD Assistant Superintendent Edith Moore and HISD Director of Employment Irene Kerr. The HISD had several continuing contract teachers who, while being deficient in the classroom, were slippery, and they were skillful in avoiding capture for their inadequacies. We put together a communication system that is laid out in the monograph that is now virtually an education industry standard. The NOLPE/ELA documentation monograph had its seventh edition released in 2014. Tim Cooper assisted in the original version, and Janet Horton lent her assistance in the later versions.[94]

A long-term best-seller for the Council of School Attorneys (COSA) has been the monograph Jeff Horner, Dick Bump of Colorado, and I wrote on *Investigating Alleged Wrongdoing by Employees in the School Setting*. Dick Bump and I conceived of this monograph while sitting in front of the old federal courthouse in New Orleans' French Quarter after a COSA seminar. (Carmela and Linda were busy looking at antiques.) This 1990 NSBA/COSA publication was rewritten in 2005, and it was expanded and reissued in 2007. The techniques set out on investigations have met the tests of the changing legal times.[95]

The collection of all this material and the resulting articles led to my desire to prepare a book on Texas public school law to be used by trustees, administrators, and students of education law. The first attempt was with my friend Dr. Alvin Cannady, who taught education law at The University of Texas-Pan American in Edinburg. Alvin was also in the citrus business, and Carmela and I bought some groves in the Rio Grande Valley which Alvin tended. At the time, citrus ownership offered tax depreciation and capital gains. (Although we sold all our Valley citrus after the 1983 and 1989 freezes, we have six citrus trees in our Houston yard.) Alvin retired, left the Valley, and the HISD desegregation case consumed my time, so the effort to write a book was put in one of those brown Bracewell file boxes.

Jeff Horner resurrected the concept of publishing "The Book" when he became active in NOLPE/ELA, and we secured a commitment from ELA to publish and market "The Book," with ELA receiving any profits. David Thompson helped get the Texas Association of School Administrators, through its Executive Director Johnny Veselka, to assist in marketing "The Book." Virtually everyone in Bracewell's School Law Section produced a chapter. Other lawyers outside the firm—such as Rick Peebles of Baytown, who had the famous search and seizure case of *Horton v. Goose Creek ISD*, and Vianei Lopez Robinson, then of Abilene—participated. Professor Bill Camp of North Texas University served as a co-editor. "The Book"—*Texas School Law: A Practical Guide*—got published in 1996, and the second edition was published in 2004. It sold fairly well considering the advent of the electronic age and the proliferation of online materials. To me there is just something special about a piece of paper, especially if the papers are in a book. Appendix-G lists the articles I authored or co-authored.

We school lawyers always borrow ideas from each other. When we use someone else's materials in a speech or article, we are careful to give the other lawyer credit. I recall only two instances when other lawyers used my original materials as their own. One was at a NSBA/COSA presentation when the speaker used the context and conclusion of my *University of Houston Law Journal* article on search and seizure law as his seminar paper. There was chatter among the members about his doing so, and he never repeated his plagiarism. The other was at an Austin seminar where a lawyer used the material of the ELA documentation monograph as his own. I was in the audience and talked with him about the impropriety of what he had done. To my knowledge, he never did so again.

Writing Editorials

While I have avoided becoming involved in making policy decisions for school boards, I have felt compelled to write opinion editorials on critical educational policy issues, and, on occasion, legal ethical matters. I found that what I observed and learned, and my overall exposure in so many settings, needed to be laid on the public table. On some occasions, media representatives suggested that I write.

My first foray into the editorial world was on March 26, 1995 when the *Houston Chronicle* published "Fiddling While Schoolhouse Burns." This piece urged the legislature and schools to focus on matters that counted, including student behavior, effective teaching and employment, and parental responsibility. I closed with, "Leave the politically popular issues to a time after we have secured the classroom for education. Our children deserve no less."

After a long respite, largely to serve as Bracewell's managing partner and president of the State Bar of Texas, I felt compelled to remind readers of what caused the challenges of schooling children today and why Houston must make education a priority if we are to succeed as a region. In "To Restore Schools, Learn from the Past," *Houston Chronicle*, January 9, 2011, I implored the nonprofit community to check their personal interests at the door and to collaborate in a collective effort to achieve the common goal of providing our children with a quality education.

When then Senator Dan Patrick introduced his voucher bill in 2012, I wrote "Constitutionally, Vouchers Are Dead on Arrival" for the *Houston Chronicle* that was published on December 9, 2012. This editorial was a simple, straight legal shot at what, if enacted, would inflict a giant wound on Texas public education's ability to educate all children. When I wrote this piece, I was confident that the Texas Supreme Court would agree that vouchers violate the Texas Constitution. After the Court's May 2016 school finance decision—where the Court punted without overruling the legal precedent of twenty-five years and where Justice Willett in dicta seemed to invite the legislature to approve vouchers—I have some concerns. Have the members of the court just lost their courage, or has the court become just another political body?

David Thompson and I revisited the voucher issue in our February 18, 2015 *Houston Chronicle* editorial "Frels/Thompson: Vouchers don't meet constitutional requirement of 'public free schools.'" This voucher piece addressed more legal issues than my 2012 piece and concluded with an interesting question: "If home schooling is a legally acceptable private school, would not a person on welfare be able to claim he or she is home schooling a child and be entitled to a voucher?"

My most challenging editorial venture was in response to numerous requests from community people and *Houston Chronicle* staffers. All asked, "How can we fix our schools"? I took a shot at a partial answer in "To Rebuild Our Schools, We Must Do More than Paint the Façade," *Houston Chronicle*, April 26, 2015. I opined that current "reforms" were focused on superficial, politically popular issues of accountability without boring down to the fundamental changes necessary to improve educational quality. I laid out three essential steps: (1) hire and pay good teachers who are motivated and are led by directed leaders like my example, Principal Gordon Cotton; (2) institute early childhood education, which is essential to have students from poverty be able to read; and (3) engage all parents to be active in their children's education. These are three essential steps I believe must be taken. To attract and keep talented teachers, it is going to take money, and, while our state leaders laud the great teachers they had as children and young adults, I have little confidence that these leaders and the members of the Texas Legislature will approve the funds needed. The behaviors and recent statements of several of our state leaders, including the support of some for vouchers, raise the question of whether some of them are actually hostile to public education.

The possible takeover of the HISD by Commissioner Mike Morath through replacing the HISD Board prompted me to offer an alternative, addressing the governance issue by changing how the trustees are elected. The *Houston Chronicle* published "HISD Board Should Represent Everyone" on July 15, 2018. I opined that rather than having all trustees elected from single-member districts, a hybrid board of at least four at-large trustees, with the remaining trustees elected from single-member districts, would go a long way to address the governance of the HISD Board. This governance issue that results from all trustees being elected from single-member districts, as well as the issue of gerrymandering, is addressed in more detail in a subsequent section of these reflections.

All seven of these editorials are included as Appendix-H to these reflections. I am certain I will write more, possibly on some of the topics I have introduced in these reflections, and especially those that follow this topic. No longer having clients is a loss, because I really enjoyed the relationships and the feeling that I was helping education and contributing to a better society. That fed my energies for almost forty-five years. On the other hand, no longer having to be concerned about how my expressing heartfelt opinions on education policy issues might be discomfiting to someone is my new freedom. I intend to be sensitive in my writing, but I will no longer hold back when I feel that the quest for justice or furthering educational quality for all our children needs expressing. I have never been appointed to a state board by any politician, and I suspect my demonstrated independence will prevent me from ever getting a call. Likewise, I have never served on a board that paid me a stipend. Accordingly, I feel it is important for me to speak out as an independent voice on issues I feel are important to the education of all our children.

Schools in Economically Diminished Areas

One of our society's pressing needs is to recognize and fix the schools in economically diminished areas. School choice, including the availability of magnet schools, private schools and charters, and especially motivated parents moving their residences, have all contributed to a greater separation of students based upon wealth than we have ever experienced. Interestingly, this is not just an urban occurrence, but it is also reflective of rural Texas schools where inter-district transfers are now common. (Until recently, the statewide desegregation order severely limited inter-district transfers.)

When you drive through the Kashmere area of Houston and similar neighborhoods, you will find neighborhoods with many vacant lots, abandoned or decaying buildings, and few active businesses. If there are any large businesses in the neighborhoods, most are led or owned by individuals who live outside the neighborhoods, so there is an absence of available, active business leadership. (North Forest ISD, now a part of the HISD, where there was an absence of effective business leadership for many years, is the best large geographic example in the Houston area.) In other words, many of those who one would normally find in a leadership role do not live in the neighborhoods. These neighborhoods generally lost the children of many motivated parents, as well as parents with the financial ability to have their children attend a school of choice or to move to other neighborhoods where the schools are perceived as being better.

I have struggled in my search for answers to improving educational opportunities in these economically diminished neighborhoods. Without a doubt, the answer requires more than fixing the schools, which need adequate funding to attract and retain quality, motivated teachers led by knowledgeable, dedicated leaders. People need hope to succeed, and education is a critical basis of that hope. Some factors which I will flesh out a bit more below are laid out in the op-ed piece I wrote for the *Houston Chronicle*, "To Rebuild Our Schools, We Must Do More than Paint the Façade," April 26, 2015.

Looking beyond this op-ed, I believe the entire community must engage in creating a culture that education matters to the future of these and all children and to our society, especially to the preservation of our democracy. Education is everybody's business. I feel our larger community has a moral obligation to provide an adequate and effective education for the children of these communities who continue to attend school in the neighborhoods. Can we create a catalyst like the post-World War II GI Bill that established a culture where getting educated was important in becoming successful?

Parents are the first and most important teachers, and we must focus on their role as teachers. Motivated parents tend to seek the educational opportunities they feel will provide the best opportunities for their children. Parenting programs, especially those offered through pediatricians, hospitals and others in the medical profession, must become universally available and focused. Daycare centers and agencies have a role in developing responsible parenting for children whose brain is 80% developed by the time they are 3 years of age. Some parents, for a variety of reasons, will fail in adequately being their child's first teachers, and it is to these children who our community must provide a parental supplement.

How to fulfill children's early education when the parents do not or cannot do so is proving to be vexing and challenging. How do we create a culture that fosters the development of motivated parents? Clearly, childcare facilities where parents entrust their children have an opportunity—and, in my opinion, a duty—to supplement the parents' first-teacher responsibilities. Would a parent mentoring program be part of the answer for parents and children alike? It also seems that the resources of agencies such as the Texas Workforce Commission, Head Start, nonprofits, and religious groups committed to this stage of children's development must collaborate, then coordinate their efforts, before children even reach the pre-K programs.

Early childhood education, especially for children from economically disadvantaged backgrounds, is an essential step in the learning process. It is here that children's learning skills can be better developed and they can begin learning to read, a skill that is essential to success in our economy and in the furtherance of our democracy. Children who can read by the end of the third grade have a real chance of succeeding in school.

Houston-area schools are participating in a collaboratively developed, Greater Houston Partnership-led, early childhood program. The many participants in this program have checked their individual interests at the door and have locked arms to achieve a common goal. The focus is to further the area's efforts to enhance early childhood learning, from birth through the third grade, with its initial focus being to secure state funding and to enhance quality pre-K. In my opinion, pre-K, like kindergarten in the 1970s, needs to be funded for all children as a part of the school funding allotment so school districts will have consistent funding to ensure quality programs and parents will have confidence that the programs will be available for the future.

I suggest other strategies for enhancing the educational chances of children from economically deprived backgrounds in several succeeding topics of these reflections. Some of the answers that evolve may seem to be radical departures from traditional education. We should also recognize that all strategies and programs must be adequately financially supported by the state, and not just the local taxpayers. A political and policy commitment is required for us to reach this goal!

Governance – Fewer Business Leaders Now Serve as Trustees

The 1970s brought a rash of student and employee lawsuits against school districts using 42 U.S.C. §1983 to access the federal courts. Since school districts could not be sued directly, lawyers sued employees and trustees in their "official" capacities to secure jurisdiction over their school districts. Crafty plaintiffs' lawyers then began suing administrators and trustees in their "individual capacity" in attempts to secure money damages from them. This development spooked many sitting trustees, and it became a major reason businesspeople, professionals, and other community opinion leaders have avoided serving on school boards. People of means became wary of exposing their assets to suits resulting from service on school boards.

The insurance companies began to offer officers and directors insurance, as well as errors and omission coverage, and the question became whether school district funds could be used to pay the insurance premiums. Was the expenditure for a "public purpose" and "reasonably necessary" in the operation of the public schools? The School Law Section of the State Bar urged the Attorney General to answer these questions in the affirmative, which he did. Having insurance was a positive for school trustees, but the fear of being sued and having to spend time in depositions and defending lawsuits was also a turn-off to many would-be trustees.

Another factor in businesspeople and professionals avoiding school board service was the extensive and long hearing process before school boards required for school employees who had a grievance, or for those employees who were proposed for termination or other discipline. Section 11.13 of the Texas Education Code, and the arcane rule of the Texas Education Agency,

"Procedures for Hearings and Appeals," required these due process school board hearings. Employee hearings, which were generally held at night after the workday, could easily last for three to four hours, with some lasting all night. As noted earlier, I had an administrator's termination hearing in the Houston Independent School District that lasted for eighty hours, and, under due process standards, at least a quorum of the same board members had to be present for all of the hearing. (Fortunately, legislative changes now allow for personnel hearings to be conducted before hearing officers.)

Many school districts, especially the urban districts, were also undergoing a new phenomenon in the early 1970s, the desegregation of their schools, which meant students and faculty were being racially mixed. School attendance boundaries were changed, and in some districts there was busing of students between schools to achieve racial integration. Some people who would have been outstanding trustees opted to place their children in private schools, and others moved to what they considered a "safe" school district, generally a growing suburban district, to escape the turmoil. The flight of whites and minorities with the economic means from urban school districts undergoing desegregation to private and other schools was a significant drain of business people and opinion leaders. People could escape having to deal with what they considered turmoil and uncertainties by moving to school districts they considered to "be in the best interests" of their children.

Trustee elections have become more politicized, and many have taken on partisan characteristics. Increasingly, school trustees use their positions as stepping stones to other political offices. Greater politicization has resulted in trustees being regularly "put on the spot." Many businesspeople did not want the hassle, while others feared that their businesses would be adversely affected by decisions they would make while serving as a school trustee. Several former trustees have told me their business did suffer due to their school board service. Interestingly, in today's world, many businesspeople and professionals serve on 501(c) (3) charter school boards as well as on boards of educations' special interest organizations.

Governance – Total Single-Member Districts: Has Their Time Passed?

Prior to the application of the Voting Rights Act of 1965, school districts and community colleges elected their seven or nine trustees using an at-large system of voting. While the at-large process usually provided a board of businesspeople and other opinion leaders, boards were largely made up of white males, with a few women and only an occasional African-American or Hispanic.

To insure that African-Americans could choose fellow African-Americans to serve, the Houston Independent School District in 1975 asked the Texas

Legislature to change the specially drawn law under which the district's trustees were elected, Article 2774(b),[96] from seven members elected at-large to seven single-member districts. This resulted in two African-American members being elected to the HISD Board. As the number of Hispanics in the HISD increased, the Texas Legislature, again at the request of the HISD Board, enlarged the board to nine members in 1981, and, with re-drawn trustee boundaries, two Hispanics were elected to the board. Many other Texas school districts changed their election process to single-member districts upon threat of a lawsuit under the Voting Rights Act of 1965, or upon being ordered by a federal judge to do so.

Single-member districts served the Voting Rights Act's purpose by having the minority residents of a single-member district elect a person of their choosing to represent them. The result has been an increase in the number of African-Americans and Hispanics serving on many Texas school district and college boards. Most of the school districts and colleges who elect trustees by single-member districts (generally in urban areas) have experienced significant demographic changes over the last forty years, with many, if not most, now having a majority minority population.

Many trustees represent single-member districts with small populations, and many are elected by a very small number of voters who turn out for school board elections. A trustee so elected is usually beholden to that small group of voters, yet the trustee serves on a board that is responsible for the education of all the school district's students. This narrowness of representation is exacerbated when districts are gerrymandered so the voting constituency's focus by race, ethnicity, or political philosophy is narrowed even more.

A narrowed constituency can insure that by doing the bidding of a small group of voters, a trustee can have a "safe" seat for so long as the trustee votes their ideological dictates. This phenomenon results in the disenfranchisement of many voters who no longer have a choice of candidates. After all, who would run against such an established incumbent? Unfortunately, gerrymandering, many times done under the guise of complying with the Voting Rights Act, has led to political polarization—an enemy of governance in a representative democracy. The inability of members of our U.S. Congress to work together and govern is exhibit A.

My experience has been that boards with trustees who are focused on their small, single-member districts often do not take the school district as a whole into account in their decision making. Some trustees refer to schools and teachers in their geographic district as "my" schools and "my" teachers, rather than "our" schools and "our" teachers. Single-member district trustees who do focus on the entire district are often conflicted that by focusing on the needs of the entire district, their single-member constituents may feel the trustees are not paying enough attention to them. Many times a series of individual fiefdoms develop and single-member district trustees trade votes with each other to further parochial or narrow political goals, rather than a focus on the broader educational objectives that serve all the school district's children. One dramatic exception I will always remember and cherish was an African-American community college trustee who, after the 1990 Census, told me, "Let's not draw the lines of my district so the voters look and think alike. I need diversity so I will be free to make the decisions I feel are right for the entire college."

I believe it is the time for many school districts currently electing all trustees from single-member districts to discontinue the practice. Students attending schools in today's diverse demographic settings, especially in the urban districts with a majority minority population, can be better served by an election system with some trustees elected at-large and some elected through larger, single-member districts. (There are probably school districts where an all single-member district configuration may be necessary to protect the voting rights of minority citizens.) This change to a mixed at-large, single-member district system could be accomplished by a phase-in—just like was done when some districts converted from at-large to all single-member districts. The sitting trustees with the shortest time remaining on their terms could become the at-large trustees, then could choose to run at-large. For example, a district could elect four (three) at-large trustees and five (four) trustees from single-member districts.

In school districts with majority minority populations, having trustees in at least some positions elected at-large would serve the purpose of the Voting Rights Act because African-American and Hispanic voters could elect trustees of their choice. In the city of Houston's mixed at-large and single-member district system, African-Americans and Hispanics are regularly elected to at-large positions.

Some will surely propose just adding at-large positions to the seven or nine single-member districts. That is the easy way out, but it is not a positive for an improved governance structure. It does not deal with the problems inherent in single-member districts. While this idea might avoid sitting trustees' opposition, it is not a positive for good governance. A school superintendent does not have independent powers like city mayors. Superintendents must have a consensus of at least a majority of the trustees on the board to pass any issue. More than seven, and certainly more than nine trustees, would stymie even the most politically facile superintendent in developing the necessary consensus, and that would be bad for effective governance. What capable superintendent candidates would be interested in serving in an urban district with its trustees elected by single-member districts, especially with a large board?

The electoral system should be changed in this way to increase the probability that school trustees will focus on the whole, and not just small parts, of a school district. Having the support of the African-American and Hispanic communities to accomplish this would diminish concerns about racial isolation or discrimination. Our children and their future deserve a change in the governance structure of school districts. While I hold out hope, I am pessimistic that this will occur, because officeholders are reluctant to risk giving up their offices, even when it would benefit the education of all the district's children.

On the larger stages of the state of Texas and nationally, extreme gerrymandering has disenfranchised an enormous body of voters and has led to governing paralysis on matters of great significance. Most of the gerrymandering of representative and senate districts in Texas and nationally was initially done ostensibly to comply with the Voting Rights Act of 1965. It wasn't far into the redistricting process when districts began to be "packed" with African-Americans and Hispanics, and politicians in both parties soon realized gerrymandering for Voting Rights Act compliance could be effectively used to consolidate political strength and create "safe" seats for a political party.

Once a person is elected to a safe seat, the representative is virtually immune from a challenge of someone in his or her own party, and certainly someone from the other party. So, the representative is elected time and time again by 50-plus percent of the voters in the representative's political party primary. Gerrymandering, therefore, effectively disenfranchises all others who live in the district. Realistically, that representative can stay in office for so long as his or her votes satisfy a small voting group of a party's primary voters.

"We the People," especially those of us who are independents, have become casualties of gerrymandering. Predictably, the safe seats of opposing parties create ideological polarization, which leads to governance paralysis where ideological issues are addressed, but the core issues of infrastructure, education (at the state level), and matters of general welfare like health care and immigration get little attention. Securing power for a political party, rather than governing and serving the needs of the people of the nation or a state, has become the political goal. This extreme gerrymandering has resulted in our two-party system not serving our representative democracy well!

Leadership Counts

The success of any organization begins with a clearly stated and understood mission and capable leadership. This is certainly true of school districts and community colleges. Boards made up of leaders committed to the mission of providing quality education for all students will almost always hire a like-minded superintendent with leadership skills. These skills and commitments of the leader then become the norm for all school administrators, principals, and teachers. As a result, everyone in the district has a basis to understand his or her role in providing quality education.

A prominent example of the positive effects of leadership is the Houston area's Aldine Independent School District. The Aldine ISD's Board was once made up of seven white men. That board now reflects the racial, ethnic, and gender makeup of the community. This transition in school board composition was accomplished because board members led the movement to change rather than fighting it—all without resorting to having trustees elected by single-member districts. In fulfilling their commitment to a consistent educational philosophy, the trustees know that the board must be a team and individuals must sometimes compromise their views for the good of the whole.

When I was helping Aldine complete its many-years-old desegregation case with the United States Department of Justice, the issue of educational quality arose. The Justice Department lawyer assigned to the case could not believe that a largely majority minority student body whose children were overwhelmingly from economically deprived backgrounds could perform so well on standardized tests. After the Justice Department lawyer visited Aldine and conducted her own investigation, she understood that the test results were real, and the Justice Department agreed to the dismissal of the desegregation case.

Good school governance exists in the Houston area and throughout Texas. These boards effectively work with their communities in defining the district's mission and in establishing goals and objectives that are clear and understandable. Policies based upon these objectives and standards follow. The boards provide the needed resources and support, then the members stay out of administrative issues. The board members effectively communicate with and hold the superintendent responsible.

The Difference Between Schools in the 1950s and Today

People, especially those who graduated from high school before the 1970s, continually ask me why we can't have the same "quality of education" in public schools today that they remember from their school days. The bottom line is that our society has changed substantially, and, as a society, we are more inclusive of who is educated in our public schools than in years past. Today's curriculum is deeper and wider to reflect our expanded knowledge base. In short, our schools are a reflection of our society, and our society has changed.

It is valuable to look back at some of the post-World War II societal characterizations and developments. The GI Bill after World War II made access to higher education possible for many who could never have afforded to attend college, and in the process created a culture that made receiving an education very important, with the belief that education matters. These newly minted college graduates fed a developing workforce and a post-war consumer economy that expanded. Public education became a cultural focus for their children because every parent (and two-parent families were pretty much the norm) wanted his or her child to have a better life than the parent. Fewer children were born to single mothers than today, and a divorce was difficult to get. A substantial majority of the population practiced a religion, or at least claimed one. There was no active war being waged, but the Cold War with the Soviet Union was very real; while a distraction, the U.S.S.R. gave us an "enemy" against whom we could competitively unite in our earthly endeavors and in the race to space. Getting an education was a part of the community and national culture. People took pride in having an education—something no one could take away from them.

Viewing life and education in America through an African-American's eyes in post-World War II America, however, was quite different. Many of the country's schools, especially those in the South, were, by law, segregated by race, and the two school systems, white and black, were not equal. I don't recall ever having any African-American who graduated from high school before the 1970s say that schools separated by race were great and that we should return to that era. That is not to say there were not outstanding black schools, with excellent black teachers and administrators, but these good schools were achieved despite receiving lower funding, generally being in lesser facilities, and often using hand-me-down textbooks that were sometimes out-of-date and no longer used in the white schools.

Today's public schools educate a diverse student body, many of whom would never have attended post-World War II-era schools. There were no locally based in-school programs in the 1950s and 1960s to educate students with disabilities. If you could not do the work offered in the classes, you failed, and when you failed, you ultimately dropped out. Children with mental disabilities either stayed at home or became residents of special schools or institutions. Children with physical handicaps who could not function in a traditional school setting likewise did not attend neighborhood schools. Today, public schools provide a free and appropriate education for students with all types of mental and physical disabilities.

In those post-WWII days, students who did not speak English either learned English or they did not attend school. A few school districts created separate schools for students who spoke Spanish. Today, there are as many as ninety different languages spoken in the homes of HISD students. Students whose home language is not English attend public schools and are taught in bilingual or English as Second Language classes.

Students of the 1950s and 1960s who misbehaved were generally punished by corporal punishment or detentions. If the misbehavior was severe, a student could be summarily suspended or expelled for the remainder of a semester without being afforded any procedural due process to determine if the misbehavior actually occurred as alleged. Many expelled students never returned to school—they just dropped out. Since no educational programs were provided during the suspension or expulsion period, the student returned to school generally having to repeat the grade. Today's state law and constitutional due process protections afford students procedural due process before long suspensions or expulsions occur, and the school district has a detailed student conduct code that provides written notice of the rules of conduct and the consequences of misbehavior. Schools must provide alternative educational services during the time of suspension or expulsion to avoid a student falling too far behind.

Records of students who dropped out of school for whatever reason in this earlier era were not kept, so we do not know how many students did not finish high school. The largely manual labor work of the era absorbed most of those without high school educations, the military took others, and many married and became homemakers. In today's world, the economy has far fewer jobs which do not require a high school education and training or education beyond that. Few ditches are dug by hand, cotton is picked by machines, and vehicles are largely assembled by robots. The list goes on. Unemployed young people without an education and useful skills, who lack hope in their future, are not positive in any society, especially in a democracy like ours. This factor alone is ample reason to provide a meaningful education to all our children.

The school curriculum of the 1950s and 1960s focused on reading, writing and arithmetic, the knowledge necessary for success in life and business at that time. Advances—largely through science, mathematics, and technology—have significantly expanded our knowledge base and its availability through the internet and other forms of communication. This knowledge evolution continues at a rapid pace. Preparing students for success in today's workforce and life requires that schools broaden and deepen their curriculum and adapt to different approaches to "teaching." Adapting and anticipating future changes is challenging when students have instant access to the same data as their teachers.

The parents of this post-World War II era did not move about as much as they do today in our mobile society that features open housing, rental deals, better roads, increased access to transportation, etc. Students of yesteryear tended to live in one location longer, while today's students tend to move from one school to another more often. There are inner-city schools in Houston where some classrooms experience greater than 100% mobility (student turnover) during a single school year. When students continually move and change schools, not only are their lives disrupted, but so is their learning environment. Increasing numbers of students are "homeless"—not having a regular physical location where they regularly stay or sleep at night. The number of homeless students increases significantly in districts affected by a natural disaster, such as Hurricanes Katrina and Harvey.

Today's students are much more likely to come from single-parent homes or from homes where both parents work. Likewise, today's children are more likely to come from economically disadvantaged homes. The percentage of students from homes where the income level is currently below the poverty line is 60% statewide in Texas and 80% in the HISD. The Coleman study, which was liberally cited by the Texas Supreme Court in the 2016 school finance case, and other researchers have documented that children from lower socioeconomic backgrounds are at an educational disadvantage when compared with those from more affluent homes. Also, a child who comes to school hungry is not going to be as attentive and engaged as a well-fed student. The number of children who have medical concerns or have uncorrected vision problems, because the parents do not recognize the condition or cannot afford care, is on the increase. If you cannot see, you cannot read, and if you cannot read, how can you learn?

As our society has changed, parents, legislators, and others have looked to our public schools to take on additional responsibilities beyond what was once viewed as the schools' basic education mission. Many parents and grandparents, who are the child's first teachers, look to the schools to provide the basics that the parents cannot or do not provide at home.

Expecting public schools to provide quality education in today's environment is expecting much more than was expected of the schools in the 1950s and 1960s. State funding for public schools has decreased from around 75% in the 1950s to about 38% in 2018. Many school districts, like the Houston ISD, the Spring Branch ISD, and the La Porte ISD, fund their operations from local property taxes without any net state funding. In fact, all three school districts send millions in local property tax funds to the state's general fund. Yet, the state continues to mandate programs and expenses which have to be funded through local property taxes, and the expense of increased security measures is an increasing concern.

Today's curriculum is wider and deeper than in the 1950s and 1960s, and the amount of information available via the internet continues to dramatically increase. Schools and their teachers must prepare students for the jobs of the future and introduce them to becoming lifelong learners. The teachers themselves must be technologically adept and committed to preparing students for future jobs and lifelong learning. One's education is not complete with high school graduation.

Teachers in our classrooms today experience a stress-filled environment with many students whose parents do not show support for their children receiving a quality education, whether from not realizing the value of education or other reasons. In years past, parents more actively supported the teacher and school authorities—the teacher was always right—while today, parents often jump to defend the actions or failures of their children without even hearing the teacher's side of the story.

Recruiting and retaining talented teachers now are more difficult tasks because we do not pay teachers competitively with what they can get in the business world—especially recognizing their role in preparing students to function in an ever-changing world where lifetime learning is required. Increasingly, teachers do not earn a living wage. Until the 1980s, when women more fully entered the business and professional worlds, school districts had access to women teachers who graduated from college at the top of their classes. Women's career opportunities before the 1980s were pretty much limited to teaching, nursing, or secretarial positions. Schools thrived on this "female subsidy," a factor that no longer exists. In addition to competitive pay and benefits with business, we must offer real-world training and find ways to create school environments that are less stressful to teachers and are more conducive to order, where learning can take place. Job satisfaction is important to retain talent in any job, and teaching is no exception. Unfortunately, I have no comprehensive answer for changing the current teaching environment and creating one conducive to teacher satisfaction in the public schools.

Texas charters, which are funded directly by the state, have been given leeway by the legislature to operate more like the schools of the 1960s. Charters have much greater flexibility in many areas of school operation than other public schools. While I do not think charters offer the solution to educating all students, such schools are now a part of the mosaic that is evolving in education. Hopefully, the positive experiences of different types of schools will be shared and lead to better outcomes for all schools. Some of the pros and cons of charters are addressed in the next section on charter schools.

Charter Schools

Charter schools began in 1995 with the development of the Knowledge is Power Program (KIPP) in the Houston Independent School District by Teach for America colleagues Mike Fineberg and Dave Levin. An early KIPP charter school was located in temporary buildings in the parking lot of the HISD administration building at 3830 Richmond Avenue. Former HISD Superintendent Billy Reagan supported the venture that was designed to provide a different and more intensive learning environment for largely minority children from economically disadvantaged backgrounds. The ultimate goal was for the children to graduate from high school and go on to college. It was HISD's hope that successes from this concentrated learning experience could be replicated in other HISD classrooms.

KIPP had longer school days, with classes from 7:30 a.m. to 5:00 p.m., plus after-school activities and some Saturday classes, so there was longer time on task for students. Teachers visited students' homes, and parents, students, and teachers were required to sign a KIPP commitment of excellence. The parties agreed to specific responsibilities, so participation required that the parents and the student be motivated to do what they could for the student to succeed in the goal of going to college.

The number of open enrollment charter schools funded by the state of Texas has increased. The growth has been fueled by parents who are motivated to seek out educational opportunities offered by the charters that parents feel are good choices for their children. Charters operate with fewer legal restrictions and regulations than regular public schools. For example, charters are not required to follow the Texas Education Code-prescribed discipline laws applicable to traditional public schools. Open enrollment charter schools must adopt their own codes of conduct, but the consequences for student misconduct are not as limited. As a result, a misbehaving child can be dismissed for any reason identified in the school's code of conduct. Children who do not perform well academically in charters often return to their neighborhood schools.

Charter schools are operated as nonprofits, with their trustees appointed rather than elected by the voters. One view of this governance arrangement is that these hand-chosen trustees bring needed talents to the table and are able to focus on educational and management matters, without getting dragged into distracting political issues. Another view is that having board members who are not politically elected limits their accountability for the expenditure of public funds. Interestingly, many of the charters' nonprofit board members have similar characteristics with those who served as public school trustees in the 1950s and 1960s—a time before the Constitution fully came to the campus and before major changes occurred in society generally. Although charters are subject to the Texas Open Meetings Act and the Texas Public Information Act, their operations seem to attract little scrutiny from public watch and advocacy groups. Based upon studies and test score analysis conducted to date, charters are a lot like other public schools; some produce good results and others do not.

Open enrollment charter schools are subject to the authority of the Texas Education Agency (TEA) under Chapter 12 of the Texas Education Code. Charters also receive services from and participate in the activities of the Regional Education Services Centers. (Region IV provides those services in the Houston region.) It will be interesting to see how and to what extent the TEA will ultimately exercise its oversight of the increasing number of charters.[97] More on charters is included in "The Commercialization, Monetization and Privatization of Public Education" section of these reflections.

Motivated and Involved Parents

The Coleman Report of 1966 found that the most significant indicator of how a child performs in school is the socioeconomic status of the child's parents. Coleman found that the children of wealthier parents (higher socioeconomic status) perform better academically than the children of parents who are in a lower socioeconomic status. Over the years, subsequent studies have supported Coleman's findings of a correlation between the wealth of the parents and student performance.

There is, however, another indicator of student success which I believe may be as significant in student performance: the existence and role of motivated or engaged parents. Motivated parents can be found in every community, and they exist in all wealth, racial, and ethnic groups. Motivated parents act to ensure that they are doing what is within their power for their children to succeed in school and in life. These folks usually take their role as first teachers seriously, and they seek out the schools and educational programs they believe are in their children's best interests.

Although I did not recognize it at the time, parental motivation to do what they thought best for their children was a contributing factor in some parents leaving the HISD to attend private schools and schools in suburban districts when the HISD was under a comprehensive desegregation order in late 1969 and 1970. (Admittedly, as the HISD's desegregation lawyer, I was not pleased to see these parents leave.) At the same time, motivated parents were the ones who put their children on HISD buses or transported them so they could attend the magnet schools of the HISD beginning in 1975. Motivated parents who seek a religious component in education choose parochial or church-sponsored private schools. Some parents are motivated to educate their children through home schooling. Many motivated parents with the economic ability, who do not choose public schooling, seek out quality private schools. I am convinced that the public charter school movement was launched largely to meet the desires of motivated parents who did not have the financial wherewithal for private school tuition and did not feel their neighborhood public schools offered what they felt was best for their children.

Empirically measuring parental motivation or engagement is impossible, but you know it when you see it. As I opined in my first *Houston Chronicle* opinion editorial in 1995, any school principal will tell you that having motivated and involved parents is a huge factor in the success of any school. Even in schools where not every parent is motivated or engaged, the whole student body benefits by the motivated parents' involvement. Engaged and involved parents also stimulate the school's teachers and other staff to excel. Dedicated teachers tend to thrive in a school with motivated parents, while less-committed teachers will likely leave.

So, if the children of motivated parents fare better educationally, what about the children whose parents are not motivated or engaged for whatever reason? Some children lack parents or even a parental figure, and we all know of numerous reasons why parents lack motivation or do not get involved. These reasons include preoccupation with putting bread on the table, having multiple jobs, fear of deportation because they are undocumented, feelings of inferiority, lack of an appreciation for the value of an education, language issues, incarceration, and the list goes on. By and large, children of unmotivated parents attend neighborhood schools, and, because of the unsupportive home life, children may not attend school regularly or may attend many schools during any given year. As stated in the section "Schools in Economically Diminished Areas," meeting the challenge of educating these children is vexing and the solutions uncertain. (That section includes several possible action steps.)

While we are properly focused on directing resources and attention to closing the achievement gap between children from lower socioeconomic backgrounds and the children of the more affluent, attention must be given to the educational needs of the "other" students, especially the "average" and "above average" students of any background. A lack of attention to the educational needs of these other students risks messaging to their parents, many of whom are motivated and involved, that the public schools consider them less important. These parents will then become more receptive to the increasingly directed messages of charter and private schools that they care about these students. Once these motivated parents—who historically have been the backbone of school board leadership and parent support groups like the PTOs and PTAs, and who provide political support for public school funding—are no longer in the public schools, their support for public education will be lost. When this support diminishes, the divide between the haves and have-nots will be exacerbated, and educating all children will become even more challenging.

I feel our entire community, including our elected and appointed state leaders, must engage in creating a culture that education matters to the future of all children and to our society, ultimately to the preservation of our democracy. I also believe our Texas Constitution and state laws mandate that we provide an adequate and effective education for all our children, not just those with motivated parents.

Imposing criminal or civil sanctions to compel parents to be involved with their children is not a viable answer. Instead, shouldn't we approach the challenge by educating the larger community on the issues of parenting, then convince our community that "Education Matters – It's Everybody's Business," like we did in our successful 2002-2003 campaign to improve Houston's air quality? An essential element of this culture must be that parents have to assume a responsibility for their children, and that our community will support them in doing so. One component in encouraging parents to be more involved could involve mentoring. Not until we get the general public motivated and engaged in creating and enforcing a culture that education matters will we be able to effectively move toward the goal of having more motivated parents who will make a difference in the education of all children.

The Commercialization, Monetization, and Privatization of Public Education

School curriculum historically was developed by teachers and administrators working in school districts. With the advent of the Regional Service Centers in Texas, some of the curriculum planning became more centralized at the Regional Service Centers, with school district teachers working with the Center's curriculum writers. School districts used state-adopted text books with local supplements. The state-adopted textbooks were developed by companies under the watchful eyes of the Commissioner of Education, Texas Education Agency, and the State Board of Education. Since enormous sums of money were involved, numerous state laws were passed in the early years of Texas public education in an effort to insure the integrity of the textbook adoption process. When I read these statutes as a new lawyer in 1970, I thought the restrictions were pretty elaborate, but with today's greater commercialization and monetization of education I now understand why the statutes were passed. Now I wonder if there are sufficient safeguards to ensure the integrity of the textbooks' adoption process and the preparation of commercially produced educational materials.

With the passage of the Elementary and Secondary Education Act (ESEA) in 1965, a part of President Lyndon Johnson's War on Poverty, Congress pumped large sums of money into the states' education systems. ESEA has been reauthorized over the years: in 2001, under President George W. Bush, as No Child Left Behind, and in 2015, under President Barack Obama, as The Every Student Succeeds Act. The federal government is now entrenched in providing funds to our nations' public schools, and with federal money comes federal regulatory control. The availability of these substantial sums of money has attracted entrepreneurs who have received contracts to develop and provide curriculum, materials, texts, and tests; much of this material was historically prepared by active teachers. (Lexile level analysis of some of the tests produced by these companies show that the tests are written at a higher reading level than the students are capable of reading.) American education has been substantially commercialized.

Large national and multinational companies have become huge commercial enterprises by capitalizing on the availability of contracts to provide tests and other commodities to states and school districts. Like our handheld devices, new versions of the programs and products that require additional purchases are common. Are the procurement laws and quality standards currently in effect sufficient to insure quality products, protect the public interest, control conflicts of interest, and insure that public funds are properly expended?

The charter school effort has now evolved into what some feel is a force "privatizing" some Texas' public schools. Many choice advocates, and some politicians, are messaging to parents that if you care about your child, you will remove your child from public school and seek a charter. The loss of parents who are influenced by this message and remove their children from public schools will further reduce political support for public education.

Charters that receive public funds and operate as nonprofits have established a separate organizational framework for education with a different structure and very different rules. As we are now finding out, the performance of many charters is not different from low-performing public schools, and financial problems plague many. As the number of public charter schools grows, it is becoming increasingly clear that the charter movement has created a separate system of public schools. We must remain vigilant to avoid charters becoming a vehicle for economic, racial, and ethnic isolation, especially when comparing children attending charters with those who attend traditional public schools.

State law provides that charters are to be held accountable through the Texas Education Agency (TEA). It is important that the TEA provide sufficient oversight and that it ensure the charter school system and the public school system do not become constitutionally unequal. Charters were the subject of my July 28, 2016 op-ed piece with David Thompson (Appendix-H) , and more is said about charters in several preceding reflection sections.

Full choice through state-funded vouchers poses the real threat to the vitality of public education. Lt. Governor Dan Patrick and his cadre of voucher supporters have and will continue to not only sell the concept of vouchers, but will relentlessly pursue legislative approval. The lieutenant governor's efforts to provide vouchers is now supported by President Trump's Secretary of Education and Texas' United States Senator Ted Cruz. Our outstanding private schools do not have space for more students, and, even with voucher money, these schools are too costly for anyone other than people of means. With vouchers, would we have an increase in the opening of new private schools built by eager entrepreneurs, developers, and contractors who contribute freely to politicians? My op-ed piece of December 9, 2012, and the one I wrote with David Thompson on February 18, 2016 (Appendix-H) lay out in more detail the dangers vouchers pose to public schools and our democracy itself.

The desire of parents to do what is best for their children's education is understandable, and I support and encourage parents to do what they believe is in their children's best interest. The existence of choices for parents results in many of the choice schools benefiting by getting the talented students whose parents are motivated to seek out what they feel are the best educational programs for their children. Increasingly, traditional public school systems appear to be adopting successful practices and programs developed by schools of choice, a trend that they must continue. Whether charters will adequately provide the costlier educational programs for children with disabilities or programs for those children who are not proficient in English remains an open question. Whatever the parents' choice school is—charter, magnet, neighborhood, private, parochial, or home schooling—if public funds or facilities are used in its support, the school's operation must be transparent, and it must be publicly accountable.

I believe the ultimate test of societal education accountability is whether we have designed and funded programs that will satisfy our moral and constitutional responsibility to provide adequate resources so "all" our state's children, 90-plus percent of whom attend traditional public schools, have access to a quality public free education. This includes children from all backgrounds and with a variety of needs.

Advice for Law Practice and Life

Bits of advice have been dispensed through school cases or school lawyers over the years. Here are a few of the tidbits that have withstood the test of time:

- "Pigs get fat and hogs get slaughtered" and "Don't violate the pig principle." Origin – East Texas. This applies to virtually everything in life, but especially when negotiating settlements or in asking for concessions. (Some of our elected representatives should be reminded of this.)

- "Don't write anything you wouldn't want to appear on the front page of your local newspaper." This applies to business in general, but especially to those who work for or provide advice to public entities. I have been in temporary injunction hearings where the "other side" has attempted to introduce as evidence one of my "confidential" opinion letters. This admonition applies with even greater force in these days of electronic communication, where little thought is often given to tweets and emails which may be disclosable under the Public Information Act.

- "Treat people like you would expect to be treated if you were in their positions." The Golden Rule stated a little differently has never lost its viability. This is especially applicable in the employee/employer relationship where one has power over the future of another.

- "If you lose your good name, it's hard to get it back." If one lies, cheats, or engages in similar behavior, it is difficult to regain one's good name and the attendant respect.

- "Disagreements are inevitable, but you can disagree without being disagreeable."

- Communication through emails, texts and the use of technology may be efficient, but listening to one another is conducive to achieving understanding.

- Speaking badly about someone is like driving a nail in a piece of wood. Even when you pull the nail out (apologize), the hole is still there.

- If a client demands that you misrepresent a matter or take an unconscionable position, tell the client the position is wrong, and if the client insists, suggest that the client get another lawyer, then resign.

- If you have a weak fact, present it before the other side does. In other words, if you have a skunk, put it on the table so you have more control of the odor.

- "A misrepresentation or lie that is told enough times without refutation with the truth may be taken by others as a 'fact'."

- "If there is no law to guide you, use common sense."

- Education is valuable, and once you have it, nobody can take it away. "Education Matters – It's Everybody's Business."

- When no one worries about who gets credit for something, more is likely to get done.

- "Apply the smell test." If something doesn't smell good, there is usually something wrong.

- A role of the lawyer representing a school district is to represent the school district while keeping the interests of the overall public in focus and helping the client, trustees, and administrators remember that public interest.

- Representing the interests of the client is what matters in the attorney-client relationship. Lawyers must never allow their personal interests to complete with or rise above the interests of their clients.

- "Bring people together, don't drive them apart." Good lawyers look out for their client's best interests and not the lawyer's personal interests.

By Kelly Frels

- If a lawyer calls you with a complaint about a teacher or administrator, ask if the parent or the lawyer has talked with the teacher or administrator. Problems get solved when people talk with each other.

- "You catch more flies with honey than vinegar." A humble, respectful approach to others is more likely to engender a positive response than a brisk or condescending approach. One can be strong and polite at the same time.

- "Respect everyone because today's adversary may be tomorrow's friend, relative or client." Especially in the political world of school districts, today's plaintiffs may be on the school boards of tomorrow—and they hire the lawyers. If you treat adversaries and friends alike with respect, you will generally be treated with respect in return. Lawyers continually tell me, "You may not remember, but we had a matter (or case) against each other years ago. You helped me resolve it."

- "If one eats at the federal trough, one must use federal manners." If you take federal money, you must comply with federal laws and regulations.

- "When you get into a pen with pigs, you will get mud on yourself" and "When you cozy up with skunks, you will acquire their odor."

- While a lawyer has an ethical responsibility to advise a client that a proposed action is illegal or unconstitutional, a good lawyer helps the client find a legally acceptable way to achieve the desired policy objective.

- School lawyers, regardless of who they represent, must remember that education is about children, their future, and the health of our representative democracy.

- "Find ways to preserve another's personal dignity." This is especially true in employer/employee relationships where the supervisor has power over the employer. Don't belittle another or back the person into a corner—leave a respectable way out so the person can avoid humiliation.

- Remember that the school district lawyer is the face of the district in litigation and negotiations. The school district is judged by the lawyer's representation.

- When trying to locate the school district administration building in a small Texas school district, look for the football stadium lights. The superintendent's office shouldn't be far away.

- "Change is inevitable, so anticipate it and take advantage of it." When changes occur, someone will benefit, so plan for change and be the winner.

Which Projects Were the Most Fulfilling?

As I have drifted into retirement, people have asked me what projects were the most fulfilling. As evidenced in these reflections, I was involved in numerous client-related issues and handled many matters that were cutting edge. The most fulfilling projects were those endeavors where I helped others create something that made a significant and positive impact on people. The first was my role in doing the legal work associated with creating the Houston Community College as a part of the HISD in 1970-1971, only a little over a month after I had been sworn in as a Texas lawyer.

A second memorable project was the development of the construction management system of fast track bidding to renovate HISD schools in 1974. This particular system of bidding and construction had never been used anywhere before. I knew nothing about construction law when Harry Patterson got shot as he walked in on the chicken restaurant robbery. Without Harry's presence, I had to take over this important project for the HISD.

The third, and probably the most significant legal work was in creating the legal framework for the comprehensive system of magnet schools with HISD Superintendent Billy Reagan in 1974. These magnet schools were at locations throughout the HISD, and they replaced court-ordered busing and completed HISD's desegregation plan. In the process, the magnets provided quality, integrated education that has had a lasting effect on the HISD.

These three projects were demanding, and the work was stress-filled. In each situation, much was riding on the outcome of our efforts. These matters all involved using legal skills and creativity to meet the HISD's needs. Successfully achieving the client's policy goals in a legally acceptable manner on each of these occasions was, and continues to be, greatly satisfying.

School law involves three practice components: governmental (policy and regulation), business, and litigation. These projects are examples of all three. Creation of the HCC was governmental; the creation of the fast track bidding system using the construction manager was business; and the development of the comprehensive magnet school system, the first in the nation, was litigation-related. I defended the actions of school clients many times over the years, and I helped boards and administrators strategize meaningful solutions to legal and policy issues. As noted in these reflections, having school clients with challenging needs afforded me many opportunities for personal and professional fulfillment.

From Bracewell to Thompson & Horton and Beyond

Over the years, school law was a staple of Bracewell's practice. As the firm grew and opened offices in other cities, the firm became more diversified. The business side of the practice expanded nationally and internationally, and with that growth came greater specialization, with an increased overhead and higher hourly rates. School districts, community colleges, and other local governmental bodies are limited in the rates they can pay for legal services. There were other Texas law firms that could effectively represent schools at the lower hourly rates. Dallas partner Lynn Rossi Scott recognized that the continuation of a school district practice at Bracewell was going to be challenging. After discussions and evaluation, Lynn resigned from Bracewell, and, with two associates, she joined the Fort Worth firm of Brackett & Ellis, where she has continued her thriving school practice.

After discussions among the school lawyers and Bracewell firm leaders, the decision was made for the school law practitioners to leave Bracewell and form their own firm. Bracewell's Managing Partner Mark Evans and firm leaders assisted in the transition of Bracewell's school lawyers to Thompson & Horton L.L.P., with the new firm leasing space in Pennzoil Place that was controlled by Bracewell for its first two years. Thompson & Horton is now located in the Phoenix Tower in the Greenway Plaza area off Buffalo Speedway and the Southwest Freeway. Philip Fraissinet is the managing partner of the forty-plus lawyer operation with other offices in Austin and Dallas.

Bracewell, through partner Jarvis Hollingsworth and other lawyers, continues to represent the Houston Community College and other community colleges, as well as providing special counsel to other school districts when their regular lawyers have conflicts. From time to time, I have served as a mediator in desegregation and complex school disputes where my years of school law experience have been helpful in bringing the parties together. Bracewell now focuses on providing full services in public finance through thirty-three lawyers and five paralegals in Houston, Dallas, Austin, San Antonio, and Washington D.C. I am happy to say that our son, Jonathan, is among the public finance partners. He now makes trips to many of the same school districts, colleges, and cities I represented during my active practice years.

Farewell to Jeff Horner

Jeff Horner did much more than shepherd the development of the book on Texas school law. He represented clients well, and he developed deep, trusting relationships with them. He led the firm's basketball team, taking half-court shots, and was always telling people to "towel off" if they got too excited. His speeches were value-filled, and he had a knack for humor and witticisms.

Most of all, he was a friend who was part brother and part son. His death in March 2011 was shockingly difficult for all of us, and adjusting to life without Jeff was slow. Giving his eulogy at his funeral mass at St. Michael Catholic Church, while cathartic, was not an easy task.

Thank You, Carmela

When reflecting as I have, it is appropriate to recognize my wife, Carmela's, involvement and support during nearly 50 years of practicing law and involvement in so many school projects and endeavors. Too many times in our marriage, I have failed to recognize her for being more than an equal part of this team.

Representing school districts was a family affair in the 1970s and early 1980s. Carmela knew and spent time with board members, superintendents, and other administrators. She attended NOLPE, COSA, TASB, and client events as a part of the group. She proofed and edited my articles and sat through many of my early speeches. Sometimes people would ask her for political advice, and on occasion she would be asked about legal issues. We have been a team.

Carmela and I have laughingly (sometimes) lived our marriage with two myths. First, during the Westheimer dispute, "It will get better next week." Secondly, "We don't have to be the last ones to leave this function." I believe the sabbatical of 2006 and the wake-up calls of my strokes in 2004 and my bypass surgery in 2016 have changed our perspective some. I certainly know that my retirement in 2014 has made a huge difference in the number of events we attend and how late we stay. Thank you, Carmela, for your love and support.

The Future

The school law practice in Texas and across the country has matured, and it has become even more of a broad, general practice that is focused on one business, education. School law is truly a specialized general practice that involves litigation, business, and government. School lawyers engage in constitutional issues, employment, civil rights, criminal law, family issues, student discipline, open records, open meetings, construction, real estate, finance, technology, intellectual property, and any other legal issues that impact our society. The state legislature delegates powers to school boards, and the legislature, along with Congress, has weighed in on what our schools should provide and how they should function. Immunities from liability for schools and their employees have proliferated legislatively and through constitutional interpretation in the federal courts. Yes, courts have even been more consistent in abstaining from being involved until the policy maker (school board) has had the opportunity to rule.

Lawsuits in federal court involving significant constitutional issues are becoming rare, as major constitutional questions first raised in *Brown v. Board of Education, Tinker*, and other cases have been decided. Most cases in federal courts today involve applying and interpreting acts of Congress or government regulations.

While school desegregation by race has basically been wrapped up, segregation by wealth or lack thereof has emerged as a vexing challenge. I will not be surprised if some creative lawyer finds a set of facts that can show that state action caused discrimination by wealth or the lack thereof in the education setting. If wealth or the lack thereof becomes accepted as a classification for Equal Protection Clause analysis, a cause of action is possible. The separation of people and communities by wealth is becoming too prevalent and severe for this cause of action not to ultimately emerge. The close nexus between race and ethnicity and wealth makes a strong statement. As long as there is real or perceived inequality in providing education, by race, ethnicity or wealth, there will be conflict, some of which will be resolved politically, but some will ultimately reach our courthouses.

Running the schools is more political today than in the twentieth century, although school operation is still dictated by the rule of law, primarily through statutes enacted by the legislative branches. Said another way, the Constitution, laws, and lawsuits drove school policies in the 1970s and 1980s, whereas policies and politics drive laws and lawsuits today. School administrators and board members are now featured on the 24-hour news cycle and in the print and social media, while school lawyers are seldom mentioned.

One of my continuing ethical concerns for today's school lawyers involves lawyers and school administrators recognizing that the lawyer's client is the school district as a public entity represented by the elected school board. While the superintendent is a part of the client school district, the superintendent is not the ultimate client, even for in-house counsel. If the superintendent proposes an illegal action and no legal alternative can be fashioned, the lawyer must so advise, and should the superintendent persist in going forward, the lawyer has a duty to advise the board. (I was faced with this dilemma once and had to warn the board of an unconstitutional proposal.) If the school board declines legal advice that an action is illegal and wants the lawyer to move forward, the lawyer must resign. Sometimes fulfilling this responsibility is difficult because superintendents wield great influence in who school boards hire as the districts' lawyers, and in-house counsel is a part of the superintendent's administrative team. It is tempting for school district lawyers who have loyalty to the superintendent to put that loyalty above the lawyers' duty to the district as represented by the board of trustees.

The number of independent lawyers currently willing to make the time and energy commitment to being effective school lawyers seems to have leveled off or perhaps declined. School districts require much attention to maintain relationships, especially as board members and administrators come and go. It is not economically feasible to represent school districts unless a lawyer regularly represents a number of districts. Lawyers marginally involved in school representation seem to be gradually moving to more narrowly defined practice areas where they can more easily keep up with the legal issues involved and client relationships. More large and mid-sized districts are utilizing in-house counsel who serve as a part of the management team, and I believe the trend will continue.

Representing a school district can best be described as a broad and general practice for a specific client. Because the school law practice covers many broad topics involving a very diverse group of lawyers, I do not want to have school law become a legal specialization certified by the State Bar of Texas. Interestingly, the percentages of Texas lawyers employed directly by government (11%) and corporations in-house (10%) have been increasing.

Conclusion

I hope you have found these reflections informative and enjoyable to read. Just to have all these events in writing satisfies my basic need to have a history available for those who will follow. Dramatic changes in our society have occurred over my nearly 50 years as a school lawyer, and change will inevitably occur in the future. Since our schools are a reflection of our society, schools and school lawyers will be involved, whatever changes occur.

I feel fortunate to have practiced during what I feel has been a "Golden Age of Lawyering," especially for a school lawyer. My school lawyering has been professionally and personally fulfilling, and I appreciate having the opportunity to work with so many wonderful clients and lawyers along the way. I have had the unconditional support of my wife, Carmela, and the support and understanding of our children, Jonathan and Catherine.

It has been rewarding to have practiced with the quality lawyers and staff of my law firm, Bracewell, and to have had Bill Wilde as a mentor. Bill taught me to be a lawyer, and he supported my endeavors to establish school law as an identifiable practice area. While we are all obviously thankful to be citizens of the United States, I have been fortunate to have lived and practiced in Houston, a city of opportunity in the great state of Texas, where it does not matter where you were born or who your parents were. If you have skills and are willing to put forth the effort, Houston is a great place to live and work.

I have enjoyed writing about these events—it has been a healthy endeavor. I thank my many friends and colleagues whose suggestions and fact-checking have enriched these stories. Jim Walsh reviewed two drafts along the way and was kind in making many constructive suggestions. I especially appreciate the diligence of Bracewell's Jo Nell Cass, Judy Conner, Elaine Edon, and Michelle Newton, who patiently made many changes as the stories evolved. Education Law Association Executive Director Cate Smith and Publications Specialist Pamela Hardy were vital in taking these stories to publication. While there are many other cases and issues that deserve reflection, doing so would make these ramblings far too long and would detract from the importance of the events recounted.

List of Appendices

Appendix A – Listing of Important Supreme Court Decisions on the Desegregation of Public Schools and All Cases and Orders Involving the Houston Independent School District Related to Desegregation (1954-1989); *Delores Ross et al v. Houston Independent School District* (C.A. No. 10444), United States District Court, Southern District of Texas / 138-144

Appendix B – Presidents of NOLPE/Education Law Association / 144-145

Appendix C – Chairs of the School Law Section of the State Bar of Texas / 146

Appendix D – Chairs of the Council of School Attorneys of the National School Boards Association / 147

Appendix E – Chairs of the Council of School Attorneys of the Texas Association of School Boards / 148

Appendix F – Listing of Reported Cases of Kelly Frels – Lead, Co-Counsel, or Amicus Curiae / 149-151

Appendix G – Listing of Published Articles of Kelly Frels / 152-157

Appendix H – Copies of Published Opinion Editorials Written by Kelly Frels / 157-173

APPENDIX A

THE HOUSTON INDEPENDENT SCHOOL DISTRICT DESEGREGATION CASE

DELORES ROSS, ET AL. V. HOUSTON INDEPENDENT SCHOOL DISTRICT

(NO. 10444, S.D. TEX., HOUSTON DIVISION)

1954-1989

Set out below are the most significant decisions of the United States Supreme Court related to the desegregation of public schools and all decisions, reported and unreported, involving the Houston Independent School District in *Delores Ross, et al. v. Houston Independent School District* (No. 10444, S.D. Tex., Houston Division):

1. *Brown v. Board of Education of Topeka, Kansas*, 347 U.S. 483, 74 S.Ct. 686 (1954). This is the original desegregation case and is commonly referred to by the courts as Brown I.
2. *Brown v. Board of Education of Topeka, Kansas*, 349 U.S. 294, 75 S.Ct. 753 (1955). This is the second Brown case wherein the plaintiffs sought further relief, and it is referred to by the courts as Brown II. The court approved the lower court ordering remedies which were to be accomplished with "all deliberate speed."
3. *Ross v. Rogers*, (S.D. Tex., No. 10444, October 15, 1957). This is the original action in the current *Ross v. Eckels* case which was filed in December 1956 after Delores Ross, Benita Williams and other black students were denied admission to a white school nearer to their homes.
4. *Ross v. Peterson*, (S.D. Tex., No. 10444, August, 1960). The cases and information in this particular order involve the Board of Education's adoption of the grade-a-year plan of desegregation. This plan was affirmed by the Fifth Circuit Court of Appeals on September 6, 1960 at 282 F.2d 95.
5. *Ross v. Dyer,* 312 F.2d 191 (5th Cir., 1963). The Fifth Circuit held that the brother-sister rule could not be applied where its effect in many situations was to compel continued attendance at a racially segregated school.
6. *Ross v. Eckels*, Decree of September 5, 1967. This Decree was the "freedom of choice" plan of desegregation under which the Houston Independent School District operated until the ultimate plan was effectuated in August-September 1970.
7. *Broussard v. Houston Independent School District*, 395 F.2d 817 (5th Cir. 1968). The Circuit Court refused to enjoin the Houston Independent School District from proceeding with its plan of school building construction.
8. *Green v. County School Board of New Kent County, Va.,* 391 U.S. 430, 88 S.Ct. 1689 (1968). *Green* held a particular "freedom of choice" plan to be

impermissible and placed the burden on the school board "to come forward with a plan that promises realistically to work, and promises realistically to work now."

9. Judge Ben C. Connally's Verbal Preliminary Ruling of July 23, 1969. This Preliminary Ruling sets forth in detail the ground rules for hearings which led to the eventual plan of desegregation which was modified by the Fifth Circuit to include the pairing of some elementary schools. The pairings were replaced by the Magnet School Plan in July 1975. This Preliminary Ruling is perhaps the most informative document regarding desegregation in the Houston Independent School District.

10. *Singleton v. Jackson Municipal Separate School District*, 419 F.2d 1211 (5th Cir. 1970). After the Supreme Court decided *Green v. County School Board of New Kent County*, the Fifth Circuit Court of Appeals considered a number of desegregation cases, and the entire Fifth Circuit Court announced general rules it would follow in future desegregation cases. All court ordered plans of desegregation in the Fifth Circuit are based almost entirely upon the guidelines established in *Singleton*.

11. *Ross v. Eckels*, 317 F.Supp. 512 (S.D. Tex., May 30, 1970). Judge Connally found that the Houston Independent School District operated a dual-school system and ordered an equidistant school zoning plan for all levels of instruction.

12. *Ross v. Eckels*, 434 F.2d 1140 (5th Cir., August 25, 1970). The plaintiffs appealed Judge Connally's decision wherein the Fifth Circuit ordered a geographical capacity plan for the secondary schools and the pairing, clustering, and rezoning of 25 elementary schools. The Houston Independent School District appealed this pairing order to the Supreme Court of the United States.

13. *Ross v. Eckels*, 402 U.S. 953, 91 S.Ct. 1614 (1971). The Supreme Court declined to hear the case by denying the District's application for writ of certiorari on May 3, 1971.

14. *Ross v. Eckels*, (S.D. Tex., No. 10444, September 18, 1970). After the Fifth Circuit Opinion of 434 F.2d 1140, Judge Connally entered an Amended Decree in which the August 25, 1970 opinion was adopted. This is the decree, with minor modifications, under which the Houston Independent School District operated throughout the remainder of the litigation.

15. *Swann v. Charlotte-Mecklenburg Board of Education*, 91 S.Ct. 1267 (1971). In *Swann*, the Supreme Court approved the concepts of pairing, clustering, and other "unusual" techniques to achieve desegregation together with the use of transportation (bussing) to implement.

16. *Ross v. Eckels*, (S.D. Tex., No. 10444, May 24, 1971). [Intervention of Narcisco Rodriguez, Jr., et al., on Behalf of Mexican Americans and Motion of the Houston Independent School District for an Alternate Pairing Plan.] Judge Connally denied the motion of the Mexican Americans to intervene as plaintiffs in the main suit and denied the motion of the Houston Independent School District to substitute an alternate plan of pairing for the one ordered by the Fifth Circuit Court of Appeals.

By Kelly Frels

17. *United States of America v. State of Texas, et al.* (E.D. Tex., C.A. No. 5281, July 13, 1971, as amended by Orders of August 9 and 15, 1973). [Statewide Modified Ordered pursuant to the Order of the Fifth Circuit Court of Appeals.] This Order restrained the Central Education Agency and all state agencies from discriminating in: (1) student transfers; (2) changes in school district boundaries; (3) school transportation; (4) extracurricular activities; (5) faculty and staff assignment; (6) student assignment; and (7) curriculum and compensatory education. The Order provided for complaints and grievances and set forth the jurisdiction of the United States District Court for the Eastern District of Texas. The Order also prescribed conditions for the transfer of property in Section J.
18. *Ross v. Eckels*, (S.D. Tex., No. 10444, August 6, 1971). [Intervention of the Almeda Civic Club.] Judge Connally denied the motion of Thompson, et al. (the Almeda Civic Club alleging to represent the interests of white parents in the Almeda area) to intervene in the case.
19. *Ross v. Eckels*, 468 F.2d 649 (5th Cir. 1972). The Fifth Circuit affirmed the denial of intervention by Thompson, et al., on behalf of the Almeda Civic Club, and remanded the question of the intervention of Narcisco Rodriguez, Jr., et al., on behalf of Mexican Americans, back to the District Court. There was never a finding made by a court that Hispanics had been intentionally discriminated against by the Houston Independent School District.
20. *Ross v. Eckels*, (S.D. Tex., No. 10444, December 19, 1971). [Intervention of Hap Farhart.] The intervention sought by Hap Farhart to change the University Scholastic League rules regarding one year residency requirements was denied by Judge Ben C. Connally. No appeal was taken.
21. *Ross v. Houston Independent School District*, (S.D. Tex., No. 10444, April 4, 1973). [Creation of the proposed Westheimer ISD.] After the State Board of Education approved the creation of the Westheimer ISD, Judge Ben C. Connally, on motion of the Houston ISD, enjoined the district's creation.
22. *Keyes v. School District No. 1, Denver, Colorado*, 93 S.Ct. 2686 (1973). The Supreme Court found Mexican Americans to be a separate minority and established certain guidelines for determining when there is unconstitutional segregation in states where there is no state statute requiring separate facilities. It was after this decision that the HISD Board recognized Hispanics as a separate ethnic group for remedial purposes, but the Board did not admit that Hispanics had even been discriminated against.
23. *Ross v. Houston Independent School District*, (S.D. Tex., No. 10444, July 22, 1974). This is a letter from Judge Ben C. Connally notifying the District that he will approve a 10% (elementary) and 15% (secondary) faculty variance. Also attached is the Order entered by Judge Connally changing the faculty variance from 5% to 10% at the elementary level and 15% at the secondary level. Judge Connally retired, and the case was transferred to Judge James Noel.
24. *Lau v. Nichols*, 414 U.S. 463, 94 S.Ct. 786 (1974). This is a suit by non-English-speaking Chinese students in San Francisco. The Supreme Court held that the school's failure to provide English language instruction for a substantial number of non-English-speaking students denied them a meaningful opportunity to participate in public educational programs in

violation of Title VI of the Civil Rights Act of 1974. This case is the bilingual education case.

25. *Milliken v. Bradley,* 418 U.S. 717, 94 S.Ct. 3112 (1974). This is the cross-district busing case involving the Detroit School Distract. The Court found that it was improper to impose a multi-district remedy for single-district de jure segregation in the absence of finding that the other included districts had failed to operate unitary school systems or had committed acts that affected segregation, the absence of any claim or finding that school district boundary lines were established with the purpose of fostering racial segregation, and without affording a meaningful opportunity for the included neighboring districts to present evidence or to be heard on the priority of the multi-district remedy or on the question of constitutional violations by those districts.

26. *Ross v. Houston independent School District*, (S.D. Tex., No. 10444, July 11, 1975). Judge Noel entered an agreed Order Amending Decree allowing the Houston Independent School District to unpair the schools paired by the Fifth Circuit Court of Appeals in 1970 and allowed the District to implement the Magnet School Plan to replace the pairings.

27. *Ross v. Houston Independent School District*, (S.D. Tex., No. 10444, August 8, 1975). The area north of the Southwest Freeway originally zoned to Poe Elementary was ordered to be returned to Poe Elementary commencing with the 1975-76 school year.

28. *Delores Ross & United States of America & Nick Estrada, et al., v Houston Independent School District, et al.* (C.A. No. 14444, February 24, 1976, S.D. Tex. [Bi-Racial Committee Composition]). The original Plaintiffs and the Houston Independent School District agreed that the Court appointed Bi-Racial Committee would be composed of four African-Americans, four Anglos, and two Hispanics until such time as the Plaintiffs'-Intervenors' Complaint in Intervention was heard by the Court and findings of fact and conclusions of law were made and entered. No finding of intentional discrimination against Hispanics was ever made.

29. *Pasadena City Board of Education v. Spangler*, 96 S.Ct. 2697 (1976). Absent acts of further discrimination, school districts are not required to annually reassign students in order to accommodate changing residential patterns. The case also relates to parties, mootness, and the remedial power of federal courts.

30. *Milliken v. Bradley*, 97 S.Ct. 2749 (1977). This case relates to the remedial power of a federal court to order remedial educational plans, including bilingual education, and the responsibility of the state to pay for additional costs of education. The case generally relates to the remedial power of the federal courts related to past discriminatory acts.

31. *Dayton Board of Education v. Brinkman*, 97 S.Ct. 2766 (1977). For the first time since *Swann*, the court speaks to the remoteness in time of past segregative acts. The court remands the case to the lower courts for further findings concerning the specific segregative action and the determination of an appropriate remedy. Like *Milliken, Brinkman* relates primarily to the fashioning of an appropriate remedy for past intentional discrimination.

32. *Delores Ross et al. v. Houston Independent School District, et al.* (Proposed Westheimer ISD), 559 F.2 937 (5th Cir. 1977). The courts reversed Judge

Noel's orders related to the proposed WISD and remanded the case for further proceedings. In doing so, the court specified the burdens which the proposed WISD would have in a trial on the merits. The court dismissed as moot the Houston Independent School District's application for writ of mandamus to disqualify Judge Noel. Judge Noel had taken senior status, and the case was reassigned to Judge Finis Cowan.

33. *Delores Ross et al. v. Houston Independent School District, et al.* (Proposed Westheimer ISD, No. 10444, December 8, 1977). Judge Cowan permanently enjoined the proposed WISD from proceeding further toward the creation and implementation of a splinter school district.
34. *Delores Ross et al. v. Houston Independent School District, et al.* (Proposed Westheimer ISD, No. 10444, December 19, 1977). Judge Cowan entered these Findings of Fact and Memorandum Opinion in support of the Injunction Decree of December 8, 1977. The Findings of Fact and Memorandum Opinion were filed on December 19, 1977, but were read in draft form from the bench on December 8, 1977.
35. *Delores Ross et al. v. Houston Independent School District, et al.* (C.A. No. 10444, December 19, 1977). Judge Cowan entered an Order relating to the composition and activities of the court's Tri-Ethnic Committee.
36. *Delores Ross. et al. v. Houston Independent School District, et al.*, C.A. No. 10444. Judge Cowan entered his Order of June 9, 1978, requiring the filing of a plan, setting hearing, and defining duties and procedures of Tri-Ethnic Committee. He stated that the Houston Independent School District was either unitary or it was not. If not unitary, further remedies would be ordered.
37. *Delores Ross et al. v. Houston Independent School District, et al.*, C.A. No. 10444. Judge Cowan's Order of October 3, 1978, established a schedule for achieving unitary status. The District took the position that it was unitary in that it had done all that was practical in the circumstances to remedy the effects of past discrimination.
38. *Delores Ross et al. v. Houston Independent School District, et al.* (Proposed Westheimer ISD), 583 F.2d 712 (5th Cir., 1978). Decision of the District Court of December 1977, affirmed in part, vacated in part by the Fifth Circuit. Judge Cowan returned to private practice, and the case is assigned to Judge Robert O'Conor.
39. *Delores Ross, et al. v. Houston Independent School District, et al.* (Proposed Westheimer ISD), C.A. No. 10444, June 4, 1979). Judge O'Conor ordered that the Houston Independent School District recover from Westheimer ISD and its Board of Trustees, interim or permanent, attorneys' fees and costs of court incurred by the Houston Independent School District in this action. No action was ever taken to collect because there were no funds available.
40. Judge O'Conor's Order of September 28, 1979, directing the Texas Education Agency to make a study of identifying and evaluating the educational challenges faced by the Houston Independent School District and other urban school districts. Report of the study was to be filed with Court by April 1, 1980.
41. *Columbus Board of Education v. Penick*, 443 U.S. 449, 99 S.Ct. 2941 (1979). In a case involving Columbus, Ohio, the Court sustained the lower court's decisions that the school district's conduct before and at the time of trial

was prompted by an unconstitutional, segregative purpose, and it also had a current segregative impact that was sufficiently system-wide to warrant the remedy ordered. The case primarily relates to burdens of proof and evidence of intent or racial motivation in non-southern school districts. At page 2948, the Court refused to consider evidence of discriminatory acts in rentals which were found to constitute impermissible motivation. The foreseeable effect standard may be utilized as one of the several kinds of proofs from which an inference of segregative intent may be properly drawn.

42. *Dayton Board of Education v. Brinkman*, 443 U.S. 406, 99 S.Ct. 2971 (1979). This case involves the Dayton, Ohio school system. In another non-southern district, the Court found intentional discrimination based upon past discrimination not being corrected, and that the school board's failure to fulfill its affirmative duty and other conduct tended to perpetuate or increase segregation on a system-wide basis.

43. *Delores Ross, et al. v. Houston Independent School District, et al.* (S.D. Tex., C.A. No. 10444, June 10, 1980). Judge O'Conor denied the motion of the United States to add party defendants and for leave to file an amended complaint in intervention. The Justice Department had attempted to add the 22 surrounding Harris County school districts, the State of Texas, the Texas Education Agency, the City of Houston, and the Harris County Department of Education as parties' defendant to make this interdistrict desegregation case.

44. *Delores Ross, et al. v. Houston Independent School District* (S.D. Tex., C.A. No. 10444, June 11, 1980). Judge O'Conor denied the plaintiff Delores Ross' Motion to Amend Pleadings and to add parties' defendant for the same reason stated in the Court's Memorandum and Order of June 10, 1980.

45. *United States v. State of Texas*, 506 F.Supp. 405 (E.D. Tex., C.A. No. 5281, January 12, 1981). Judge Justice found that the State of Texas had discriminated against Mexican Americans as an ethnic group in education based upon the Fourteenth Amendment and the Equal Education Act of 1972 but not under Title VI of the 1964 Civil Rights Act. Judge Justice then ordered the State to develop a comprehensive bilingual educational plan to remedy this discrimination.

46. *United States v. State of Texas* (E.D. Tex., C.A. No. 5281, April 17, 1981). Judge Justice followed up on his March 9, 1981 Order by requiring a comprehensive bilingual plan for the State of Texas. The comprehensive plan is set out in this order.

47. *Delores Ross, et al. v. Houston Independent School District* (S.D. Tex., C.A. No. 10444, June 17, 1981). In this Memorandum and Order, Judge O'Conor found that the Houston Independent School District had done all that was practical in the circumstances and declared the school district to be unitary. The Court placed the case on an inactive docket and indicated that he would review the case again in three years. If no segregative acts had been taken by the District to disturb this unitary status, the case would be dismissed. At Page 33, the Court again denied the motions of the Justice Department and the NAACP Legal Defense & Education Fund to add parties, for protective order, and for supplemental relief as it relates to a metropolitan interdistrict remedy.

48. *Delores Ross, et al. v. Houston Independent School. District*, 699 F.2d 218 (5th Cir. 1983). The Fifth Circuit affirmed Judge O'Conor's finding that the

Houston Independent School District was unitary and that the Court was correct in denying the motion to make the case a metropolitan one under Rules 19 and 20 at this late date. A separate suit could be filed wherein the test would be whether the Houston Independent School District actively participated with other school districts in intentional segregative acts. The case was to remain on the inactive docket for three years. Judge O'Conor returned to the private practice, and the case was assigned to Judge John V. Singleton.

49. *Delores Ross, et al. v. Houston Independent School District.* (Settlement Agreement). (S.D. Tex., C.A. 10444, September 10, 1984). The parties settled the litigation involving the desegregation of the Houston Independent School District. After a hearing before Judge Singleton, language relating to the monitoring committee was added as a stipulation. This Settlement Agreement lasted five years, but could have been extended by agreement of the parties.
50. *Delores Ross, et al. v. Houston Independent School District.* (S.D. Tex., C.A. 10444, November 27, 1984). The Settlement Agreement was approved by the Court. The Court dismissed the case with prejudice with enforcement action to be taken only as provided in the Settlement Agreement.
51. *Delores Ross, et al. v. Houston Independent School, District.* (S.D. Tex., February 19, 1985). The parties agreed on the attorneys' fees to be paid to the plaintiffs' attorneys for the desegregation case and entered into a settlement agreement. By this time, the original plaintiffs' attorneys, Weldon Berry and Francis Williams had died, and no claims for attorneys' fee were made by their estates.

Delores Ross, et al. v. Houston Independent School District. (S.D. Tex., March 29, 1985). The settlement agreement concerning attorneys' fees was approved by Judge Singleton, thus concluding the Court's active involvement in the case. The case ended without further court action at the conclusion of the settlement agreement on September 10, 1989.

APPENDIX B

PRESIDENTS OF NOLPE/EDUCATION LAW ASSOCIATION

Titles reflect the positions held at the time of the presidents' terms.

1955-56	Madaline Kinter Remmlein, National Education Association, VA
1957	Eugene S. Lawler, Florida State University, FL
1958-59	Reynolds C. Seitz, Marquette University, WI
1960	Edward C. Bolmeier, Duke University, NC
1961	Marion A. McGhehey, U.S. Office of Education, VA
1962	Walter L. Hetzel, Ames, Iowa Schools, IA
1963	Marlin M. Volz, University of Louisville, KY
1964	Lloyd E. McCann, University of Arizona, AZ
1965	Lee O. Garber, University of Pennsylvania, PA
1966	Henry E. Butler, Jr., University of Rochester, NY
1967	E. Edmund Reutter, Jr., Columbia University, NY
1968	Martha L. Ware, National Education Association, VA
1969	Joseph E. Bryson, University of North Carolina, NC

1970 John Philip Linn, University of Denver , CO
1971 Manny S. Brown, Attorney at Law, Racine, WI
1972 Thomas A. Shannon, Deputy Supt. and School Attorney, VA
1973 Roger M. Shaw, Kent State University, OH
1974 Robert E. Phay, University of North Carolina, NC
1975 M. Chester Nolte, University of Denver, CO
1976 Irving C. Evers, Attorney, Hackensack, NJ
1977 August W. Steinhilber, National School Boards Association, MD
1978 Philip K. Piele, University of Oregon, OR
1979 Kelly Frels, Bracewell & Patterson, LLP, TX
1980 Burton R. Shifman, Shifman & Goodman, PC, MI
1981 Floyd G. Delon, University of Missouri, MO
1982 William F. Paton, Oconomowoc Public Schools, WI
1983 Ralph D. Stern, Whitmore & Kay, CA
1984 Dale Gaddy, National School Boards Association, VA
1985 Martha M. McCarthy, Indiana University-Bloomington, IN
1986 John F. Lewis, Squire Sanders & Dempsey, OH
1987 D. Parker Young, University of Georgia, GA
1988 William C. Bednar, Jr., Eskew, Muir & Bednar, TX
1989 Marvyn D. Jaffe, Staples High School, CT
1990 Stephen B. Thomas, Kent State University, OH
1991 Joseph C. Beckham, Florida State University, FL
1992 James C. Ullman, Jennings, Strouss & Salmon, AZ
1993 Steve W. Batson, West Virginia State College, WV
1994 Nelda Cambron-McCabe, Miami University of Ohio, OH
1995 Ivan Gluckman, National Association of Secondary School Principals, VA
1996 Perry A. Zirkel, Lehigh University, PA
1997 Richard Dickinson, Ohio School Boards Association, OH
1998 Jeffrey J. Horner, Bracewell & Patterson, LLP, TX
1999 Charles J. Russo, University of Dayton, OH
2000 Terrence Leas, Valley Community College, MN
2001 Ralph D. Mawdsley, Cleveland State University, OH
2002 R. Craig Wood, McGuireWoods LLP, VA
2003 Allan G. Osborne, Jr., Snug Harbor Community School, MA
2004 Philip T.K. Daniel, Ohio State University, OH
2005 P. Tyson Bennett, Reese & Carney, LLP, MD
2006 Lois F. Berlin, Falls Church City Public Schools, VA
2007 M. David Alexander, Virginia Tech, VA
2008 Christopher P. Borreca, Bracewell & Patterson, LLP, TX
2009 Kathleen Crume, Academy School District, CO
2010 Brad Colwell, Bowling Green State University, OH
2011 Edwin C. Darden, Appleseed, VA
2012 Susan G. Clark, University of Akron, OH
2013 William E. Thro, University of Kentucky, KY
2014 Kenneth E. Lane, Southeastern Louisiana University, LA
2015 Patrick D. Pauken, Bowling Green State University, OH
2016 R. Craig Wood, University of Florida, FL
2017 Lynn Rossi Scott, Brackett & Ellis, PC, TX
2018 Suzanne E. Eckes, Indiana University-Bloomington, IN
2019 Wayne Haglund, Haglund Law Firm, TX

By Kelly Frels

APPENDIX C
SCHOOL LAW SECTION – STATE BAR OF TEXAS CHAIRS

1972-1973	Cecil A. Morgan	Fort Worth
1973-1974	Warren Whitham	Dallas
1974-1975	Grant Cook	Houston
1975-1976	Ralph Langley	San Antonio
1976-1977	Morris A. Galatzan	El Paso
1977-1978	Kelly Frels	Houston
1978-1979	Tanner T. Hunt, Jr.	Beaumont
1979-1980	William H,. Bingham	Austin
1980-1981	William C. Bednar, Jr.	Austin
1981-1982	Robert B. Cox	Odessa
1982-1983	Nathan E. White, Jr.	McKinney
1983-1984	Marion J. Borchers	New Braunfels
1984-1985	J. W. Gary	Corpus Christi
1985-1986	Joe Hairston	Austin
1986-1987	Jeffrey Davis	Houston
1987-1988	Paul Lyle	Plainview
1988-1989	Janet Little Horton	Houston
1989-1990	Charles Thompson	Atlanta
1990-1991	Blake Hansen	Odessa
1991-1992	Thomas (Tom) Carr	Fort Worth
1992-1993	Jefferson K. Brim III	Austin
1993-1994	Judith C. G. B. Underwood	Austin
1994-1995	Merri Schneider-Vogel	Houston
1995-1996	Tom Garner, Jr.	Port Lavaca
1996-1997	Edgar Oran Coble, Jr.	Fort Worth
1997-1998	Nan P. Hundere	San Antonio
1998-1999	Myra Chickering Schexnayder	Houston
1999-2000	Neal W. Adams	Grapevine
2000-2001	Roger Dean Hepworth	Austin
2001-2002	Denise Hays	Austin
2002-2003	Lisa A. Brown	Houston
2003-2004	Lynn Rossi Scott	Fort Worth
2004-2005	Lonnie F. Hollingsworth, Jr.	Austin
2005-2006	Wayne Haglund	Lufkin
2006-2007	Kevin Lungwitz	Austin
2007-2008	Shellie Hoffman Crow	Austin
2008-2009	Miles T. Bradshaw	Nacogdoches
2009-2010	Elneita Hutchins-Taylor	Houston
2010-2011	Joy Surratt Baskin	Austin
2011-2012	Joey W. Moore	Austin
2012-2013	S. Anthony Safi	El Paso
2013-2014	Michael Currie	Austin
2014-2015	Juan Cruz	Laredo
2015-2016	Ellen Spalding	Houston
2016-2017	Fred Stormer	Amarillo
2017-2018	Julie Leahy	Austin
2018-2019	Mark Tilley	Austin
2019-2020	Marney Collins Sims	Houston

APPENDIX D
PAST NATIONAL SCHOOL BOARDS ASSOCIATION COUNCIL OF SCHOOL ATTORNEYS CHAIRS

1967-1970	Thomas A. Shannon	CA
1970-1971	H. Rollin Allen	MI
1971-1973	Robert T. Baker	OH
1973-1975	Benjamin L. Craig	CO
1975-1977	Allen D. Schwartz	IL
1977-1978	Kelly Frels	TX
1978-1979	Charles E. Keller	MI
1979-1980	Malcolm Kitt	MD
1980-1981	Edgar H. Bittle	IA
1981-1982	Ralph D. Stern	CA
1982-1983	James F. Clark	WI
1983-1984	R. Dean Jollay	OH
1984-1985	E. Freeman Leverett	GA
1985-1986	Gerald A. Caplan	CO
1986-1987	George T. Register, Jr.	NC
1987-1988	William Fearen	A
1988-1989	David M. Pedersen	NE
1989-1990	Patricia Baker	KS
1990-1991	Donald B. Sweeney, Jr.	AL
1991-1992	James C. Hanks	IA
1992-1993	Jean B. Arnold Dodge	VA
1993-1994	John G. Moyer, Jr.	OK
1994-1995	John S. Aldridge	TX
1995-1996	David B. Rubin	NJ
1996-1997	Benjamin J. Ferrara	NY
1997-1998	Gary R. Thune	ND
1998-1999	Ann L. Majestic	NC
1999-2000	James T. Maatsch	
2000-2001	Martin Semple	CO
2001-2002	Cynthia Lutz Kelly	KS
2002-2003	Margaret A. Chidester	CA
2003-2004	Nancy Fredman Krent	IL
2004-2005	Anthony G. Scariano	IL
2005-2006	David A. Farmelo	NY
2006-2007	Deryl W. Wynn	KS
2007-2008	Jay Worona	NY
2008-2009	Sam S. Harben, Jr.	GA
2009-2010	A. Dean Pickett	AZ
2010-2011	Thomas E. Wheeler, II	IN
2011-2012	Patrice McCarthy	CT
2012-2013	Elizabeth Eynon-Kokrda	NE
2013-2014	Allison Schafer	NC
2014-2015	Gregory J. Guercio	NY
2015-2016	Justino D. Petrarca	IL
2016-2017	Andrew M. Sanchez NM	
2017-2018	Pilar Sokol	NY
2018-2019	Diane Marshall-Freedman	CA
(1968-1997)	August W. Steinhilber, NSBA General Counsel and Associate Executive Director	

By Kelly Frels

APPENDIX E
TEXAS SCHOOL BOARDS ASSOCIATION COUNCIL OF SCHOOL ATTORNEYS CHAIRS

1979-1980	James Deatherage
1980-1981	Kelly Frels
1981-1982	Kelly Frels
1982-1983	Bill Bingham
1983-1984	Bill Bingham
1984-1985	Tanner Hunt
1985-1986	Tanner Hunt
1986-1987	Robert Cox
1987-1988	Robert Cox
1988-1989	John Hardy
1989-1990	John Hardy
1990-1991	J. W. Gary
1991-1992	Nan Seidenfeld
1992-1993	Richard Peebles
1993-1994	Jim Walsh
1994-1995	Jeff Horner
1995-1996	Ann Manning
1996-1997	Wayne Haglund
1997-1998	Blake Hansen
1998-1999	Gus Acevedo
1999-2000	Janet Horton
2000-2001	Judy Brown
2001-2002	M. Kaye DeWalt
2002-2003	S. Anthony Safi
2003-2004	Bill Armstrong
2004-2005	Alan Rhodes
2005-2006	Elneita Hutchins-Taylor
2006-2007	Lisa Brown
2007-2008	Tom Myers
2008-2009	Dorcas Green
2009-2010	Cheryl Mehl
2010-2011	Juan Cruz
2011-2012	Merri Schneider-Vogel
2012-2013	Lynn Rossi Scott
2013-2014	Mia Martin
2014-2015	Ellen Spalding
2015-2016	Miles Bradshaw
2016-2017	David Backus
2017-2018	Christine Badillo
2018-2019	Leticia McGowan

APPENDIX F
KELLY FRELS CASES
LEAD, CO-COUNSEL OR AMICUS CURIAE
(Reported Cases Only)

Carr v. Stripling and Houston Independent School Dist., No. 13-03-00248-CV, Court of Appeals of Texas, Thirteenth District, Corpus Christi, 2005 Tex. App. Lexis 1395, February 3, 2005, Decided. Petition for Review Denied June 10, 2005, Reported at: 2005 Tex. Lexis 455

Morris v. Dearborne, No. 98-40488, United States Court of Appeals for the Fifth Circuit, 181 F.3d 657; 1999 U.S. App. Lexis 16042, July 16, 1999, Decided, Rehearing *En Banc* Denied September 14, 1999, Reported at: 1999 U.S. App. Lexis 25463

Bell v. Katy Independent School Dist., No. 01-97-01134-CV, Court of Appeals of Texas, 1st District, Houston, 994 S.W.2d 862; 1999 Tex. App. Lexis 4160, June 3, 1999, Opinion Issued

Doe v. Santa Fe Independent School Dist., 933 F.Supp. 647 (S.D.Tex., 1996); 171 F.3d 1013 (1999); 5th Cir. See *Santa Fe Independent School District v. Doe*, 530 U.S. 290, 120 5th Cir. 2266 (2000)

Becerra v. Asher, (No. 96-20401) United States Court of Appeals for the Fifth Circuit, 105 F.3d 1042, 111 F.3d 894, 1997 U.S. App. Lexis 6632, April 7, 1997, filed, *Certiorari* Denied October 6, 1997, Reported at 1997 U.S. Lexis 4801

Jackson v. Katy Independent School Dist., 951 F.Supp. 1293, 116 Ed. Law Rep. 214 (S.D.Tex., June 08, 1996) (NO. CIV. A. H-95-0280)

Johnson v. Houston Independent School Dist., 930 F.Supp. 276, 111 Ed. Law Rep. 243 (S.D.Tex., May 13, 1996) (NO. CIV.A. H-93-2588)

Fowler v. Szostek, 905 S.W.2d 336, 103 Ed. Law Rep. 519 (Tex.App.-Hous. (1 Dist.), Aug 03, 1995) (NO. 01-94-01136-CV)

Massey v. Houston Baptist University, 902 S.W.2d 81, 101 Ed. Law Rep. 1260 (Tex.App.-Hous. (1 Dist.), June 08, 1995) (NO. 01-94-01276-CV)

Edgewood Independent School District v. Meno, No. 94-0152, Supreme Court of Texas, 893 S.W.2d 450; 1995 Tex. Lexis 4; 38 Tex. Sup. J. 188, May 25, 1994, Argued, January 30, 1995, Delivered, As Corrected. Second Correction May 4, 1995

Hispanic Educ. Committee v. Houston Independent School Dist., 886 F.Supp. 606, 100 Ed. Law Rep. 1062 (S.D.Tex., Dec 27, 1994) (NO. CIV. A. H-94-1065)

Cox v. Galena Park Independent School Dist., 895 S.W.2d 745, 99 Ed. Law Rep. 647 (Tex.App.-Corpus Christi, Dec 01, 1994) (NO. 13-93-481-CV)

Jones v. Clear Creek Independent School Dist., 977 F.2d 963, 61 USLW 2341, 78 Ed. Law Rep. 42 (5th Cir.(Tex.), Nov 24, 1992) (NO. 89-2638)

Mitchison v. Houston Independent School Dist., 803 S.W.2d 769, 65 Ed. Law Rep. 1329 (Tex.App.-Hous. (14 Dist.), Jan 10, 1991) (NO. B14-90-278-CV)

Swanson v. Houston Independent School Dist., 800 S.W.2d 630, 64 Ed. Law Rep. 1267 (Tex.App.-Hous. (14 Dist.), Nov 15, 1990) (NO. A14-89-00943-CV)

Houston Independent School Dist. v. Houston Chronicle Pub. Co., 798 S.W.2d 580, 64 Ed. Law Rep. 293 (Tex.App.-Hous. (1 Dist.), Aug 09, 1990) (NO. 01-90-00116-CV)

Houston Chronicle Pub. Co. v. Mattox, 767 S.W.2d 695, 53 Ed. Law Rep. 312 (Tex., Mar 22, 1989) (NO. C-7911)

Continental Cas. Co. v. Hall, 761 S.W.2d 54, 50 Ed. Law Rep. 906 (Tex.App.-Hous. (14 Dist.), Oct 20, 1988) (NO. A14-86-00873-CV, A14-86-00688-CV)

League of United Latin American Citizens v. Pasadena Independent School Dist., 672 F.Supp. 280, 45 Fair Empl.Prac.Cas. (BNA) 177, 45 Empl. Prac. Dec. P 37,802, 42 Ed. Law Rep. 1122, 2 IER Cases 1143 (S.D.Tex., Jul 31, 1987) (NO. CIV. A. H-87-935)

League of United Latin American Citizens v. Pasadena Independent School Dist., 662 F.Supp. 443, 43 Fair Empl.Prac.Cas. (BNA) 945, 43 Empl. Prac. Dec. P 37,098, 2 IER Cases 40 (S.D.Tex., Apr. 14, 1987) (NO. CIV. A. H-87-935)

Lopez v. Houston Independent School Dist., 817 F.2d 351, 39 Ed. Law Rep. 21 (5th Cir.(Tex.), May 26, 1987) (NO. 86-2569)

Houston Federation of Teachers, Local 2415 v. Houston Independent School Dist., 730 S.W.2d 644, 40 Ed. Law Rep. 533 (Tex., Apr 22, 1987) (NO. C-5729)

Houston Independent School Dist. v. Houston Federation of Teachers, Local 2415, 715 S.W.2d 369, 34 Ed. Law Rep. 957 (Tex.App.-Hous. (1 Dist.), May 22, 1986) (NO. 01-86-0110-CV)

Neubauer v. City of McAllen, 766 F.2d 1567; 1985 U.S. App., Aug 08, 1985, (NO. 83-2553) (Trial court lead counsel for City of McAllen)

Voorhies v. Conroe Independent School Dist., 610 F.Supp. 868, 26 Ed. Law Rep. 233 (S.D.Tex., June 04, 1985) (NO. CIV. A. H-83-1958)

Heaney v. U.S. Veterans Admin., 756 F.2d 1215 (5th Cir.(Tex.), Apr 11, 1985) (NO. 84-1348)

Mathews v. Houston Independent School Dist., 595 F.Supp. 445, 36 Fair Empl. Prac.Cas. (BNA) 110, 21 Ed. Law Rep. 187 (S.D.Tex., Aug 23, 1984) (NO. C.A. H-83-4044)

Wells v. Hico Independent School Dist., 736 F.2d 243, 18 Ed. Law Rep. 225 (5th Cir. (Tex.), Jul 16, 1984) (NO. 82-1468)

U.S. v. CRUCIAL, 722 F.2d 1182, 15 Ed. Law Rep. 92 (5th Cir.(Tex.), Dec 29, 1983) (NO. 82-1444)

Burris v. Willis Independent School Dist., Inc., 713 F.2d 1087, 13 Ed. Law Rep. 13 (5th Cir. (Tex.), Sep 06, 1983) (NO. 82-2204); 537 F.Supp. 801, 4 Ed. Law Rep. 501 (S.D.Tex., Apr 19, 1982) (NO. CIV. H-80-1450)

Cruce v. Brazosport Independent School Dist., 703 F.2d 862, 31 Fair Empl. Prac.Cas. (BNA) 938, 31 Empl. Prac. Dec. P 33,561, 10 Ed. Law Rep. 85 (5th Cir.(Tex.), Apr 25, 1983) (NO. 82-2035)

U.S. v. State of Tex., 680 F.2d 356, 5 Ed. Law Rep. 141 (5th Cir.(Tex.), Jul 12, 1982) (NO. 81-2196, 81-2310, 81-2330)

Sessum v. Houston Community College, 94 F.R.D. 316, 32 Fair Empl.Prac.Cas. (BNA) 1172, 29 Empl. Prac. Dec. P 32,929, 5 Ed. Law Rep. 455 (S.D.Tex., Jun 07, 1982) (NO. C.A. H-77-404)

Rogers v. Kroger Co., 669 F.2d 317, 28 Fair Empl.Prac.Cas. (BNA) 404, 28 Empl. Prac.Dec. P 32,510 (5th Cir.(Tex.), Mar 05, 1982) (NO. 80-2090)

Houston Independent School Dist. v. Houston Teachers' Ass'n, 617 S.W.2d 765 (Tex. Civ. App.-Hou. (14 Dist.), May 27, 1981) (NO. B2665)

Doe v. Plyler, 628 F.2d 448 (5th Cir.(Tex.), Oct 20, 1980) (NO. 78-3311)

Ross v. Houston Independent School District, 699 F.2d 218 (5th Cir. 1983); 81 F.R.D. 532 (S.D.Tex., Feb 01, 1979) (NO. CIV 10444); 583 F.2d 712 (5th Cir. (Tex.), Nov 06, 1978) (NO. 78-1576); 457 F.Supp. 18 (S.D.Tex., Dec 19, 1977) (NO. CIV. 10444); Civil Action No. 10,444, in the United States District Court for the Southern District of Texas Houston Division, 1977 U.S. Dist. Lexis 15463, June 13, 1977; Civil Action No. 10,444, in the United States District Court for the Southern District of Texas Houston Division, 1977 U.S. Dist. Lexis 15566, June 6, 1977, as amended June 16, 1977, June 20, 1977 and June 30, 1977. (Numerous unreported decisions and orders were entered from 1970 through the end of the desegregation case in 1984)

Kite v. Marshall, 454 F.Supp. 1347 (S.D.Tex., Jul 27, 1978) (NO. CIV. H-78-1171)

Hernandez v. Houston Independent School District, 558 S.W.2d121 (Tec.Cir. App. – Austin 1977, - Writ ref'd n.r.e.)

Wright and Meyers v. Houston Independent School Dist., 569 F.2d 1383, 21 Fair Empl.Prac.Cas. (BNA) 647, 16 Empl. Prac. Dec. P 8186 (5th Cir.(Tex.), Mar 27, 1978) (NO. 76-1017)

Wright v. Houston Independent School Dist., 366 F.Supp., 1208 (S.D. Tex. 1972), aff'd; 486 F.2d 137 (5th Cir.(Tex.), 1973), cert. denied 94 S. Ct. 3173 (1974)

Sullivan (Paul Kitchen) v. Houston Independent School District, 333 F.Supp. 1149 (S.D.Tex. 1971), reversed 475 F.2d 071 (5th Cir. 1973)

APPENDIX G
KELLY FRELS PUBLICATIONS

"**Exhaustion of the Educational Institution's Remedies - Teachers, Students and the Federal Courts**," 1 *NOLPE School Law Journal* - No. 2, Spring 1971

"**Teacher Employment and Termination**," 19 *Texas School Board Journal*, No. 2, December, 1972

"**Student Suspensions and Procedural Due Process**," 11 *Texas Study of Secondary Education Research Journal*, No. 1, Winter 1972-73

"**Corporal Punishment in Texas Schools**," 19 *Texas School Board Journal* - No. 4, June, 1973

"**Teacher Employment in Texas**," 36 *Texas Bar Journal* 499, No. 6, June, 1973

"**Procedural Due Process and the Suspension of Students**," 19 *Texas School Board Journal*, No. 5, September, 1973

"**Search and Seizure in the Public Schools**," 11 *Houston Law Review* 876, No. 4, May, 1974

"**Corporal Punishment - 1975 Style**," 4 *NOLPE School Law Journal* 149, No. 2, 1974

"**Teacher Consultation in Texas - The Last Frontier or a New Horizon**," 27 *Baylor Law Review* 233, No. 2, Spring 1975

"**1975: The Status of Search and Seizure in the Public Schools**," *New Directions in School Law*, NOLPE, 1976

"**Corporal Punishment: Update 1976**," *Policymaking A Challenge for School Board Members* 17, TASB, Spring 1976

"**A Comprehensive Look at the Houston Plan**," *Magnet Reporter* 5, National Conference on Magnet Schools, May, 1976

"**Teachers' Rights: They've Come a Long Way**," 39 *Texas Bar Journal* 509, No. 6, June, 1976

"**Teachers' Rights: Latest Signposts**," IX *TEPSA Journal* 6, No. 14, December, 1976

"**Perspective: What is a Property Right**," 23 *Texas School Board Journal* 16, No. 1, March, 1977

"**Dismissal of Public Employees: Procedural Considerations in View of *Bishop v. Wood***," *Current Legal Issues in Education* 163, NOLPE, 1977

Frels and Robertson, "**Privacy**," *The Courts and Education*, Chapter XI, p. 273, National Society for the Study of Education, Univ. of Chicago Press, 1978

"**Burden of Proof - The Controlling Principle in Applying the First and Fourteenth Amendments**," *School Law Update* - 1977, NOLPE, 1978

"**Burden of Proof - The Controlling Principle in Applying the First and Fourteenth Amendments**," *School Law Seminar Proceedings*, NSBA Council of School Attorneys, 1978

"**Suits for Damages and Attorneys' Fees Against School Districts and School Officials**," *Contemporary Legal Issues in Education* 1, NOLPE, 1979

"**Student Discipline: Yesterday, Today and Tomorrow**," 25 *Texas School Board Journal* 4, No. 2, June, 1979

Frels and Cooper, "**Effective Documentation for Employee Improvement or Termination**," 26 *Texas School Board Journal* 28, No. 2, June, 1980

"**The Management of Student Records Under Federal Legislation and Regulation**," NSBA Council of School Attorneys *School Law Seminar Proceedings* 1980 172, 1980

"**Metropolitan Desegregation Remedies: Interdistrict Relief**," *School Law for a New Decade*, NOLPE, 1981

"**Burden of Proof – the Controlling Principle in Applying the First and Fourteenth Amendments,**" *Preventing and Defending Employee Civil Rights Suits*, NSBA Council of School Attorneys Coursebook 1981, rev. 1984; Editor

"**1981 Supplement to Burden of Proof - The Controlling Principle in Applying the First and Fourteenth Amendments**," *School Law in Changing Times* 220, NOLPE, 1982

Frels and Cooper, ***A Documentation System for Teacher Improvement or***

Termination, NOLPE monograph, 1982, 2nd ed. 1984, 3rd ed. 1988, Janet L. Horton co-author beginning with 4th ed. 1994, 5th ed. 2003, 6th ed. 2007

Frels and Cooper, "**Documentation of Employee Performance**," *Legal Issues in Public School Employment*, Phi Delta Kappa, 1983

Frels and Horner, "**The Negligent Deprivation of Liberty Interests Under 42 U.S.C. § 1983; *Flores v. Edinburg I.S.D.***," 14 West's *Education Law Reporter*, No. 4, p. 615, 1984

Frels and Cooper, **"School Discipline Policies and Procedures: A Practical Guide,"** NSBA Council of School Attorneys, monograph, 1984, rev. 1990

Frels, Cooper and Reagan, **"Practical Aspects of Teacher Evaluation,"** NOLPE monograph, 1984

"**Can a Teacher Ever Be Fired**," *Lawyers Alert Interview*, 3 Lawyers Alert 14, April 30, 1984

Frels and Horner, "**The Interrelationship of Tort Liability, Governmental Immunity and the Civil Rights Statutes**," 16 *St. Mary's Law Journal* 851, 1985

Frels and Schneider-Vogel, "**The First Amendment and School Employees: A Practical Management Guide**," NOLPE, 1986

Frels and Horner, "**The Death Knell to the Negligence Cause of Action Under 42 U.S.C. 1983**," 34 West's *Education Law Reporter*, No. 1, p. 1, 1986

"**How to Advise a School District on Disciplining Students,**" *Lawyers Alert Interview*, 6 Lawyers Alert 10, March 9, 1987

"What Schools, Police Departments, and Other Public Employees, Should Do About the New 'Wrongful Discharge' Claim," *Lawyers Alert Interview* 17 7 Lawyers Alert 18, June 27, 1988

"Student Discipline in the Public Schools," *Current Municipal Problems*, 1988

"Documentation for Teacher Improvement or Termination," *Principal's Handbook--Current Issues in School Law* 175, NOLPE, 1989

Bump, Frels and Horner, **"Investigating Alleged Wrongdoing by Employees in the School Setting,"** NSBA Council of School Attorneys, April 1990

"Legal Aspects of Site-Based Management," *School Law in Review*, 1992

Brown and Frels, **"Investigating and Preventing Claims of Sexual Harassment,"** *Inquiry & Analysis*, NSBA Council of School Attorneys, July 1992

"Legal Aspects of Site-Based Management," 31 *Kansas School Board Journal* 3, August 1992

Brown and Frels, **"Investigating and Preventing Claims of Sexual Harassment,"** *Sexual Harassment in the Schools: Preventing and Defending Against Claims* (rev. ed.), NSBA Council of School Attorneys, March 1993

Frels, **"Fiddling While Schoolhouse Burns,"** *The Houston Chronicle*, guest editorial, March 1995.

Frels, et al., ***Texas School Law: A Practical Guide***, Education Law Association, 1996, 2nd ed. 2004

"Legal Aspects of Site-Based Management," *School Reform: The Legal Challenges of Change*, NSBA, April 1996

"Documentation of Teacher Performance," *Termination of School Employees: Legal Issues and Techniques*, NSBA, April 1997

Frels and Brown, **"Dangerous Liaisons: It's Up to the Supreme Court to Decide School District's Liability for Sexual Harassment of Students,"** *Texas Lawyer*, January 26, 1998

"Pro Bono Controversy Resolved--Now What?" *Texas Lawyer,* June 8, 1998

Frels and Brown, **"Free Speech in the Classroom: Courts Don't Agree on Analysis in Academic Freedom Cases,"** *Texas Lawyer*, August 17, 1998

"Partnerships Reflect a Changing Profession," *Texas Lawyer*, January 25, 1999

"Courthouse Stories," *The Houston Lawyer*, September/October 1999, Vol. 37, Number 2

"Practice in the New Millennium," *The Houston Lawyer,* March/April 2000, Vol. 37, Number 5

"Representing School Districts," NSBA's *A Word On*, Spring 2000, Vol. XVI, Number 1

"Balancing Students' Rights and Schools' Responsibilities," *Houston Law Review*, Spring 2000, Vol. 37, Number 1

"The Role of Lawyers," Houston Young Lawyers Association, Pocket Parts, Vol. LXVII, No. 2 p. 10 (2003)

"The State Bar Helps Teach Democracy in Romania," *Texas Bar Journal*, Volume 67, Number 2, pp. 664-667 (2004)

"Allow Judgment Without Fear – Attacks on Judges Erode a Free Society," *The Houston Chronicle* (April 17, 2005)

"Have We Forgotten Our Civics Lessons?" *West University Examiner*, Vol. 5, Issue 16 (April 20, 2005)

"Documentation," *The Principal's Legal Handbook*, Education Law Association, 3rd ed. 2005, 4th ed. 2008, 5th ed. 2013

Frels, ***"Reflections of a School Lawyer,"*** 2007

Bump, Frels and Horner, **"Investigating Alleged Misconduct by Employees,"** NSBA Council of School Attorneys, monograph (May 2005, rev. October 2007) – a revision of **"Investigating Alleged Wrongdoing by Employees in the School Setting,"** NSBA Council of School Attorneys, monograph (April 1990)

Smaby and Frels, **"Twenty Years of the Texas Center for Legal Ethics,"** Vol. 72, No. 10 *Texas Bar Journal* 838 (November 2009)

Willett and Frels, **"Lawyer's Creed Curbed 'Sharp Practices,'"** *The Houston Chronicle*, Section B, page 10 (November 22, 2009)

Frels, **"To Restore Schools, Learn from the Past,"** *The Houston Chronicle*, Section B, page 10 (January 9, 2011)

Frels, **"Constitutionally, Vouchers are Dead on Arrival,"** *The Houston Chronicle,* Section B, page 8 (December 9, 2012)

Frels, **"Clean Air and Quality of Life – Business Leads,"** The Heart of

Houston – Lessons in Servant Leadership, pp 32-36, Bright Sky Press (2013)

Frels, Horton, McBride, Feldsherov, ***A Documentation System for Teacher Improvement or Termination,*** Education Law Association monograph, 7th ed. (2014)

Frels and Thompson, **"Vouchers Don't Pass Constitutional Muster,"** *The Houston Chronicle*, Section B, page 11 (February 19, 2015)

Frels, **"To Rebuild Our Schools, We Must Do More Than Paint The Façade,"** The Houston Chronicle (April 26, 2015)

Frels and Thompson, **"Should Charters and ISD's Share More?"** *The Houston Chronicle* (July 28, 2016)

Frels, "**HISD Board Should Represent Everyone**," *The Houston Chronicle* (July 15, 2018)

APPENDIX H

GUEST EDITORIALS OF KELLY FRELS

The Houston Chronicle, **"Fiddling While Schoolhouse Burns"** (March 26, 1995) / 158

The Houston Chronicle, **"To Restore Schools, Learn from the Past"** (January 2, 2011) / 160

The Houston Chronicle, **"Constitutionally, Vouchers are Dead on Arrival"** (December 2, 2012) / 164

The Houston Chronicle, **"Vouchers Don't Pass Constitutional Requirement of 'Public Schools'"** (February 18, 2015); co-authored with David Thompson / 165

The Houston Chronicle, **"To Rebuild Our Schools, We Must Do More Than Paint The Façade"** (April 24, 2015) / 167

The Houston Chronicle, **"Should Charters and ISD's Share More?"** (July 28, 2016); co-authored with David Thompson / 169

The Houston Chronicle, **"HISD Board Should Represent Everyone"** (July 15, 2018) / 171

Fiddling While Schoolhouse Burns

Houston Chronicle – March 26, 1995

By Kelly Frels

Singling out no-pass, no-play as the educational issue of the day is like fiddling while the schoolhouse burns.

Come Sept. 1, the education laws of Texas will expire. The Legislature faces the formidable task of rewriting the entire code of laws governing education before the September deadline. For the first time in more than a decade, the public and the state lawmakers have a meaningful opportunity to address the needs of our schools.

Unfortunately, the public debate over the popular political football—the no-pass, no play rule—has obscured the real education issues that must be addressed. The current discussion detracts from important matters such as the control of students, the quality of teaching in the classrooms, and the responsibility of parents for the development of their children's character and academic performance.

The public must press legislators to address these and other fundamental issues as they consider proposals such as Senate Bill 1, the state Senate's version of the comprehensive education law rewrite. The focus on highly politicized issues such as no-pass, no-play, where everyone seems to have an opinion, threatens the quality of the remaining legislation, much of which is vitally important to the future of Texas education. Issues that should receive attention include the following:

Student discipline. The ability of teachers and principals to control students' behavior was significantly watered down in 1984 with the reforms of House Bill 72. Student disciplinary laws are again the subject of a possible dilution this session. Some have proposed depriving schools of the ability to use short-term suspensions and emergency removals of students. While this effort is well-intentioned, it is not very practical What is a principal of a 2,500-student high school supposed to do with a student who has brought a gun to school, or when a student has assaulted another student, during the time the principal must give legal notice of an expulsion hearing to parents (if any are around) and conduct a hearing if requested? (The police and juvenile authorities will detain a disruptive student for only a short time before the student is back at school, and an expulsion hearing may not be held for a week or more.) Likewise, what is a school principal to do when 200 students stage a walkout in protest of a school policy or engage in a riot or other disruption?

The public schools are among the safest of locations for our children, hut we must provide our teachers and administrators with the authority to secure and maintain a safe environment. The current legislative proposal provides that the principal must keep the student in an alternative setting pending an expulsion hearing. Is this practical, and what message does keeping such a student around send to other students? What happens when a student in an alternative placement engages in further violence?

Principals and teachers tell us that effective discipline requires a prompt, certain, and fair response. Being unable to remove a disruptive student from the school environment is neither prompt nor certain, and the continued presence of a disruptive student is not fair to other students who are in school to learn. While alternative placement after a removal and hearing is an appropriate disciplinary technique, it is but another example of an unfunded mandate by the Legislature. At present, no state funds have been appropriated by the Legislature to provide for the cost of the alternative educational program, so the local taxpayers will again have to pick up the tab.

Effective teaching and employment. Administrators and school boards must be able to remove ineffective teachers from the classroom in a timely manner. The process for termination must be fair. However, the hearing process shouldn't take a year of procedural activity, as it now does in some school districts, before the unsuccessful teacher is removed from the public payroll. The teacher should not be terminated for bogus reasons, or for reasons unrelated to teaching, but the process should not prevent the school district from terminating a teacher during the school year who cannot spell or who slaps a child; such is now the case in school districts whose teachers are employed through continuing contracts.

The Legislature, through SB1, is considering the reasons for terminating teachers and administrators, as well as the hearing process required for termination. What is decided this session concerning teacher employment will dictate whether a district can control the quality of those in its classrooms.

Parental responsibility. One issue not adequately addressed is the responsibility of parents for the development of a child's character and his or her scholastic performance and behavior at school. It is amazing how many parents of children proposed for expulsion from school for drug possession or sale, assaults, or persistent misbehavior seem surprised and attempt to justify their child's misbehavior rather than accept the responsibility for correcting it. Teachers and principals want to ask parents, "Where have you been?" The school have had quite enough of parents unloading on the schools the parents' responsibility for raising their children.

Teachers and principals tell us that good schools are in large part the result of children whose parents are involved in the general development of the child. A parent who is involved with the child at home will generally be involved at school. Schools should be given the authority to require that parents are involved in assuring student behavior at school, and that parents are involved in their children's education. Parents should not escape responsibility for their children's behavior. In fact, they should have to come to school to participate in the discipline of the child.

Principals tell us, and it mirrors my experience as a lawyer representing school districts, that most guns and other weapons come from the home; yes, the kids generally get their guns from parents and other relatives. Perhaps a state law similar to Houston's ordinance holding adults accountable for what a child does with an adult's gun would help.

The Legislature could address the abdication of parental responsibility to the schools and other social agencies by adopting a parental responsibility law with a cornerstone provision that requires a determination of parentage at birth. A child's birth is the most opportune time to determine the father and establish his personal and financial responsibility for his offspring. A parental responsibility law is essential to helping our society define our basic legal responsibilities for the children we parent.

Most of us can live with the current no-pass, no-play rules, and we will function well with whatever amendments are passed. We must encourage our elected officials to focus on the educational issues that really affect what goes on in the school, especially in the classroom where education really occurs, and in securing and maintaining the proper environment for education to take place.

Leave the politically popular issues to a time after we have secured the classroom for education. Our children deserve no less.

To Restore Schools, Learn From the Past

Houston Chronicle – January 9, 2011

By Kelly Frels

In 1970, I began my legal career representing school districts. Forty years later, I am constantly asked, "Can we fix our schools?" I am convinced the answer is yes, but to get there, we must honestly look back, even with some discomfort, to the events that shaped our schools in the '70s, '80s and '90s. While we cannot change the past, we can learn from it to take charge of our future.

With the end of the Great Depression and World War II, America focused on developing its infrastructure for its growing population. There was an increased awareness and recognition that the social and economic system did not provide equal opportunity and access for all. Nowhere was this inequity more pronounced than in the nation's segregated school systems, most notably in the southern states where segregation was mandated by state laws. The U.S. Supreme Court unanimously ruled in 1954 that such racially segregated schools violated the Constitution. Lawsuits to end segregated schools were filed all across the South. The Houston Independent School District desegregation case was filed in 1956.

The war in Vietnam escalated in the 1960s and fueled social unrest. In 1969, the Supreme Court held that First Amendment assurance of free speech protected the right of high school student John Tinker to wear a black armband at school in Des Moines, Iowa, to protest the Vietnam War. Students' and teachers' First Amendment rights became fully protected by the courts on school campuses, with little consideration given to the schools' unique environment.

Lawsuits by students and teachers against school districts, administrators and school board members became commonplace. Some court rulings required policy changes—an intrusion into the historical prerogative of elected school boards. Student dress and behavior reflected the growing community turmoil. School board meetings which had normally lasted several hours began to extend beyond midnight. Bankers, doctors, and business leaders who had historically been bulwarks on local school boards declined school board service, largely due to greater time requirements and the fear of being sued.

During these times, urbanization of America was rapidly increasing, and the improving economy gave people mobility. These economic and racial/ethnic changes in HISD students also resulted from the remarkable demographic revolution that has forever changed the composition of the Houston region. As Professor Stephen Klineberg has regularly pointed out in his annual Houston Area Survey, Anglos were pouring into Houston during the years of the oil boom. After 1982, however, the Anglo population stopped growing and virtually all the population increase in Harris County during the past 28 years has been non-Anglo growth. This is the primary reason for the increase in HISD Hispanic students from 13 percent in 1970 to 62 percent today. The students of HISD today are 27 percent African-American, 62 percent Hispanic, 8 percent Anglo and 3 percent Asian-American.

The developing Houston suburbs offered new, affordable houses with populations that were virtually all Anglo. Predictably, the Houston suburbs grew, as did their schools. With many affluent Anglos moving to the suburbs, the Houston ISD students became more predominately minority, with a growing percentage of all students becoming eligible for free or reduced meals. Today, 79.2 percent of the HISD's 202,773 students are from economically disadvantaged homes.

By Kelly Frels

Immigrant students to the Houston region have largely been of limited English-speaking ability. In 2009-2010, the HISD Home Language Survey reflected that 99 languages are spoken in students' homes, and 31 percent of HISD's 202,773 students are limited English-speaking.

Over these 40 years, the family structures of our society changed, with an ever-increasing number of single parents. Many children do not have parents with whom to live. The incarceration rate in Texas has tripled, with most of the imprisoned being dropouts or undereducated.

During the last decades of the 20th century, the community basically abandoned and neglected our public schools, especially the core city school districts such as the Houston ISD. Many leaders of all races and ethnicities who could have made a difference in the Houston schools left. It was like a football team losing many of its key players without a draft to replenish the talent loss.

The business community became less engaged in actively supporting Houston's public education. People were interested in educating "my" children, but there was little support for educating "those" children.

Teacher unions and special interest groups filled much of the influence vacuum created by this neglect and abandonment. Their enhanced presence made terminating unsatisfactory teachers, administrators and staff increasingly difficult.

We live in a competitive world economy, and to survive and prosper, we must have an educated population. Globalization and modern technology have ushered in new economic realities. An educated, trained, and skilled work force is required if the Houston region is to have a secure economic future. To do so, we must focus on providing a quality education not just for "my" children, but for "our children.

But assuring our region's economic viability is only one part of the picture. We must have an educated citizenry to support our democracy and maintain our freedom. The Texas Constitution established the public free schools with the acknowledgment that "A general diffusion of knowledge being essential to the preservation of the liberties and rights of the people ...." We must return education to its historic priority to maintain our freedom.

To fix our schools, the community must make education the central priority that is reflected in the hearts, minds, and actions of our community. Our children must be convinced that getting an education is important to their future.

The Houston business community, especially the Greater Houston Partnership, is a leader in the effort to fix our schools. Education is at the top of the Greater Houston Partnership's priorities. The Center for Houston's Future, the Hispanic Chamber of Commerce, and many other Houston business organizations and their leaders are all speaking out consistently and clearly that educating all our children is a top priority. The Texas Association of Business has established a foundation to advance quality education across the state. Many businesses and charitable foundations are making substantial financial commitments to initiatives and programs that promise to further that objective.

Excellent individual public schools exist at all grade levels in Houston, Austin, and other urban districts, notably in the neighboring Aldine ISD. All these schools are models of success. Parental involvement and consistent community support are evident at each of these schools, and they are led by outstanding principals with well-prepared and motivated teachers.

Public charter schools, such as KIPP and YES Preparatory, which educate over 9,000 of Harris County's 811,198 schoolchildren, have also developed effective programs that are narrowing the achievement gap. And now, through the bold Apollo 20 initiative which is financially supported by charitable foundations and businesses, HISD is attempting to replicate the successes of these charters and other high-achieving public schools in a larger public school environment. Key components of these programs are committed teachers and principals who have high expectations supported by a "community of interest" along with high-dosage tutoring and more instruction time.

Significant contributors in this prioritization of education in the community can be the many leaders already involved in nonprofits and interest groups that support education. The collective effectiveness of these organizations can be enhanced through an education coalition. An education coalition can provide networking collaboration for the common goal and get community members involved without a loss of each organization's independence or purpose.

Making education the priority must begin with our community and business leaders openly and actively supporting the education of all of "our" children. The Houston region children currently number 1,216,109, with 92.8 percent attending public schools, 2.8 percent in charter schools, and 4.3 percent in private schools. As these percentages show, the focus for improving education in Houston must be on the public schools.

Can we fix our schools? The answer is yes, but we must develop and promote the community's enthusiasm and commitment to fix them. The essential first step is to make the education of our children the priority. Doing so will not be easy, but is essential; their future, our region's future, and our liberty are at stake, and time is running out.

By Kelly Frels

Constitutionally, Vouchers are Dead on Arrival

Houston Chronicle – December 9, 2012

By Kelly Frels

State Sen. Dan Patrick has proposed that the state of Texas provide vouchers to help parents pay for private school tuition. Vouchers are bad public policy, and they are not permitted by the Texas Constitution.

Ronald L. Trowbridge, who worked for President Ronald Reagan and then served as chief of staff for Chief Justice Warren Burger, explained why vouchers are not good for private schools in "Reject vouchers for schools" (Page B11, Sept. 18). He noted that established and reputable private schools do not have space for greater numbers of students. Private school leaders know that with government funds come government rules that would change how they operate. When one eats at a government table, one must use government manners. In a second article on Oct. 25, "Proposed school voucher system won't work in Texas," (Page B9), he focused on how few students would be affected by vouchers and stressed again that ultimately political strings would follow the state's money.

I wish to focus here on two other reasons vouchers are a bad idea for Texas. First, vouchers are bad public policy because they would be another distraction from our mission to effectively educate all of our public schoolchildren. Vouchers would divert funds from this education mission. Second, vouchers, in my opinion, are not permitted by the Texas Constitution.

From a public policy perspective, assume that Texas adopts a voucher system. Will all private schools that benefit from state voucher money be required to accept any child who appears at the school's door, or will the private school be able to continue to pick and choose from those who apply? Will such private schools be required to offer bilingual education and to provide an appropriate, free education for students with disabilities? Or will the private school be able to take the state's money for its chosen students and deny admission to those with educational challenges or those who misbehave, leaving them to the public schools to educate?

Our public schools face enormous challenges, and the system must be accountable to the public for educating our children. What we Texans too often fail to recognize is that adequately funding our schools is only the foundation. (The constitutional adequacy of the Legislature's funding of our public schools is currently being litigated in a Travis County District Court.) We must actively support public education in additional less tangible, but very significant ways—by emphasizing the importance of education to our children, and by engaging parents and our community as a whole in educating our future.

Constitutionally, vouchers are dead before they start. The Texas Constitution, Article VII, Section 1, recognizes the importance of "a general diffusion of knowledge being essential to the preservation of the liberties and rights of the people ..." Article VII, Section 1 mandates that "... it shall be the duty of the Legislature of the State to establish and make suitable provision for the support and maintenance of an efficient system of public free schools." Given this constitutional mandate, how can the state's money be used to fund private schools, even if the money follows the child to a private school?

Private schools that are sponsored by a church or a religious group face another constitutional roadblock in Section 7 of the Texas Constitution's Bill of Rights. "No money shall be appropriated or drawn from the Treasury for the benefit of any sect, or religious society, theological or religious seminary, nor shall property belonging to the State be appropriated for any such purpose." Can anyone in good conscience argue that vouchers do not benefit the private school, even if the voucher is given to the child's parents?

Many in our society have avoided the responsibility of citizenry to educate our children, and vouchers would be another convenient way to continue avoiding that responsibility. Funding vouchers would also violate the Texas Constitution. Let us all reject vouchers and focus instead on adequately funding our public schools and marshaling community support for their success. The resounding approval of the Houston Independent School District's comprehensive bond plan on Nov. 6 was a significant show of the support needed.

Vouchers Don't Meet Constitutional Requirement of 'Public Free Schools'

Houston Chronicle – February 18, 2015

By Kelly Frels and David Thompson

Our Texas Constitution imposes upon the Legislature a clear duty to establish and maintain a "system of public free schools." Public school vouchers are not good policy, and vouchers do not meet this great constitutional requirement.

First, the financial numbers simply don't add up. Voucher proposals, or taxpayer savings grants, currently pending before the Texas Legislature seek to give parents a voucher equal to 60 percent of the average cost of providing schooling to a student in public school. The problem is that the state doesn't contribute 60 percent of the average cost of a student's education. The state only pays an average of about 45 percent of the total; the remainder is paid by local property taxes.

In many Texas school districts, the state share is considerably below average. In some "Robin Hood" districts, state funding is almost nonexistent. These districts actually give local property tax revenues to the state. If the state each year contributes only $1,200 on average for every student in the Houston Independent School District, why would it make sense for the state to give a $4,000 voucher for the student to leave HISD? Isn't a child attending HISD worth as much to the state as the state would be willing to spend on a voucher?

The Legislative Budget Board determined in 2011 that taxpayer savings grants (vouchers) would cost the state hundreds of millions of dollars more than educating students in public schools. It was further estimated that Texas would lose about $1,000 in federal funds for each voucher—federal funds targeted to help educate low-income children, students with disabilities, breakfast and lunch programs, and technical/vocational education. How is that efficient or fair to the state's taxpayers?

Second, vouchers and accountability for the use of public funds don't match up. For public money spent in the constitutionally required "system of public free schools" there is accountability for what happens to public money. Districts publish test results and graduation and dropout rates. Statistics and data are available about how money is spent and how students are doing. School board meetings are open to the public, as are virtually all district records. With vouchers and private schools, this transparency and accountability for the expenditure of public funds is nonexistent.

Third, vouchers can be used to discriminate. We should always remember the experience of the 1960s, when vouchers were used in some Southern states to continue segregated schools. Could a voucher be used at a private school that discriminates in enrollment based on a student's race, ethnicity, gender, handicap, religion or family income? To date, no voucher proposal has included a workable mechanism to ensure that public funds are not used to discriminate.

Fourth, high-achieving private schools, like most acclaimed public schools, do not have the capacity to take in additional children with vouchers. Also, assuming that nondiscrimination laws would be applied to all schools taking state or federal money, providing bilingual programs and educating those with disabilities require specialized teachers and additional facilities. How many private schools are in a position to make that financial investment?

Fifth, remember that home schools in Texas are just one form of private school under a 1994 Texas Supreme Court decision. So, could a voucher be used simply to subsidize home schooling, with absolutely no accountability for the use of public funds? Could parents simply pocket thousands of state dollars and keep their kids home?

We should not forget that locally, parents have existing choices of educational programs. The HISD's magnet school program and other student-transfer options offer parents many choices for their children. Likewise, parents in HISD and other districts have the option of public school charters that are held accountable for the state funding they receive.

Our state's future depends on all our children receiving an education and possessing the knowledge and skills to compete. The time has arrived when, in Texas and nationally, we appear to have a consensus that we must find ways to meet the unique needs of economically disadvantaged children. How we answer this challenge is complex, but we should not let voucher proposals at either the state or federal levels divide and distract us.

Texans have believed since 1876 that our state's prosperity is tied to educating each generation of children within the "public free schools." Let's not let them down now.

To Rebuild Our Schools, We Must Do More Than Paint the Façade

Houston Chronicle – April 24, 2015

By Kelly Frels

How do we fix our schools? People expect a specific answer from this longtime school lawyer. After years of study and deep reflection, I feel comfortable suggesting a response. If you ask any school superintendent what makes a good school, you will likely hear, "good teachers and motivated, involved parents."

Legislative education "reforms" have come and gone, most without great measurable success. Unfortunately, most educational reforms, while well-meaning, have focused on process or procedural laws rather than the substance of quality education.

"Reforms" have suffered because we do not acknowledge that today's society is significantly changed and the responses must be fundamentally different. Increasingly, parents, the "first teachers," are not nurturing and stimulating their children to develop learning skills. In addition, an increasing number of children come from economically disadvantaged backgrounds.

Real changes in career opportunities for women have contributed to education not being able to attract a sufficient number of top-tier college graduates to teaching. Until the 1980s, quality education thrived on the "female subsidy" of women who graduated at the top of their college classes whose opportunities were largely limited to teaching, nursing and secretarial work. The great teachers of yesteryear, of all races and ethnicities, often become lawyers, doctors, engineers, or business leaders today.

There is little debate that students' academic performance is closely related to their parents' economic levels. Children from economically disadvantaged backgrounds are significantly more likely to not read at grade level by the end of the third grade, and they score lower on standardized tests. Children of poverty are much less likely to graduate from high school and go on to become a vital part of our workforce.

The answer to fixing our schools is fundamentally two-fold. First, we must create incentives to attract top college graduates to become and remain teachers and ultimately enter school leadership. Second, we must motivate parental involvement and find effective ways to provide all children with the constructive learning ingredients experienced by children who do not live in poverty. Engaged parents motivate teachers and push them to do their best.

Yes, attracting quality talent involves paying teachers at rates that are competitive with the business world. And, retaining teachers means elevating the level of respect in which teachers are held in our society. Every working person needs to feel respected to have lasting job satisfaction. Teachers and administrators must, of course, be evaluated and held accountable.

A first step to increasing teacher compensation would be to allow school districts to implement a teacher merit pay plan like the Second Mile Plan initiated in Houston under Superintendent Billy Reagan in the early 1980s. Teachers, principals, secretaries and, yes, the custodians and cafeteria workers, shared in merit pay when their collective efforts resulted in raising student test scores measured by a nationally normed test.

Educating children is a collaborative process involving many people. When the monetary rewards for success, as well as personal satisfaction and pride, are jointly shared, people will work together to achieve improved student achievement. The Second Mile Plan was replaced by a legislatively mandated plan that rewarded only individual teachers—it failed and was abandoned.

Supplementing what children from economically deprived families receive at home is complex. Effective parenting cannot be legislated. Teaching parents how to stimulate their young children is the beginning point that has primarily been a role of the medical community and social services. However, for a parent who is focused on finding a job, having a place to live, and providing food, reading to a child is not a priority. Brain development occurs early in the child's life, so early childhood education is a significant ingredient.

State funding of quality pre-K for children from economically deprived backgrounds is a first step to provide the learning stimulation that some parents do not provide. Children who can read at grade level by the end of the third grade are significantly more likely to graduate from high school and achieve further education and training. When this happens, the entire economy and our society are enhanced.

These two steps alone, attracting and keeping talented teachers and motivating positive parenting, will not fix our schools, but they will be a good start. Most important, these two "reforms" would stand as a substantive community statement that educating our children is the highest of priorities. We must rebuild the infrastructure of public education and not simply repaint the façade. Fixing our schools won't be easy, but achieving important goals usually isn't.

Should Charters and ISDs Share More?

Houston Chronicle – July 28, 2016

By Kelly Frels and David Thompson

Houston has a long history with charter schools. Houston ISD actually pioneered the concept of charter schools in Texas, well before the enactment of state laws on the subject. Some of the most successful charter schools in Houston and Texas, such as KIPP and YES Prep, started as HISD programs to provide options to students and parents, similar to the magnet programs and campus charters available in HISD. Ideally, traditional public schools and high-quality charter schools all should be able to thrive and work together cooperatively. Accomplishing this worthy goal will require action by the Texas Legislature as well as thoughtful leadership at the local level.

One of the larger obstacles to cooperation has been an unwillingness by the Texas Legislature to follow through on the original purpose for charter schools. The goal of the 1995 legislation authorizing the creation of charter schools in Texas was never simply to create a "parallel universe" of alternative public schools with different funding, accountability and legal requirements. The goal was to create a less-regulated environment in which creative ideas could be tried, with the Legislature then giving all public schools the flexibility to adopt the best ideas. Unfortunately, this original goal has never really been embraced. Charter schools are exempt from hundreds of requirements that govern traditional public schools, such as the school calendar, employment contracts, admissions and student-discipline laws.

Charter schools are able to be more selective in the students they admit, while a traditional public school accepts and serves all students. Charter schools generally don't serve the same proportion of disabled students as traditional public schools, particularly those students with greater needs. Also, charter schools don't have to keep the students they accept, but may simply expel or "counsel out" students who don't fit or perform, with those students then returning to traditional public schools, sometimes close to state-mandated testing dates.

Traditional public schools are more regulated by the state today than at any time in the past 20 years. One recent positive development is the "district of innovation" process enacted by the Texas Legislature last year; it holds promise for traditional public schools to have much of the same flexibility and reduced regulation that charter schools enjoy. But already there are legislative discussions about pulling back some of the potential flexibility offered through this new process before school districts even have an opportunity to implement it. Simply put, for there to be more cooperation between traditional public schools and charter schools, there must be a more level playing field so that all schools have greater flexibility to make decisions at the local and campus level that are beneficial for students.

Another obstacle to cooperation has been the difference in funding between traditional public schools and charter schools. There is a much-repeated and inaccurate figure sometimes tossed around that charter schools receive $1,000 per student less than traditional public schools, when in fact the opposite is true. This number is based on the state average of annual debt payments by school districts for facilities, not on any state formulas or state aid to school districts. But these funds are mostly locally raised to pay for locally approved bonds. HISD and most other school districts in this area do not receive any state money for facilities, for example. A traditional public school that is not able to pass and pay for a bond locally is in exactly the same position as a charter school with regard to facilities.

In terms of funding to pay for teacher salaries, utilities, transportation, food services and other necessary operating expenses, charter schools are funded at a significantly higher level than traditional public schools in the Houston area. Any charter school, whether high-quality or low-quality, receives about $1,000 more per student for operations than HISD. For a 20-student classroom, that is $20,000—and it is all state money. A charter school receives over ten times as much state funding per student as HISD. And, of course, a charter school never has to send local property tax revenue to the state as "recapture," or revenue that is above a level set by the state's public education funding formula. HISD, meanwhile, is being forced to pay more than $160 million of local property taxes for the 2016-17 school year into the state's general revenue fund, which the state is not required to use for educational purposes. There is a reason why several innovative programs started by HISD have chosen to become state charter schools instead of maintaining a relationship with HISD—they receive significantly more money from the state, and they are subject to much less regulation.

Cooperation is not just about giving charter schools access to buildings belonging to traditional public schools. Cooperation should include changes to state law so that all schools have the flexibility to adapt programs to meet the needs of students and parents. Cooperation should include the ability for traditional public schools and charter schools to share accountability for students. And cooperation definitely should include fair funding; it makes absolutely no sense for a student to be able to leave HISD and go to any charter school, and for the state to pay that charter school $1,000 more than it is willing to fund HISD to serve the same student. Shouldn't a child in HISD be worth as much to the state as that child is worth in a charter school within the boundaries of HISD?

We have an opportunity in Houston to create an environment for traditional public schools and charter schools to work together for the good of all students and parents - cooperation that will be good for Houston. Let's not set our sights too low or too narrowly. Let's work together to get the legislative changes made so that all schools have the opportunity to be great.

HISD Board Should Represent Everyone

Houston Chronicle – July 15, 2018

By Kelly Frels

Changing the way members are elected will give the district a fairer means of helping kids achieve goals. Quality education in any public school system begins with the leadership of its board of trustees. A pattern of failing schools has compelled Commissioner of Education Mike Morath to focus his attention on HISD, and he has the option of replacing the current board. But a state takeover won't repair the fundamentally broken nature of HISD. What we need is a long-term fix: Change the system for electing HISD trustees. Replace the nine district seats with a combination of at-large and single-member districts.

Public school governance is admittedly a controversial subject. People have been reluctant to advance possible solutions, probably for fear of offending sitting board members. But with the possibility of a state takeover, the time has come to put the proposal on the table.

It is apparent that HISD's current system of electing its trustees through all single-member districts is not conducive to effective governance. The results speak for themselves. HISD's current electoral system can and must be changed so its board members will focus on the entire district, rather than individual single-member geographic districts.

By Kelly Frels

But first, we have to understand why board looks the way it does. The story begins in 1975, when the board at the time rightfully sought a legislative change to replace seven at-large positions with single-member seats. Given the demographics at the time, single-member districts were the only way to insure African-Americans could be elected to serve on the board. At-large elections would dilute the African-American vote, denying this key political entity fair representation.

Change came again in 1981, when the HISD Board asked the Legislature to add two single-member district positions so the growing Hispanic population would have the opportunity to be represented as well.

The demographics of the city of Houston and the HISD have changed substantially since 1981. Today, the adult and student population is majority-minority. African-Americans and Hispanics have been regularly elected to at-large City Council positions and countywide seats. The same could happen at HISD. Single-member districts have served their intended purpose, and it is now time to focus on governance.

Many single-member trustees are elected by a small number of voters. It is natural for these trustees to feel beholden to this group of supporters. Trustees risk focusing on the affairs of their small electoral district at the expense of the school district as a whole. Pay attention to board meetings, and you'll find it is common for trustees to refer to schools and teachers in their geographic area as "my" schools and "my" teachers rather than "our" schools and "our" teachers. Looking out for "all" of "our" children gets lost.

Single-member trustees who properly focus on issues of the entire school district end up in a tight spot. By making issues of the entire district a priority, they risk not properly paying enough attention to their supporters, the ones who get them elected. The blame for a narrowly focused board doesn't necessarily rest with the trustees themselves—the entire election system contributes to less effective governance.

So, how can we change this? HISD's controlling law is a narrowly drawn statute, Article 2774b, which is not actually found in the Texas Education Code. Instead, you have to look through what are known as the Education Ancillary Laws. That statute should be amended to provide for at least four at-large positions and five larger single-member districts for the nine-member board. This hybrid system of at-large and single-member districts, already utilized in the city of Houston, would provide a near majority of trustees with district-wide views on issues. The remaining five or fewer single-member district trustees would have a much larger constituency and hopefully broader views. This combination configuration should lead to more consistent district-wide decisions.

It might be tempting to merely add two or three at-large positions to the current nine-member board. After all, that change would leave today's board untouched and avoid agitating them into opposition. But simply growing the current board wouldn't solve the governance problem; it would make it worse.

First, adding positions does nothing to eliminate the inherent problems with small single-member districts.

Second, school superintendents do not have the same sort of independent powers as a city mayor. Consequently, superintendents have to work with board members to develop a consensus on policy and other issues that come before the board. The more trustees a superintendent has to work with, the more difficult developing consensus becomes.

Few, if any, highly capable superintendent candidates would accept a position as superintendent in a large urban school district with more than nine board members, especially if many of them were elected by single-member districts. There's a reason why superintendents of large school districts with single-member boards have such short tenures.

Good school governance exists in the Houston area. These boards effectively work with their communities in defining the district's mission and in establishing goals and objectives that are clear and understandable. Policies based upon these objectives and standards follow. The boards provide the needed resources and support, then the members stay out of administrative issues. The board members effectively communicate with and hold the superintendent responsible. None of them have nine-member, single-district boards.

The HISD board has faced challenges before, and voters found solutions. Whatever Morath decides, only changing how we elect trustees will serve as a step toward a long-term solution. The time to act is now. Our children's education and the quality of our future workforce depend on our making this change.

Endnotes

1 347 U.S. 483 (1954); and 349 U.S. 294, 75 S.Ct. 753 (1955). / 1

2 98 Stat. 241, Pub L. 88-352, 42 U.S.C. 2000 et seq. (1964). / 1

3 79 Stat. 437, Pub L. 89-110, 52 U.S.C. 1010 et seq. (1965). / 1

4 393 U.S. 503, 895 S.Ct. 733 (1969). / 1

5 148 S.W. 2d 460 (Tex. Civ. App. – Galveston 1941 writ dism'd judgment correct) Interestingly, J.S. Bracewell, the firm's founder, was the plaintiffs' lawyer in *Fromen*. / 4

6 148 S.W. 2d (Tex. Civ. App. – San Antonio 1938 writ ref'd n.r.e.). / 4

7 430 F.2d 852 (5th Cir. 1970). / 4

8 Nicholson, Patrick J, *In Time, An Anecdotal History of the First Fifty Years of the University of Houston*, Pacesetter Press, Houston, Texas, (1977), Library of Congress No. 77-071492. / 6

9 *Shepherd v. San Jacinto Junior College District*, 363 S.W.2d 742 (1962). / 9

[10] *Sullivan (Paul Kitchen) v. Houston Independent School District*, 333 F.Supp. 1149 (S.D. Tex. 1971) rev'd 475 F.2d 711 (5th Cir. 1973). *Sullivan et al v. Houston Independent School District*, 307 F.Supp. 1328 (S.D.Tex. 1969) led to the adoption of the new disciplinary rules in the HISD. / 11

[11] *Wright v. Houston Independent School District*, 366 F.Supp. 1208 (S.D. Tex. 1972) aff'd.; 436 F.2d 137 (5th Cir. Tex.) 1973, cert. denied 94 S.Ct. 3173 (1974). / 11

[12] Sec. 21.904, Tex. Ed. Code (1973). / 12

[13] Tex. Rev. Civ. Stat. Article 5154(c). / 12

[14] *See* "Teacher Consultation in Texas – The Last Frontier or a New Horizon," 27 Baylor Law Review 233, No. 2, Spring 1975. / 13

[15] A complete compilation of all the HISD desegregation orders, published and unpublished, along with Supreme Court decisions on desegregation are in two bound volumes in my office. A summary of these cases and orders is included as Appendix "A." / 13

[16] 349 U.S. 294, 75 S.Ct. 753 (1955). Commonly known as *Brown II*. / 14

[17] 391 U.S. 430, 88 S.Ct. 1689 (1968). / 14

[18] 419 F.2d 1211 (5th Cir. 1970). / 15

[19] *Guild v. HISD*, (C.A. No. 70-H-1102, U.S. Dist. Ct. S.D. Tex., December 28, 1970). / 26

[20] 370 U.S. 421 (1962) New York state composed prayer recited in public schools. / 26

[21] 374 U.S. 201 (1963) School sponsored bible readings in Pennsylvania and reciting the Lord's Prayer (Madalyn Murray O'Hair). / 26

[22] Special Act of 1923 Creating the Houston Independent School District, 38th Legislature; Chapter 91, S.B. 402 (1923). / 27

[23] Gilmer-Aiken Act, Senate Bills 115, 116, and 117, 50th Legislature (1949). The Gilmer-Aiken Act created the Foundation School Funding through which the state provided 80% of the cost of public schools with local school districts providing 20%. Minimum teachers' salaries were set, and the concept of average daily attendance was introduced along with a school year of 175 days over nine months. / 27

[24] Tex. Local Gov't. Code, Chapter 171.000 et seq. 70th Legislature Ch. 149 (Effective Sept. 1, 1987). / 27

[25] Policy BBFA (Legal), Texas Association of School Boards Policy Service. / 28

[26] Section 11.13, Texas Education Code (1969). / 40

[27] Procedures on Hearings and Appeals; Rule, State Board of Education (Amended 1972). / 40

[28] Tex. Rev. Stat. Anno. Art. 5154(c). / 40

[29] 430 F.2d 842 (5th Cir. 1970). / 40

[30] 408 U.S. 564, 92 S.Ct. 2701 (1972) and 408 U.S. 593 (1972). / 40

[31] Eventually the hearing rules were changed and the appeal of disputes from local school boards were held before TEA hearing officers rather than the Commissioner of Education. The Commissioner now reviews the record before the hearing officer and renders a decision which can be appealed to state district court. / 40

[32] 411 U.S.1 (1973). / 42

[33] 487 P.2d 124, 5 Cal. 3d 584 (1971). / 42

[34] See *Neeley v. W. Orange-Cove Consol. Indep. Sch. Dist.*, 176 S.W.3d 746 (Tex. 2005) (West Orange-Cove II); *W. Orange-Cove Consol. I.S.D. v. Alanis*, 107 S.W.3d 558 (Tex. 2003) (West Orange-Cove I); *Edgewood Indep. Sch. Dist. v. Meno*, 917 S.W.2d 717 (Tex. 1995) (Edgewood IV); *Carrollton-Farmers Branch Indep. Sch. Dist. v. Edgewood Indep. Sch. Dist.*, 826 S.W.2d 489 (Tex. 1992) (Edgewood III); *Edgewood Indep. Sch. Dist. v. Kirby*, 804 S.W. 2d 491 (Tex. 1991) (Edgewood II); *Edgewood Indep. Sch. Dist. v. Kirby*, 777 S.W.2d 391 (Tex. 1989) (Edgewood I). / 42

[35] 490 S.W.3d 826 (2016). / 42

[36] Tex. Const. art. VII § 1. SUPPORT AND MAINTENANCE OF SYSTEM OF PUBLIC FREE SCHOOLS. / 42

"A general diffusion of knowledge being essential to the preservation of the liberties and rights of the people, it shall be the duty of the legislature of the State to establish and make suitable provision for the support and maintenance of an efficient system of public free schools."

[37] TEX. CONST. art. VIII, § 1-3. TEX. CONST. art. VIII, Section 1-e "No state ad valorem taxes shall be levied upon a property within the state." / 42

[38] James S. Coleman et al., Equality of Educational Opportunity (U.S. Office of Education 1966).

[39] The Elementary and Secondary Education Act of 1965, P.L. 89-10, 799 Stat. 27. / 43

[40] *See* "Economically Diminished Schools," page 111, "Leadership Counts," page 117, "The Gordon Cotton Principalship – An Example of School Leadership," page 89, and "The Difference Between Schools in the 1950s and Today," page 118. / 43

[41] 470 F.2d 659 (5th Cir. 1972). / 45

[42] 460 F.2d 607 (5th Cir. 1972), (El Paso ISD). / 45

[43] 519 F.2d 273 (5th Cir. 1975). / 45

[44] School authorities who permit student walkouts for some causes with which they agree and not for others with which they do not agree subject school districts to claims of viewpoint discrimination under the First Amendment. / 46

[45] 519 F.2d 273 (5th Cir. 1975). / 47

[46] 588 F.2d 96 (5th Cir. 1979). / 47

[47] Tex. Educ. Code Ann. §21.031 (Vernon Supp. 1981). Prior to the 1975 Amendment of §21.031, Attorney General John Hill opened that excluding alien children would violate the United States Constitution. Atty. Gen. Op. H-586 (1975). / 49

[48] See *Hernandez v. Houston Independent School District*, 558 S.W.2d121 (Tex. Civ. App. – Austin 1977 – writ ref'd n.r.e. / 49

[49] *In Re Alien Children Litigation*, 501 F. Supp. 544 (S.D. Tex, 1980). / 50

[50] *Doe v. Plyler*, 458 F. Supp. 569 (E.D. Tex 1978). Aff'd 628 F.2d448 (5th. Cir. 1980). / 50

[51] 457 U.S. 202 (1982). / 50

[52] *League of United Latin American Citizens v. Pasadena Independent School District*, 662 F.Supp. 443 (S.D. Tex. 1987). / 50

[53] 562 S.2d 844 (Tex. 1978). / 51

[54] Chapter 101, Texas Civil Practice and Remedies Code. / 51

[55] 610 F.Supp. 868 (S.D. Tex. 1985). / 51

[56] 436 U.S. 658 (1978). / 51

[57] 451 U.S. 527 (1981). / 51

[58] Tex. Rev. Civ. Stat. Ann. Article 6252-17 (1973); Now Tex. Govt. Code Ann. §551.001 et seq (codified 1993 and as amended). / 52

[59] Tex. Rev. Civ. Stat. Ann. Article 6252-17a (1973); Now Tex. Govt. Code Ann. §552.001 et seq (codified 1993 and as amended). / 52

[60] The Attorney General's Open Meetings Handbook is online at: www.texasattorneygeneral.gov./files/OMA_handbook 2016 pdf / 53

[61] Tex. Govt. Code. Ann. §552.001 et seq (codified 1993 and as amended). / 53

[62] 20 U.S.C. §1232g; 34CFR Part 99 (1974). / 53

[63] The Attorney General's Public Information Handbook is online at: www.texasattorneygeneral.gov/files/PIA_handbook 2016 pdf / 54

[64] Tex. Edu. Code §23.26 (1969). / 55

[65] Tex. Edu. Code §21.301 (1969). / 55

[66] *Sullivan et al v. Houston Independent School District*, 307 F. Supp. 1328 (S.D. Tex. 1969). / 55

[67] *Sullivan (Paul Kitchen) v. Houston Independent School District*, 333 F. Supp. 1149 (S.D. Tex. 1971) rev'd 475 F. 2d711 (5th Cir. 1973). / 55

[68] 419 U.S. 565 (1975). / 55

[69] Art. 1142, Tex. Penal Code (1973) Article 1142 provided: Article 1142 Lawful Violence. "Violence used to the person does not amount to an assault or a battery in the following cases: 1. In the exercise of moderate restraint or correction given by law to the parent over the child, the guardian over the ward, the master over the apprentice, *the teacher over the scholar*" Tex. Edu. Code Chapter 37, §37.001 et seq (2017). emphasis added. Also, see Tex. Edu. Code Section 22.0512 (2003). / 56

70 "Search and Seizure in the Public Schools", *Houston Law Review* 876, No. 4, May 1974. Also see: "1975: The Status of Search and Seizure in the Public Schools." *New Directions in School Law*, NOLPE, 1976. / 57

71 *Horton v. Goose Creek Independent School District*, 690 F. 2d 470 (5th Cir. 1982). Also, see *New Jersey v. TLO*, 469 U.S. 325 (1985). Search of students' purse by assistant principal for drugs and drug paraphernalia reasonable. / 58

72 Tex. Edu. Code Chapter 37, §37.001 et seq (2017). / 58

73 *Kite v. Marshall*, 454 F.Supp. 1347 (S.D. Tex., Jul. 27, 1978). / 60

74 H.B. 72, 68th Leg., 2nd Called Session (1984). / 61

75 695 S.W.2d 556 (Tex. 1985). / 63

76 PL 94-142 (1975). / 65

77 PL 101-476, 104 Stat. 142 20 U.S.C. § 1400 et seq. (1990). / 66

78 After the La Porte hearing, Bill Bednar began negotiating with the Bureau of Education for the Handicapped (as it was then called) at the U.S. Office of Education, which was then part of the Department of Health, Education and Welfare. In 1978, these negotiations resulted in the first set of TEA rules for special education hearings, which, with some modifications, survive to the present day. / 66

79 PL 93-112, 87 Stat. 355 29 U.S.S. §701 (1973). / 67

80 843 S.W.2d 41 (Tex. Civ. App – Ft. Worth) aff'd Tex. S.Ct. 0893 S.W.2d 423 (Tex. 1991). / 68

81 "Exhaustion of the Educational Teachers, Students and *NOLPE School Law Journal* – Institution's Remedies – the Federal Courts." No. 2 Spring 1971. / 69

82 *Houston Federation of Teachers, Local 2415 v. Houston Independent School District*, 730 S.W.2d 644 (Tex. 1987). / 70

83 20 U.S.C. § 1681 et seq. (1972). / 79

84 413 U.S. 189, 93 S.Ct. 2686 (1973). / 83

85 430 F.2d 852 (5th Div. 1970); 408 U.S. 564 92 S.Ct. 2701 (1972); and 408 U.S. 593, 92 S.Ct. 2694 (1972). / 87

86 569 F.2d 1383 (5th Cir. 1978). / 89

87 *Santa Fe Independent School District v. Doe*, 530 U.S. 290, 120 S.Ct. 2766 (2000). / 92

88 Texas Family Code, Chapter 261.000, 74 Leg., 1995 especially Section 261.101 requiring reporting of suspected child abuse. School personnel are held to a higher standard to report. Effective April 20, 1995. / 93

89 369 U.S. 186, 82 S.Ct. 691 (1962). / 95

90 *Houston Chronicle Publishing Co. v. Mattox*, 767 S.W.2d 695 (Tex. 1989) and *Houston Independent School District v. Houston Chronicle Pub. Co.*, 798 S.W.2d 580 (1990). / 97

91 *U.S. v. Texas* (C.A. No. 5281, E. D. Tx., Tyler – numerous orders and opinions). / 103

92 *U.S. v. Crucial*, 722 F.2d 1182 (5th Cir. 1983). / 103

93 "*Friday Night Lights: A Town, a Team and a Dream*," H.G. Bissinger (original printing 1988); Da Capo Press Paperback Edition (2004). Football in Texas' segregated black schools was placed on Thursday or Saturday nights, see "*Thursday Night Lights: The Story of Black High School Football*," Michael Hurd, University of Texas Press (October 2017). / 103

94 Frels, Horton, McBride, Feldsherov, "A Documentation System for Teacher Improvement or Termination," ELA Monograph 2014, 7th Ed. / 108

95 Bump, Frels, Horner, "Investigating Alleged Wrongdoing by Employees in the School Setting," NSBA Council of School Attorneys (May 2005, revised October 2007). / 108

96 Tex. Rev. Stat. Anno. Art. 2774(b); 52nd Legislature Chapter 339 (1951); amended 64th Legislature, Chapter 717, H.B. 313 (1975), amended, 67th Legislature, Chapter 3451 H.B. 510 (1981). See Tex. Edu. Code Section 11.052 for general law provisions for at-large and single-member districts. / 115

97 For more information on charters, see *The Houston Chronicle*, "Should Charters and ISD's Share More?" (July 28, 2016); co-authored with David Thompson, Appendix H, page 169. The 84th Texas Legislature provided some legal flexibility for public school district operations through Districts of Innovation, Tex. Edu. Code, Chapter 12A and Tex. Adm. Code Chapter 102, Subchapter JJ (2015). / 123

Acknowledgements

My gratitude to all the people and associations listed in this book and appendices — friends, colleagues, clients, leaders, adversaries, and loved ones — who have been part of my professional life story and have influenced the history and development of school law.

The names in the following list appear as they do in the book. Some of the organization leaders listed were before my time and I did not know them; however, they established the foundation that made my career possible.

Acevedo – Gus Acevedo
Adams – Neal Adams
Aldridge – John S. Aldridge
Alexander – Blue Alexander
Alexander – M. David Alexander
Alexander – Marquis Alexander
Allen – H. Rollin Allen
Ammerman – Dan Ammerman
Anderson – David Anderson
Anthony – Judge Marsha Anthony
Armstrong – Bill Armstrong
Arnett – Richard Arnett
Atkins – Mike Atkins
Backus – David Backus
Badillo – Christine Badillo
Baker – Robert T. "Bob" Baker
Baker – Hines Baker
Baker – Patricia Baker
Barlow – Jim Barlow
Baskin – Joy Surratt Baskin
Baskin – Stanley Baskin
Batson – Steve W. Batson
Beckham – Joseph C. Beckham
Bednar – Bill Bednar
Bennett – P. Tyson Bennett
Berlin – Lois F. Berlin
Berry – Weldon Berry
Bertelsen – Elmer Bertelsen
Bingham – Bill Bingham
Bischoff – Susan Bischoff
Bittle – Ed Bittle
Blue – Monte Blue
Boehm – Don Boehm
Bohn – Susan Bohn
Bolmeier – Edward C. Bolmeier
Borchers – Marion J. Borchers
Borreca – Chris Borreca
Bowns – Carmella Bowns
Bracewell – Fentress Bracewell
Bracewell – Searcy Bracewell
Bracken – Hazel "Shug" Bracken
Bradshaw – Miles Bradshaw
Brand – Mayor Othal Brand
Braun – Steve Braun
Brim – Jay Brim
Brim – Jefferson K. Brim III
Broesche – Travis Broesche
Brooks – Senator Chet Brooks
Brown – Judy Brown
Brown – Lisa Brown
Brown – Manny S. Brown
Broyles – Bill Broyles
Bryant – Faye Bryant
Bryson – Joseph E. Bryson
Bucek – Michael Bucek
Bump – Dick Bump
Burton – Les Burton
Bush – Governor/President George W. Bush
Butler – Henry E. Butler, Jr.
Butler – Joe Kelly Butler
Butler – Susan Butler
Byer – Von Byer
Byrnes – Don Byrnes
Cambron-McCabe – Nelda Cambron-McCabe
Camp – Bill Camp
Cannady – Alvin Cannady
Cannon – Ernie Cannon
Cantu – Norma Cantu
Caplan – Gerald A. "Jerry" Caplan
Carlson – James Carlson
Carr – Jackie Carr
Carr – Tom Carr
Cass – Jo Nell Cass
Castillo – John E. Castillo
Champagne – Joseph Champagne
Chedester – Margaret A. Chidester
Childs – Ken Childs
Clark – James F. "Jim" Clark
Clark – Judge Charles Clark
Clark – Susan G. Clark

Clifton – Ruby Clifton
Coats – Bill Coats
Coble – Edgar Oran Coble, Jr.
Collins – Gary Collins
Colwell – Brad Colwell
Connally – Judge Ben C. Connally
Conner – Judy Conner
Cook – Grant Cook
Coolidge – Joel Coolidge
Cooper – Tim Cooper
Cotton – Gordon Cotton
Cowan – Judge Finis Cowan
Cox – Robert B. "Bob" Cox
Craig – Benjamin L. "Ben" Craig
Crow – James B. Crow
Crow – Shellie Hoffman Crow
Crume – Kathleen Crume
Cruz – Juan Cruz
Cruz – Senator Ted Cruz
Currie – Michael Currie
Daniel – Philip T.K. Daniel
Darden – Edwin C. Darden
Dasher – Susan Dasher
Daves – Larry Daves
Davidson – Judge Mark Davidson
Davis – Jeff Davis
Davis – Judge Paul Davis
Day – Jonathan Day
Dean – Don Dean
DeAnda – Judge James DeAnda
DeAnda – Ricardo DeAnda
Deatherage – Jim Deatherage
Delon – Floyd G. Delon
DeWalt – Kaye DeWalt
DeWitt – Chip DeWitt
Dickinson – Richard Dickinson
Dies – Martin Dies
Dodge – Jean Harshbarger Dodge
Dolcefino – Wayne Dolcefino
Dollar – Barry Dollar
Downey – Judge Dan Downey
Doyal – Tom Doyal
Driscoll – Mike Driscoll
Dundas – Bob Dundas
Dutton – Dolores Dutton
Dykes – W. I. Dykes
Eckes – Suzanne E. Eckes
Edgar – J.W. Edgar
Edon – Elaine Edon
Englehardt – Judge Kirk Englehardt
Equia – Rev. L. E. Equia
Evans – Mark Evans
Everett – Rev. D. Leon Everett
Evers – Irving Evers
Eynon-Kokrda – Elizabeth Eynon-Kokrda
Fallon – Gayle Fallon
Farmelo – David A. Farmelo
Faubus – Governor Orville Faubus
Fearen – William Fearen
Feldman – David Feldman
Feldman – DeDe Feldman
Ferrara – Benjamin J. Ferrara
Fineberg – Mike Fineberg
Fisher – Mike Fisher
Fraissinet – Philip Fraissinet
Franklin – Ron Franklin
Frels – Carmela Madden Frels
Frels – Catherine Frels
Frels – Jonathan Frels
French – Larry French
Fry – Pat Fry
Gaddy – Dale Gaddy
Galatzan – Morris Galatzan
Garber – Lee O. Garber
Garcia – Bobby Garcia
Garcia – Juliet Garcia
Garner – Tom Garner
Garver – George Garver
Gary– J. W. Gary
Garza – Gonzalo Garza
Gilbert – Chris Gilbert
Glass – Frank Glass
Gluckman – Ivan Gluckman
Godley – Gene Godley
Green – Dorcas Green
Gregory – Gwen Gregory
Grossberg – Marc Grossberg
Guercio – Gregory J. Guercio
Gunter – Randy Gunter
Haglund – Wayne Haglund
Hairston – Joe Hairston
Hall – Robert E. "Bob" Hall
Handke – Jonathan Handke
Hanks – James C. Hanks
Hansen – Blake Hansen
Harben – Sam S. Harben, Jr.
Hardy – John Hardy
Hardy – John Hardy III
Hardy – Pamela Hardy
Harwell – Bill Harwell
Hays – Denise Hays
Heinen – Erwin Heinen
Hendrickson – Preston Hendrickson
Hensel – Bill Hensel
Hepworth – Roger Dean Hepworth
Herman – Erwin Herman

Herolz – Trudy Herolz
Hetzel – Walter L. Hetzel
Hightower – Richard Hightower
Hile – Dickie Hile
Hill – John Hill
Hinsley – J. C. Hinsley
Hodgins – David Hodgins
Hoffman – Philip Hoffman
Hofheinz – Mayor Fred Hofheinz
Holden – Orbry Holden
Hollingsworth – Jarvis Hollingsworth
Hollingsworth – Lonnie Hollingsworth
Holtz – James Holtz
Hook – Al Hook
Horn – Don Horn
Horner – Jeff Horner
Horton – Janet Horton
Hughes – Judge Lynn Hughes
Hundere – Nan P. Hundere
Hunt – Tanner Hunt
Hutchins-Taylor – Elneita Hutchins-Taylor
Jaffe – Marvin Jaffe
Jamail – Joe Jamail
James – Kim Brooks James
Johnson – Dick Johnson
Johnson – Karen Johnson
Johnson – Orrin Johnson
Johnson – President Lyndon Johnson
Jollay – Dean Jollay
Jones – Woodie Jones
Jordan – Senator Barbara Jordan
Justice – Judge William Wayne Justice
Kacal – Jerry Kacal
Kacal – Linda Kacal
Keller – Charles E. "Chuck" Keller
Kelly – Cynthia Lutz Kelly
Kelly – Jim Kelly
Kelly – Judge Joe Kelly
Kent – Judge Sam Kent
Kerr – Irene Kerr
Kirk – George Kirk
Kitchen – Paul Kitchen
Kite – Greg Kite
Kitt – Malcolm Kitt
Knowles – Lonnie Knowles
Krent – Nancy Fredman Krent
Kreunen – Warren Kreunen
Kronzer – Jim Kronzer
Landrum – H. M. Landrum
Lane – Kenneth E. Lane
Langley – Ralph Langley
Lanier – Mayor Robert C. Lanier
Lawler – Eugene S. Lawler
Lawson – Rev. Bill Lawson
Leahy – Julie Leahy
Leas – Terrence Leas
Leverett – Freeman Leverett
Levin – Dave Levin
Lewis – John Lewis
Linn – John Philip Linn
Lopez – David Lopez
Luna – Earl Luna
Lungwitz – Kevin Lungwitz
Lyle – Paul Lyle
Maatsch – James T. Maatsch
MacDonald – John MacDonald
Majestic – Ann L. Majestic
Mallett – Ed Mallett
Malonson – Roy Malonson
Manning – Ann Manning
Markowsky – Bishop John L. Markowsky
Marshall – Diane Marshall-Freedman
Marshall – Larry Marshall
Marshall – V. Bailey Marshall
Martin – Attorney General Crawford Martin
Martin – Mia Martin
Martinez – Vidal Martinez
Mawdsley – Ralph D. Mawdsley
McCann – Lloyd E. McCann
McCarthy – Glen McCarthy
McCarthy – Martha M. McCarthy
McCarthy – Patrice McCarthy
McDonald – Judge Gabrielle McDonald
McGhehey – Marion "Mac" McGhehey
McGowan – Leticia McGowan
McNamara – James McNamara
Mehl – Cheryl Mehl
Meisgeier – Charles Meisgeier
Michel – Arturo Michel
Mitchell – George Mitchell
Moore – Edith Moore
Moore – Joey W. Moore
Moore – Judge Lewis Moore
Morath – Mike Morath
Morgan – Cecil Morgan
Morris – S. I. Morris
Morrison – Ray Morrison
Motley – Ron Motley
Moyer – John G. Moyer, Jr.
Mullins – John Mullins
Myers – Tom Myers
Nelkin – Carol Nelkin
Nelkin – Stuart Nelkin
Nelson – Eric Nelson
Nelson – Jim Nelson

Newton – Michelle Newton
Nicholson – Patrick J. Nicholson
Nido – Luis Nido
Noel – Judge James Noel
Nolte – M. Chester Nolte
Null – Bud Null
O'Conor – Judge Robert O'Conor
O'Hanlon – Kevin O'Hanlon
Ogden – Bill Ogden
Ollison – Chester Ollison
Osborne – Allan G. Osborne, Jr.
Oser – George Oser
Paige – Rod Paige
Pannill – Bill Pannill
Parsley – Bob Parsley
Passons – Donna Passons
Patman – Senator William Patman
Paton – William F. Paton
Patrick – Senator Dan Patrick
Patterson – Edith Patterson
Patterson – Harry W. Patterson
Pauken – Patrick D. Pauken
Pedersen – David M. Pedersen
Pederson – Tony Pederson
Peebles – Richard "Rick" Peebles
Pence – Vice President Mike Pence
Penedo – Frank Penedo
Petrarca – Justino D. Petrarca
Petruzielo – Frank Petruzielo
Phay – Robert Phay
Pickett – A. Dean Pickett
Piele – Philip K. Piele
Popovich – Peter Popovich
Pratt – Reagan Pratt
Radack – Sherry Radack
Ramirez – Abe Ramirez
Rausch – Fred Rausch
Ravkind – Sidney Ravkind
Raymond – Joan Raymond
Reagan – Billy Reagan
Redford – David Redford
Reed – Bevington Reed
Register – George T. Register, Jr.
Remmlein – Madaline Kinter Remmlein
Reutter – E. Edmund Reutter, Jr.
Reynolds – Joe Reynolds
Rhodes – Alan Rhodes
Rich – Joe Rich
Robbins – Leonard Robbins
Robertson – Judson Robertson Jr.
Robinett – Mark Robinett
Robinson – Vianei Lopez Robinson
Rock – Darci Rock
Rodriguez – Eduardo Rodriguez
Ross – Delores Ross
Rossi Scott – Lynn Rossi Scott
Rubin – David B. Rubin
Rucker – Ron Rucker
Rusk – Cecil Rusk
Russell – William F. Russell
Russo – Charles J. Russo
Ryan – Britton (Britt) Ryan
Ryan – David Ryan
Saavedra – Abelando "Abe" Saavedra
Saegert – Jerry Saegert
Safi – S. Anthony "Tony" Safi
Sanchez – Andrew M. Sanchez
Sanders – Bob Sanders
Sanders – Janet Sanders
Sanders – Judge Barefoot Sanders
Savich – Jessica Savich
Say – Michael Say
Scarcella – Mayor Leonard Scarcella
Scariano – Anthony G. Scariano
Schafer – Allison Schafer
Schexnayder – Myra Chickering Schexnayder
Schneider-Vogel – Merri Schneider-Vogel
Schwartz – Allen D. Schwartz
Schwartz – Richard Schwartz
Scott – Ron Scott
Seals – Judge Woodrow Seals
Sedgley – Dick Sedgley
Seidenfeld – Nan Seidenfeld
Seitz – Reynolds Seitz
Semple – Martin Semple
Sewell – Tom Sewell
Shackelford – Ray Shackelford
Shannon – Judge Fred Shannon
Shannon – Thomas A. "Tom" Shannon
Shaw – Roger M. Shaw
Shell – Patricia Shell
Shepard – Gene Shepard
Shifman – Burton R. Shifman
Short – Police Chief Herman Short
Sims – Marney Collins Sims
Singleton – Judge John V. Singleton
Singleton – Maureen Singleton
Smith – Cate Smith
Sokol – Pilar Sokol
Sondock – Judge Ruby Sondock
Spafford – Franklin Spafford
Spalding – Ellen Spalding
Sparks – Sam Sparks
Spencer – Tom Spencer

Stapp – Bill Stapp
Steinhilber – August “Gus” Steinhilber
Stern – Ralph Stern
Stone – Jeri Stone
Stormer – Fred Stormer
Strahan – Richard Strahan
Stripling – Kaye Stripling
Sullivan – Dan Sullivan
Sweeney – Donald B. Sweeney, Jr.
Taylor – Lynne Taylor
Thomas – Stephen B. Thomas
Thompson – Charles Thompson
Thompson – David Thompson
Thompson – Rayborne Thompson
Thro – William E. Thro
Thune – Gary R. Thune
Tidwell – Jack Tidwell
Tilley – Mark Tilley
Tinsley – Eleanor Tinsley
Torres – Isaias Torres
Tritico – Chris Tritico
Ullman – James C. Ullman
Underwood – Judith Underwood
Van Ness – John Van Ness
Vance – Carol Vance
Veselka – Ronnie Veselka
Volz – Marlin M. Volz
Wade – Chuck Wade
Walker – Billy D. Walker
Walsh – Jim Walsh
Ward – John Ward
Ware – Martha Ware
Watkins – Joe Bill Watkins
Watts – Annie Watts
Watts – Larry Watts
Watts – Robert Watts
Weber – Leona Weber
Welch – Mayor Louie Welch
Weston – Jennifer Weston
Wheeler – Thomas E. Wheeler, II
White – Governor Mark White
White – Joel White
White – Nathan E. White, Jr.
White – Ryan White
Whiteley – J. B. Whiteley
Whitham – Warren Whitham
Wilde – William Key “Bill” Wilde
Willett – Justice Willett
Williams – Francis Williams
Williams – Robert Williams
Wilson – Kenneth Wilson
Wood – R. Craig Wood (FL)
Wood – R. Craig Wood (VA)
Worona – Jay Worona
Wright – Clymer Wright
Wright – Harry Wright
Wright – Linus Wright
Wright – Rita Wright
Wynn – Deryl W. Wynn
Young – D. Parker Young
Young – Robert Young
Zindler – Marvin Zindler
Zirkel – Perry A. Zirkel

ORGANIZATIONS

American Association of School Administrators/AASA
Delta Theta Phi Professional Law Fraternity
Education Law Association/ELA (NOLPE)
Greater Houston Partnership/GHP
Houston Bar Association
National Organization on Legal Problems of Education/NOLPE (ELA)
National School Boards Association/AASA
National School Boards Association’s Council of School Attorneys/COSA
State Bar of Texas School Law Section (formerly School Law Committee of the State Bar of Texas)
Texas Association of School Administrators/TASA
Texas Association of School Boards Council of School Attorneys/TASB

By Kelly Frels

Photos

Kelly Frels' elementary school in LaWard, Texas (Industrial Consolidated Independent School District) 1949-54. It was subsequently demolished.

Irving Evers, school law pioneer and mentor, NOLPE past president (undated photo from ELA archives)

NOLPE/ELA past presidents (front l to r) McCarthy, Steinhilber, Berlin, Cambron-McCabe; (middle l to r) Horner, Frels, Borreca, Russo; (back l to r) Zirkel, Leas, Alexander (undated photo from ELA archives)

In conversation at a NOLPE/ELA conference (undated photo from ELA archives)

Tom Shannon, founder of COSA and NOLPE/ELA past president (photo from San Diego School District, 1969)

(Title page photo by Jonathan Frels)

Made in United States
North Haven, CT
11 November 2026

22197196R00104